Engineering Data Mesh in Azure Cloud

Implement data mesh using Microsoft Azure's Cloud
Adoption Framework

Aniruddha Deswandikar

Engineering Data Mesh in Azure Cloud

Group Product Manager: Niranjan Naikwadi

Publishing Product Manager: Yasir Ali Khan

Book Project Manager: Kirti Pisat

Senior Editor: Tazeen Shaikh

Technical Editor: Seemanjay Ameriya

Copy Editor: Safis Editing

Proofreader: Safis Editing

Indexer: Subalakshmi Govindhan

Production Designer: Joshua Misquitta

DevRel Marketing Coordinator: Vinishka Kalra

First published: March 2024

Production reference: 1150324

Published by Packt Publishing Ltd.

Grosvenor House

11 St Paul's Square

Birmingham

B3 1RB, UK.

ISBN 978-1-80512-078-0

www.packtpub.com

To my dear father, Ashok, and my cherished late mother, Asha, who have been guiding lights on my life's journey. To my beloved wife, Reshma, whose unwavering support and encouragement have been my constant source of strength.

Contributors

About the author

Aniruddha Deswandikar has more than three decades of industry experience working with start-ups, enterprises, and software companies. He has been an architect and a technology leader at Microsoft for almost two decades, helping Microsoft customers build scalable applications and analytical solutions. He has spent the past three years helping customers adopt and implement the data mesh architecture. He is one of the subject matter experts on data mesh and cloud-scale analytics at Microsoft Europe, helping both customers and internal teams to understand and deploy data mesh on Azure.

About the reviewer

Vinod Kumar is a customer success leader for Microsoft Global Accounts with over 25 years of industry experience delivering end-to-end cloud solutions to customers. Based in Singapore, he leads the Asia team to help customers build resilient cloud architectures, embrace digital innovation and transformation, secure their use of the cloud, and make informed decisions using AI and data solutions. He is a mechanical engineer from the College of Engineering, Guindy. He is a passionate technology leader who inspires people, embraces tech, and champions inclusion. He is an author of multiple books on SQL Server and an avid community speaker.

I'd like to thank my daughter, Saranya, and my whole family for giving me the space I needed to contribute to this book.

Table of Contents

3

Deploying a Data Mesh Using the Azure Cloud-Scale Analytics Framework   27

4

Building the Data Mesh Governance Framework Using Microsoft Azure Services   51

5

Security Architecture for Data Meshes   67

Part 2: Practical Challenges of Implementing a Data Mesh

8

How to Design, Build, and Manage Data Contracts   125

9

Data Quality Management   139

10

Master Data Management   155

11

Monitoring and Data Observability   165

Part 3: Popular Data Product Architectures

15

Big Data Analytics Using Azure Synapse Analytics   247

16

Event-Driven Analytics Using Azure Event Hubs, Azure Stream Analytics, and Azure Machine Learning   255

17

AI Using Azure Cognitive Services and Azure OpenAI   263

Preface

In 2019, Zhamak Dehghani published her whitepaper on data mesh during her time at Thoughtworks. While it caught the attention of many large corporations, adopting data mesh was not easy. Most large companies have a strong legacy of analytical systems, and migrating them to a mesh architecture can be a daunting task. At the same time, the theoretical concepts of data mesh can be confusing when you map them to an actual analytical system.

In 2021, I started working with a large Microsoft customer that was struggling with their centralized data analytics platform. The platform was based on a central data lake and a single technology stack. It was rigid and was hard for all the stakeholders to adopt. As a result, many projects were creating their own siloed infrastructure, producing islands of data, technology, and expertise. We observed the dilemma the central analytics team was facing and proposed the data mesh architecture. It seemed that data mesh would solve most of their challenges around agility and adoption, as well as opening the doors to some other challenges, such as federated governance.

In the next year, we helped onboard this customer to data mesh. It was a long journey of multiple workshops followed by a consulting engagement where we built data mesh artifacts for them. Since then, I have been engaged with multiple customers on data mesh projects. As a member of a team of subject-matter experts on data mesh at Microsoft Europe, I have also guided other Microsoft team members on how to engage, design, and manage a data mesh project.

Along the way, I have realized that translating the theory of data mesh into a practical, production-ready system can be a challenge. A lot of terms get thrown around that actually can represent large projects in themselves.

This book consolidates information on all the challenges (and their solutions) involved in implementing data mesh on Microsoft Azure, going from understanding data mesh terminology and mapping it to Microsoft Azure artifacts to all those unknown things that only get mentioned as topics for you to look up for yourself in other data mesh resources. Some of these topics, such as master data management, data quality, and monitoring, can be large, complex systems in themselves.

The driving motivation behind writing this book is to help you understand the concepts of data mesh and to dive into their practical implementation. With this book, you will focus more on the benefits of a decentralized architecture and apply them to your own analytical landscape, rather than getting caught up in all the data mesh terminology.

Who this book is for

This book is for individuals who manage centralized analytical systems built on Microsoft Azure for medium-sized or large corporations and are looking to offer more agility and flexibility to their stakeholders.

This book is also ideal for small companies that currently do not have a well-designed analytical system and want to explore the idea of building a distributed analytical system to handle future growth and agility requirements.

What this book covers

Chapter 1, Introducing Data Meshes, briefly covers the concepts from Zhamak Dehghani's original whitepaper and book on data mesh.

Chapter 2, Building a Data Mesh Strategy, guides you in evaluating your company's current maturity level where analytics is concerned, aligning the company's strategy with the business strategy, and how data mesh architecture could play a role in that.

Chapter 3, Deploying Data Mesh Using the Azure Cloud-Scale Analytics Framework, covers Microsoft's own cloud-scale analytics framework for implementing data mesh.

Chapter 4, Building a Data Mesh Governance Framework Using Microsoft Azure Services, talks about how the key to a successful data mesh implementation is managing federated governance. This chapter will cover all the aspects of data mesh governance and align it with Microsoft Azure services that can be used to implement it.

Chapter 5, Security Architecture for Data Meshes, covers how with distributed data comes security challenges. *Chapter 4* discusses network security. In this chapter, we will discuss various aspects of data security, such as access control and retention.

Chapter 6, Automating Deployment through Azure Resource Manager and Azure DevOps, looks at how with distributed data and analytics comes distributed environments and products. The key to efficiently managing your environment is automation. This chapter walks you through all the aspects of automating the deployment and management of data mesh.

Chapter 7, Building a Self-Service Portal for Common Data Mesh Operations, explores how data mesh promotes agility and innovation by democratizing data and analytical technologies. One of the ways to empower data mesh users is to give them tools to discover data and deployment environments. A common practice is to build a self-service data mesh portal. This chapter provides guidance on how to design and build a self-service portal.

Chapter 8, How to Design, Build, and Manage Data Contracts, looks at how data mesh federates data ownership. Each team is responsible for the quality and reliability of their own data. In such a scenario, how do you build trust? This chapter discusses the formal method and process of maintaining data contracts and SLAs that help build trust and increase the reliability of data mesh.

Chapter 9, Data Quality Management, explores how, as data mesh grows, data products become dependent on each other for their outcomes. Some of these products deliver key analytics that is critical to business operations. The bad data quality of one data product could impact multiple products. This chapter showcases how to build/buy an enterprise-class data quality management system.

Chapter 10, Master Data Management, looks at **Master Data Management** (**MDM**), which provides a unified, consistent view of critical data entities across the organization; this is essential for data mesh's principle of domain-oriented decentralized data ownership and architecture. In this chapter, we will look at buy-and-build options for MDM for data mesh.

Chapter 11, Monitoring and Data Observability, covers monitoring and data observability, which are crucial for data mesh as they enable real-time insights into the health, performance, and reliability of data across decentralized domains. It is also one of the most challenging features to implement. It involves monitoring data products and data. In this chapter, we will design a **Data Mesh Operations Center** (**DMOC**) to consolidate all the monitoring aspects into one pane of glass.

Chapter 12, Monitoring Data Mesh Costs and Building a Cross-Charging Model, covers how analytical systems are typically cost centers. They are investments, and there are many ways to manage and distribute costs. This chapter looks at various cost models, systems of monitoring costs, and ways of distributing the costs of shared and individual components.

Chapter 13, Understanding Data-Sharing Topologies in a Data Mesh, looks at how one of the features of data mesh is to minimize the movement of data across the enterprise. It introduces the concept of in-place sharing. However, in-place sharing has its limitations and challenges. This chapter discusses various data-sharing topologies and describes the different scenarios for using each topology.

Chapter 14, Advanced Analytics Using Azure Machine Learning, Databricks, and the Lakehouse Architecture, is a reference chapter that describes one of the most commonly used architectures for advanced analytics: the lakehouse architecture. The lakehouse architecture combines the scalable storage capabilities of a data lake with the data management and ACID transaction features of a data warehouse, enabling both analytical and transactional workloads on the same platform.

Chapter 15, Big Data Analytics Using Azure Synapse Analytics, covers how big data processing is a common scenario in most companies today. This reference chapter discusses a possible architecture with Azure Synapse Analytics.

Chapter 16, Event-Driven Analytics Using Azure Event Hubs, Azure Stream Analytics, and Azure Machine Learning, looks at how certain areas, such as social media data analysis, logistics, and supply chain, require the real-time or near-real-time analysis of data. This kind of data processing needs different kinds of services and storage. This chapter discusses these event processing components and how to lay them out in a real-time analytics architecture.

Chapter 17, AI Using Azure Cognitive Services and Azure OpenAI, looks at how AI and machine learning have very different needs when it comes to data processing. They need quick cycles of training and re-training as data and models drift with time. Large language models bring in concepts such as prompt engineering and chaining. This chapter describes modern architectures for how to build Azure Cognitive Services- and Azure OpenAI-based models for natural-language-based interactions with your corporate data.

To get the most out of this book

While having read the original data mesh materials by Zhamak Dehghani would definitely be an advantage, it's not a must. This book provides documentation references for all the Microsoft Azure services mentioned, but some working knowledge of Microsoft Azure will help you save time reading the docs.

Software/hardware covered in the book	Operating system requirements
Microsoft Azure • Azure SQL Database • Azure Synapse • Azure Data Lake Gen2 • Microsoft Purview • Microsoft Active Directory • Azure Resource Manager • Azure Log Analytics Workspace • Azure Data Explorer	NA
Great Expectations	Windows or Linux with Python 3.8 to 3.11
Profisee	Deployed using Azure Marketplace
PowerShell, Azure Command Line Interface	Windows
Python 3.8 to 3.11	Windows 11 or Ubuntu 22.04
SQL Server Management Studio	Windows 10 or Windows 11

For installation and setup of the preceding tools and platforms, please see the following references:

- Installing PowerShell: `https://learn.microsoft.com/en-us/powershell/scripting/install/installing-powershell?view=powershell-7.4`

- Installing Azure Command Line Interface: `https://learn.microsoft.com/en-us/cli/azure/install-azure-cl`

- Installing SQL Server Management Studio: `https://learn.microsoft.com/en-us/sql/ssms/download-sql-server-management-studio-ssms?view=sql-server-ver16`

- Setting up SQL Server Management Studio to query Azure SQL Database: `https://learn.microsoft.com/en-us/azure/azure-sql/database/connect-query-ssms?view=azuresql`

- Installing Python: `https://www.python.org/downloads/release/python-3110/`

- Profisee SaaS Enterprise Data Management: "https://profisee.com/#

Note that the format of *Chapters 14, 15, 16,* and *17* is different from those of the previous chapters. That is because these chapters are architectural references. The aim of these chapters is to provide guidance on how to set up analytics for a given workload. You might also observe portions of text being repeated across those chapters. This is also by design. At a later point, you might want to refer to a specific reference chapter directly. In order to make sure you have everything you need in those four chapters, we repeat some of the text in them. Each reference chapter is designed to be a quick read and lets you explore all the components of the architecture using the reference links provided.

If you are using the digital version of this book, we advise you to type the code yourself. Doing so will help you avoid any potential errors related to the copying and pasting of code.

Access the GitHub repository

The GitHub repository functions as a valuable resource for future reference, enabling you to report any issues. Furthermore, the author can upload extra updates and examples to the repository, providing ongoing support. Access the repository on GitHub at https://github.com/PacktPublishing/Engineering-Data-Mesh-in-Azure-Cloud.

We also have other code bundles from our rich catalog of books and videos available at https://github.com/PacktPublishing/. Check them out!

Conventions used

There are a number of text conventions used throughout this book.

Code in text: Indicates code words in text, database table names, folder names, filenames, file extensions, pathnames, dummy URLs, user input, and Twitter handles. Here is an example: "It sets a mask on Column01 as a default number mask, from the sixth digit to the fourteenth digit."

A block of code is set as follows:

```
1# Grant access to individual user at a Subscription Level
2  function GrantAccessAtSubscription ($userID, $roleDef, $subScope) {
3      New-AzRoleAssignment -SignInName $userID `
4      -RoleDefinitionName $roleDef `
5      -Scope $subScope
6}
```

Bold: Indicates a new term, an important word, or words that you see onscreen. For instance, words in menus or dialog boxes appear in **bold**. Here is an example: "Each Azure service comes with its own built-in roles. Azure Data Lake comes with three built-in roles: **Reader**, **Contributor**, and **Owner**."

> **Tips or important notes**
> Appear like this.

Get in touch

Feedback from our readers is always welcome.

General feedback: If you have questions about any aspect of this book, email us at `customercare@ packtpub.com` and mention the book title in the subject of your message.

Errata: Although we have taken every care to ensure the accuracy of our content, mistakes do happen. If you have found a mistake in this book, we would be grateful if you would report this to us. Please visit `www.packtpub.com/support/errata` and fill in the form.

Piracy: If you come across any illegal copies of our works in any form on the internet, we would be grateful if you would provide us with the location address or website name. Please contact us at `copyright@packt.com` with a link to the material.

If you are interested in becoming an author: If there is a topic that you have expertise in and you are interested in either writing or contributing to a book, please visit `authors.packtpub.com`.

Share your thoughts

Once you've read *Engineering Data Mesh in Azure Cloud*, we'd love to hear your thoughts! Scan the QR code below to go straight to the Amazon review page for this book and share your feedback.

`https://packt.link/r/1-805-12078-6`

Your review is important to us and the tech community and will help us make sure we're delivering excellent quality content.

Download a free PDF copy of this book

Thanks for purchasing this book!

Do you like to read on the go but are unable to carry your print books everywhere?

Is your eBook purchase not compatible with the device of your choice?

Don't worry, now with every Packt book you get a DRM-free PDF version of that book at no cost.

Read anywhere, any place, on any device. Search, copy, and paste code from your favorite technical books directly into your application.

The perks don't stop there, you can get exclusive access to discounts, newsletters, and great free content in your inbox daily

Follow these simple steps to get the benefits:

1. Scan the QR code or visit the link below

https://packt.link/free-ebook/9781805120780

2. Submit your proof of purchase
3. That's it! We'll send your free PDF and other benefits to your email directly

Part 1: Rolling Out the Data Mesh in the Azure Cloud

Part 1 starts with the theory of the data mesh architecture as described by Zhamak Dehghani in her original whitepaper (`https://www.thoughtworks.com/insights/whitepapers/the-data-mesh-shift`) and maps it to Microsoft Azure's Well-Architected Framework, Cloud Adoption Framework, and cloud-scale analytics framework. Crossing this chasm is difficult for companies. This section will make it easier to understand the theory and apply it to your Microsoft Azure-based analytical systems. Whether you already have an existing central analytical system that you wish to migrate to a data mesh architecture or you are building an analytical system from the ground up, this part of the book will help you pave the way forward to adopt the data mesh architecture on Microsoft Azure.

This part has the following chapters:

- *Chapter 1*, Introducing Data Meshes
- *Chapter 2*, Building a Data Mesh Strategy
- *Chapter 3*, Deploying a Data Mesh Using the Azure Cloud-Scale Analytics Framework
- *Chapter 4*, Building a Data Mesh Governance Framework Using Microsoft Azure Services
- *Chapter 5*, Security Architecture for Data Meshes
- *Chapter 6*, Automating Deployment through Azure Resource Manager and Azure DevOps
- *Chapter 7*, Building a Self-Service Portal for Common Data Mesh Operations

1

Introducing Data Meshes

Before we start designing and implementing a **data mesh** architecture, it is important to understand *Why consider a data mesh?* This chapter briefly walks through the history of **business intelligence** (**BI**) and analytics. We will go through the events and transitions of how analytics has evolved over the last few decades and the current challenges that make a data mesh architecture an alternative to traditional centralized analytical systems.

In this chapter, we're going to cover the following main topics:

- Exploring the evolution of modern data analytics
- Discovering the challenges of modern-day enterprises
- **Data as a product** (**DaaP**)
- Data domains
- The data mesh solution

Exploring the evolution of modern data analytics

After the advent of **databases** in the late 1970s and early 1980s, databases were treated as a central **source of truth** (**SOT**) and designed to record transactions and produce daily, weekly, and monthly financial reports. These are largely termed **online transaction processing** (**OLTP**) systems.

In the late 1980s, businesses felt the need to understand how their business was performing and investigate any changes to sales, production, revenue, or any other important aspects of the business so that they could run their businesses more efficiently. But in order to conduct this investigation, they had to run complex queries across all tables in their database and be able to slice and dice the data to dig deeper into it. They also had to aggregate values in order to find totals and averages across a period of time. A relational model that spread data across multiple tables was needed to aggregate and join data across these tables. As a result of these complex joins and aggregations, the queries started getting expensive and more demanding in terms of execution time and resources. Database engineers soon realized that they needed a new method of storing the same data so that it would be easier to query and aggregate. This was the birth of **online analytical processing** (**OLAP**) systems, and the database transformed into a **data warehouse**.

Data warehouses dominated the analytics world for over three decades and are still the analytics tool of choice for small and medium businesses.

At the turn of the millennium, as the dot-com revolution started flourishing and businesses went online, computer engineers realized that data is not always tabular and structured. The requirements of an online business changed dynamically. Formats for user profiles, product data, and user interaction data changed constantly and could not be stored against a fixed schema definition. The volumes of data that an online business needed to handle were also exponentially higher than for a traditional business. Computer hardware had also advanced, providing more compute, storage, and memory in smaller and cheaper machines that could be racked on top of each other, forming what we now call **data centers**.

The main challenge with an OLAP approach was that data had to move from storage to memory for joining tables, aggregations, and calculations. As businesses got more complex and with the advent of the internet and the dot-com boom, the amount of data collected started getting larger and structurally more fluid in nature. Engineers during this time challenged the traditional concept of moving structured data to memory and processing it in a central unit. They started experimenting with storing data as text files with a fluid structure and querying these large volumes of files using a distributed storage and compute architecture. They brought the compute to where the data was residing. Thus started the era of **Hadoop**, **MapReduce**, and **big data** processing using **Apache Spark** and **NoSQL**. These technologies split the data into smaller pieces, processed them on parallel compute nodes, and then combined the results.

This completely changed the way data was stored and processed. Storage systems used for storing these semi-structured files were called **data lakes**. They were built on a distributed file storage mechanism called **Hadoop Distributed File System** (**HDFS**).

Amazon launched the **Elastic Compute Cloud** (**EC2**) cloud platform in 2006, followed by **Microsoft Azure** in 2010. This further revolutionized the computing landscape.

Up until public cloud platforms such as **Amazon Web Services** (**AWS**) and Microsoft Azure were launched, data centers and the hardware that went into the data centers were all purchased by companies. The data center was a **capital expenditure** (**CapEx**). However, after the launch of the public cloud, servers were now available as pay-as-you-go subscriptions. Renting servers in the cloud became an **operational expense** (**OpEx**). Hardware expenditure went from CapEx to OpEx, providing practically unlimited compute and storage whenever you needed it, without having to raise a purchase order and go through procurement cycles. This also provided a boost to **artificial intelligence** (**AI**) and **machine learning** (**ML**). AI and ML further added more semi-structured and unstructured data such as images, sound, and video files. The data lake, with all this structured, semi-structured, and unstructured data, now moved to the cloud and was used to store massive amounts of data. For large enterprises, this data went into terabytes and petabytes.

The data warehouse was still a part of every enterprise. While storage and processing evolved, most of the final processed models were still stored in a data warehouse. This created a bottleneck as the performance of the data warehouse drove the speed of analytics for an enterprise. This architecture also created a lot of moving parts in terms of separate components for big data processing, the data warehouse, and real-time data processing.

For some time (around the 2010s), enterprises used a combination of a data lake for semi-structured and unstructured data and a data warehouse for structured data. It was a complex **cloud data platform** with multiple moving parts to be maintained.

Today, enterprises are moving to the **data lakehouse** architecture. A lakehouse combines the flexibility and scalability of a data lake and the modeling and analytics efficiency of a data warehouse. It maintains semi-structured data along with a log of all **Create, Read, Update, and Delete** (**CRUD**) operations and uses the combination of the data and log files to perform complex data warehouse queries without having to store the data in a relational or star-schema format. This technology provides many benefits. It's low-cost, as storing flat files is cheaper. It allows for flexibility as the table schema can change over time without having to modify the entire database design. Traditional BI and advanced ML-based analytics can be performed on the same physical data. We don't need to have separate stores for data warehouse and ML jobs.

Data lakehouses are still evolving, and enterprises are in the process of adopting this new analytics architecture.

Figure 1.1 shows a timeline of how BI and modern-day analytics evolved:

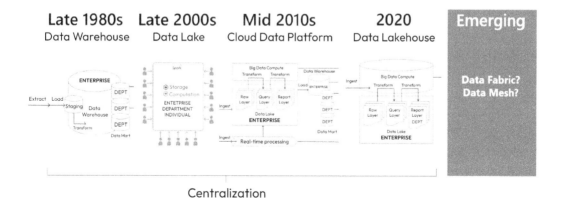

Figure 1.1 – A centralized analytics system

Next, we'll look at some challenges that enterprises face today with the traditional analytical systems described in this section.

Discovering the challenges of modern-day enterprises

As enterprises get bigger, the ability to be agile and competitive becomes challenging. Some enterprises have large departments for sales, marketing, engineering, and so on. Many large corporations split their global businesses into regions or zones. Each of these sub-organizations operates as an independent unit. They have their own business complexity, analytics needs, and speed at which analytical output is required. They choose their tools according to their requirements. But at the end of the day, they are asked to move their data to a central lakehouse or data warehouse for enterprise-wide analytics, which uses a specific set of tools and mandates a certain data format. This strategy has multiple challenges:

- The sub-organizations are forced to use the tools in the central analytical system to perform their analytics.

- The sub-organizations then start building their own local analytical platforms to speed up their analytics using tools that best suit them. These analytical islands start producing their own output and deliver it directly to the business. No one else has access to their data. Neither is the data managed under any common standards. This creates **analytical silos** all across the organization, hindering collaboration and innovation.

- The enterprise is missing out on all local innovation and is rigidly tied to what the central analytical system provides, making it less agile and competitive and hindering innovation.

A lot of organizational effort is spent on **extract, transform, and load** (ETL) pipelines and Hadoop, MapReduce modules to move data to the central data lake or data warehouse and analytical stores. *Figure 1.2* depicts what a centralized analytical system looks like in an enterprise:

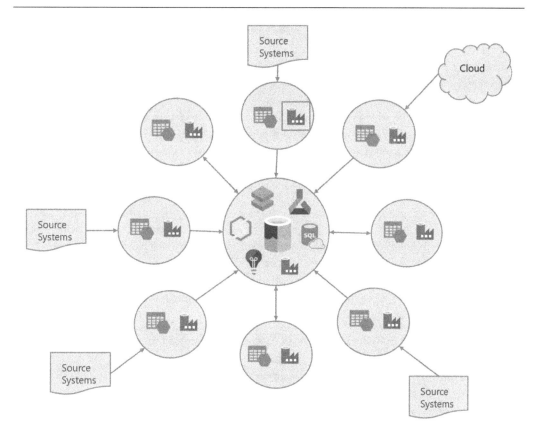

Figure 1.2 – A centralized analytical system in an enterprise

These challenges mandate a new strategy and architecture on how an enterprise should look at data analytics.

In 2019, Zhamak Dehghani, while working as a principal consultant at Thoughtworks, coined the term *data mesh* (`https://www.thoughtworks.com/what-we-do/data-and-ai/data-mesh`): a decentralized data analytics architecture that allows large, distributed organizations to scale their analytics using **domain-oriented decentralization**.

Now that you understand the current architecture of a typical centralized analytical system, in the next section, we will talk about the various challenges faced by a growing large organization and how a centralized system can hinder the speed of innovation that the enterprise needs to keep itself ahead of the curve. We will also dive deeper into different elements of a data mesh architecture and how it solves challenges faced by enterprises.

DaaP

Historically, data has always been treated as a backend. It was used by the middle tier and then surfaced to the frontend. Applications did not do a lot with the data other than aggregating and presenting it with better visuals. Relational database systems also ensured that data adhered to a schema and format and that all mandatory fields were populated. As a result, applications received quality data and had to do minimal checks on quality. But with semi-structured data, this equation changes. Semi-structured data does not comply with fixed schemas and rules of how data is formatted and populated. Advanced analytics, ML, and big data analytics need a lot of processing on the data before it's consumed by any algorithm and application. ML algorithms provide exponentially accurate output as the volume of quality data increases.

In a paper published in 2001 (`https://homl.info/6`), Microsoft researchers Michele Banko and Erik Brill showed that different ML algorithms performed equally well as long as ample quality and labeled data was provided. This paper proves that quality and quantity of data have a bigger role in determining the accuracy and performance of ML models than the models themselves. As a result, data scientists are continuously seeking quality data. This also makes the role of data engineers critical as they curate and engineer data for the data scientists.

Another aspect of modern analytics with ML is that it needs continuous training. ML algorithms are trained on historical data, and as the business collects new data, new patterns may be introduced, which starts making the trained algorithms inaccurate over time. This is typically referred to as **data drift**. There are also situations where the business requirements change that demand the models to be retuned and retrained. This is called **concept drift**. To make retraining efficient, data analytics teams build automated operations around this retraining process. This process is called **ML operations** or **MLOps** (`https://learn.microsoft.com/en-us/azure/machine-learning/concept-model-management-and-deployment?view=azureml-api-2`).

For MLOps to work consistently, the quality and availability of data used for training becomes critical. This requirement leads to versioning and **service-level agreements** (**SLAs**) on data being fed into the training process. At this point, data starts to acquire the characteristics of an application or a product. Data itself needs a DevOps-like process to ensure consistent quality and availability to ensure that all downstream processes work reliably.

And hence, the concept of DaaP was born:

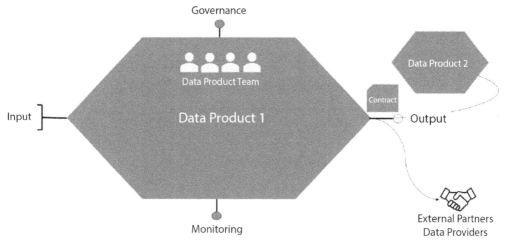

Figure 1.3 – DaaP

In the next section, we will learn about how a network of these data products creates a data mesh and all the advantages and challenges that come with it.

Data domains

One of the concepts defined in `https://www.thoughtworks.com/what-we-do/data-and-ai/data-mesh` is the concept of data domains. **Data domains** are defined as a logical grouping of data and teams aligned with certain business domains, such as sales, marketing, or production. While each of these domains may have multiple data products, all the teams and the data used to build these products fall under the same domain. This domain team is responsible for managing and maintaining the data in their domain. This is described as **domain ownership**.

However, in reality, we have found that adopting a domain as a concept could be challenging for many companies as every company has its own structure. For example, large global companies that run their business in different geological zones have sales, marketing, production, and local finance departments in every location. Each of these departments works independently based on their local market and country requirements. Clubbing all sales teams across the world into a domain is not practical. Hence, these large companies might choose to make their geographical zones their domains. And while sales teams from North America might want to get data from European sales teams to analyze similar trends, they need not belong to the same domain. This can be further complicated for companies with multiple lines of products that need to be separated but could have common domains (finance, sales) crossing the lines of products.

To simplify this, a domain could be referred to as just a logical grouping of data products that need to be managed together because they have very similar needs or access common data and resources:

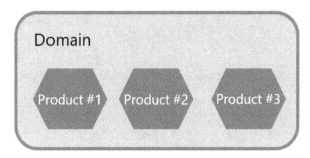

Figure 1.4 – Data domains and data products

The focus of building a data mesh architecture should be to decentralize data, centralize governance, and monitor and improve the collaboration and agility of enterprise analytics.

The data mesh solution

As we learned in the *Discovering the challenges of modern-day enterprises* section, having a central data lake or data warehouse has several disadvantages, especially for large organizations. In the previous section, we learned about changes in data processing requirements driven by ML and advanced analytics and how data now needs to be treated like a product with its own complete life cycle.

To explain a data mesh in one sentence, a data mesh is a centrally managed network of decentralized data products. The data mesh breaks the central data lake into decentralized islands of data that are owned by the teams that generate the data. The data mesh architecture proposes that data be treated like a product, with each team producing its own data/output using its own choice of tools arranged in an architecture that works for them. This team completely owns the data/output they produce and exposes it for others to consume in a way they deem fit for their data. Here are some examples.

A team from marketing gathers social media data for their products and curates it into a clean dataset that can be used by other marketing and sales teams for analytics. Instead of moving this data to a central data lake, they make the dataset available as raw JSON files in a data lake managed by this team. Other teams can reference this data, import it into their ML notebooks, or copy it into their local storage and transform it in some useful way.

Another team generates a real-time *Sales Volume by Month by Product* **key performance indicator** (**KPI**). This value is made available through an API that can be called with parameters of *Date* and *Product Identifier*.

In each of the preceding examples, the team that generates the data is responsible for the quality, consistency, and availability of the data. For other teams to reliably use their data, they need to provide some guarantees of quality and availability.

Also, the fact that the data is available for others to use needs to be announced in some way. This means that there needs to be a way for people to search for and discover this data.

These data quality and availability guarantees and the ability to discover data need to be managed centrally by some common team: a team of data governors.

In summary, a data mesh decentralizes data and data responsibilities and centralizes management and governance. Each data product team needs to maintain, manage, and provide access to their data, just like developers manage their code, build products, and provide access to these products. A data mesh brings aspects of application life cycle management, application versioning, and DevOps to the world of data.

At a high level, the data mesh architecture proposes the following:

- Decentralizing data to the department/team where it originates (data products)

- Decentralizing the decision of selecting tools used by each department/team to build their analytical output

- Decentralizing the responsibility of data quality and life cycle management to individual departments/teams (data products and data domains)

- Centralizing data access management to allow different teams to access each other's data in a secure and standardized manner

- Centralizing data governance tools such as data catalogs and common pipelines to get data from legacy and external systems

- Centralizing infrastructure deployment as **Infrastructure-as-Code** (**IaC**) to bring agility, standardization, and centralized management to the infrastructure that is deployed to the individual pools

- Providing a self-service platform for data producers and consumers to develop, manage, and share data products

Figure 1.5 shows a high-level data mesh concept sketch as depicted in Zhamak Dehghani's original text on a data mesh:

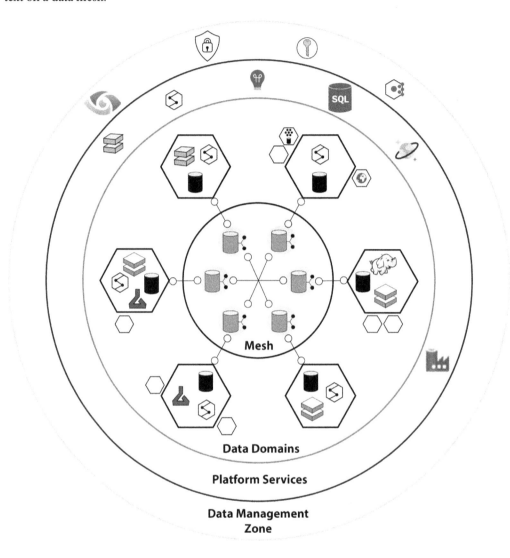

Figure 1.5 – The data mesh architecture

This architecture has the following advantages:

- Democratizes and streamlines access to enterprise-wide data, thus increasing the speed of innovation around data
- Brings agility to creating new analytical products or changing existing products

- Promotes sharing and discoverability of data

- Brings a culture of responsibility toward data quality and life cycle management

- Standardizes infrastructure deployment through centrally managed IaC templates

- Promotes the reuse of common pipelines and processing modules

- Centralizes data governance tools such as data catalogs, **master data management** (MDM) tools, and **data quality management (DQM)** tools

Decentralizing data and centralizing access management does bring about some challenges, especially around data movement. How do different teams access each other's data for their processing? Do they copy the data locally to their storage? Do they access the data directly from the source and copy it into memory structures such as DataFrames in Python?

One of the characteristics of a data mesh is to minimize data movement by keeping data at the source and accessing it directly. This is called **in-place sharing**. However, in-place sharing is not always viable as distances between producer and consumer could be far, and network latencies could make it impractical. We need to strike a balance between in-place sharing and data movement based on what is best suited for the specific scenario.

Implementing a data mesh architecture also involves a lot of non-technical changes to the organization. It's a cultural mind-shift from centralized to decentralized, from authoritative to autonomous. While it democratizes data access, it also puts a lot of responsibility on individual teams to ensure that their data is maintained, versioned, available, and reliable. The data mesh through its design and processes must build a system of trust among these teams so that they can confidently use each other's data products and accelerate innovation.

Summary

We saw in this chapter how data analytics evolved over time as technology advanced and as business needs changed. One of the main objectives of walking through this history is to realize that, once again, we are at the cusp of a change. Data-driven organizations are putting pressure on data products to deliver faster innovation to keep the company ahead of the competitive curve. We also saw how data preprocessing has become critical to modern-day analytics, which uses machine learning for accurate predictions and forecasting. Clean, curated data itself becomes like a product that other products can consume to get innovative insights. This drives the need for a more collaborative and agile analytical environment where data can be discovered and used to build data products, as opposed to the centralized dashboards and reports of the past. A data mesh is one of the ways to bring this agile and collaborative framework to life.

However, a data mesh is a long-term strategy and not a quick solution. In *Chapter 2*, we will look at building a data analytics strategy that leads to a data mesh architecture.

Building a Data Mesh Strategy

A **data mesh** may not be helpful to everybody, and adopting it as hype could be overkill. This chapter will discuss the conditions of when a data mesh is applicable and, for those who can benefit from a data mesh architecture, what should be considered before adopting it. In order to build a data mesh, a company needs to first recognize the current state of its analytical solutions and define its future state. This chapter will walk through the main strategic areas to consider when building your data analytics strategy.

In this chapter, we're going to cover the following main topics:

- Is a data mesh for everybody?
- Aligning your analytics strategy with your business strategy
- Understanding data maturity models
- Building the technology stack
- The analytics team
- Data governance
- Approaches to building your data mesh

Is a data mesh for everybody?

The answer is no. So, who should adopt a data mesh architecture?

- Medium-size companies that have autonomous departments (sales, marketing, finance, human resources) that have their own analytical needs but are forced to centralize data to a central location
- Large multi-national companies that have business across multiple geographical zones and run as independent businesses catering to local market needs
- Small companies and start-ups forecasting exponential growth that rely on data for their business

Which companies do not need a data mesh architecture?

- Small companies that don't see exponential growth in data should continue using a central data lake or data warehouse.

- Companies that by design or by regulation are prohibited from sharing data across intra-business boundaries will see benefits from some characteristics of a data mesh, but not all. For example, pharma companies working with highly sensitive patient information do not allow data to be exchanged between departments. We will discuss mesh topologies for such companies later in this book.

- Companies where the current analytics platform is providing all the required agility and innovation that the company needs. Any inefficiencies are just a matter of minor technological decisions.

In order to understand how a data mesh can help an enterprise, it is important to understand and build a data analytics strategy. The remaining part of this chapter will discuss the various aspects of building a data analytics strategy before you consider implementing a data mesh.

Aligning your analytics strategy with your business strategy

A successful data strategy is one that aligns with the business strategy, delivering business outcomes. Depending on the nature of the business and the industry it operates in, there can be different business strategies. A business operating in a very competitive space might want to have a pricing advantage, and hence reducing manufacturing or service costs might be the core strategy for the business. An online business might have a strategy around engaging its customers or marketing the right products to the right audience. It's important to ensure that the results of your data analytics are providing the right **key performance indicators** (**KPIs**) and answering the required questions for your business to align with this strategy. Because, let's face it, any technology initiative will only get buy-in when it supports the goals of the company.

Understanding and aligning your technology strategy with your business strategy is beyond the scope of this book. However, we will focus on aligning your analytics strategy, which is a crucial step to complete before building a technology strategy. You need to dig deep into your business and decide on the operating model of your analytical framework. You need to organize your stakeholders into domains. Look at their technical knowledge and understand how they will participate in your analytical process.

A traditional operating model divides the company into business and IT:

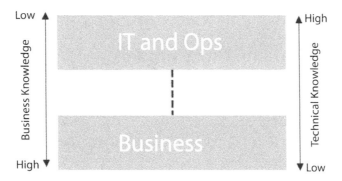

Figure 2.1 – Traditional operating model

As tools and technologies improve with natural-language interactions and friendly user interfaces, knowledge gaps become increasingly insignificant. Business analysts can build complex **online analytical processing** (**OLAP**) structures by dragging and dropping entities and columns onto a canvas, something that had to be put in as a request to a data engineer to build. As a result of this, IT teams and business teams can collaborate better and be more agile. Hence, a more modern operating model has hybrid and virtual teams overlapping business and technology knowledge:

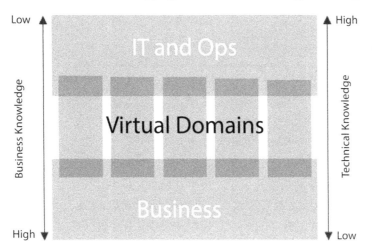

Figure 2.2 – A collaborative operating model

The operating model needs to be understood from a present and future perspective as part of the data strategy.

In the next section, we will discuss data analytics maturity models for a company so that you can analyze and understand how mature your current analytical platform is before you can start architecting your data mesh.

Understanding data maturity models

Data analytics maturity models help assess how an organization is leveraging and can leverage data to help the business make decisions. Studies have shown that organizations broadly fall into the following four stages of maturity when it comes to data analytics:

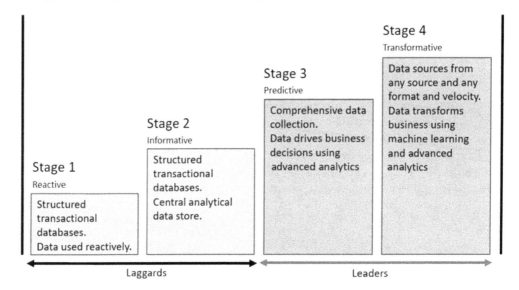

Figure 2.3 – Stages of analytics maturity

Let us learn more about these stages in the following sub-sections.

Stage 1

In this stage, companies ingest data from source systems and transform and move it to a staging area. From the staging area, it is modeled into **data marts** and served as OLAP cubes. Reporting applications read these cubes and present the data. This stage only caters to structured tabular data available in transactional and legacy sources. The pipelines are all centralized and managed. The system can quickly adapt to new sources as long as those sources provide tabular structured data:

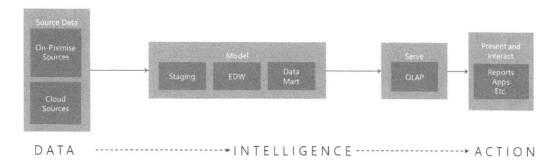

Figure 2.4 – Data maturity: Stage 1

Stage 2

Companies at this stage of maturity start collecting structured and semi-structured data into a **data lake** in a raw format. The concept of a data lake has been established. Additional pipelines are built to move the data from the data lake to the modeling system.

This main advancement at this stage is that historical data is stored in its raw format and is available at any time. This means it is possible to build new models by exploring historical data. This provides some agility for the modeling team to innovate and build new models faster:

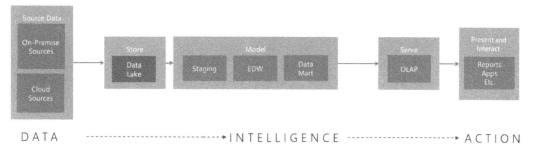

Figure 2.5 – Data maturity: Stage 2

Stage 3

In *Stage 2*, the transformation of data from the data lake to the *staging area* is still part of rigid pipelines. In *Stage 3*, the transformation and enrichment of data are separated out as a separate layer. This allows for the storage and transformation layers to scale independently. Additional tools to discover and analyze the data are added to the architecture to help do **exploratory data analysis** (**EDA**) on structured and semi-structured data. This allows for fast **proofs of concept** (**POCs**) and pilots and reduces the load on IT as data discovery and access are carried out through **self-service systems**.

At this stage, the company could also start tapping into more diverse data and ingesting real-time **internet-of-things (IoT)** and transactional data. As a result, the ingestion part of the architecture gets more sophisticated with a separate scalable and extensible platform:

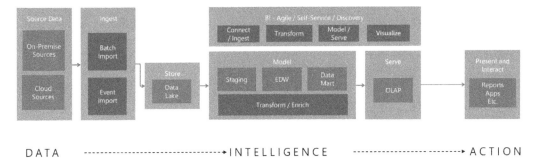

Figure 2.6 – Data maturity: Stage 3

Stage 4

Companies and enterprises at this stage leap into predictive and prescriptive analytics with data science-based advanced analytics. At this stage, the data is exploding, and hence a lot of automation needs to be brought in to manage the growth of data. This results in designing an orchestration piece with metadata management and planned workflows of how data is ingested and used in the organization:

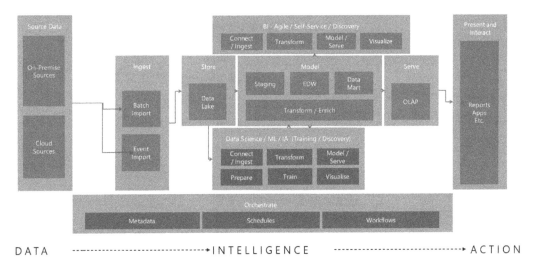

Figure 2.7 – Data maturity: Stage 4

In summary, your business could be at any of the aforementioned stages of maturity or somewhere in between. It is important to realize the stage. The stage of your data maturity and the size of your company will decide the path to build your data mesh.

In the next section, we will see how the technology stack can get complex with growing data analytics needs and how a data mesh can help ease that by decentralizing the technology stack decision.

Building the technology stack

Once you have the business strategy aligned with your data analytics strategy, you can start thinking about the technology stack you will need. Instead of going with the latest and the coolest technology available, you need to align your data analytics strategy with your technology stack. You need to look at your current data maturity and plan your target maturity model based on the analytics required now and in the future. Think about the life cycle of the data as it enters your organization right up to the output it generates – *ingestion*, *integration*, *transformation*, *processing*, *presentation*, and *archiving*.

One of the challenges of modern-day analytics is that data now comes in different formats having different processing needs and processing speeds. **Big data** has semi-structured data processed on parallel Spark nodes. **Transactional data** needs to be transformed into OLAP cubes and processed by a **massively parallel processing (MPP)** data warehouse engine such as **Azure Synapse SQL Data Warehouse (Azure SQL DW)**. **IoT data** is streamed and processed in near real time and needs very different transformation and analytics technology. Fitting all these different architectures into one central architecture becomes challenging to build and maintain.

This is where a data mesh architecture can help. A data mesh allows each **data product owner** to build their own architecture based on their data processing needs and yet provide their data product to others to use in a decentralized architecture. Each team can pick and choose their own tools for various stages of the data life cycle. A team that produces a KPI based on some legacy data can use a combination of **Azure Data Factory (ADF)** and Azure SQL DW to build their data product. A team that streams IoT data from a factory floor and produces some real-time production dashboards can use Azure IoT stack with Event Hubs and Azure Data Explorer to build their product. As long as they build the data product and make it available to consumers with quality and availability guarantees, they can choose whichever technology stack best suits their needs.

Hence, a data mesh can ease your technology strategy by making the technology stack more democratic.

With distributed data products, the obvious next thought is, what about the team structure? In the next section, we will cover the crucial topic of changes that need to be brought to your analytics teams to facilitate collaboration.

The analytics team

An agile collaborative team is one of the most critical parts of a data analytics strategy for a company. The structure of your team will play a larger role than technology in deciding the efficiency of the **analytical framework**. The structure of your team will be dependent on the *operating model* that you build. And, depending on your future data strategy, you might have to regroup teams and even create and hire new roles.

With the growing importance of **data governance**, a new role called **chief data officer** (**CDO**) is being introduced in many companies. The CDO manages the data analytics team along with the new data governance team. A CDO and their team are responsible for the governance and utilization of enterprise-wide data, along with identifying new innovative opportunities to utilize data. *Figure 2.8* shows an example of such an organizational structure with a CDO position:

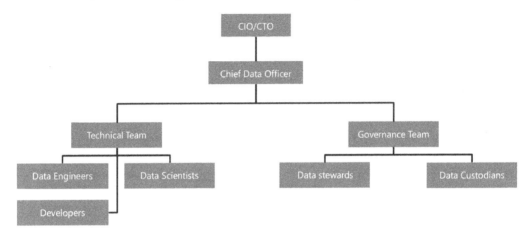

Figure 2.8 – A sample data organization structure

The left part of this organizational structure must be familiar to most of you. On the right side of the organizational structure, the *governance team* is a relatively new concept. The *data stewards* in this new team are responsible for the quality, availability, and life cycle of data and metadata. They plan, design, and maintain data contracts between various collaborative organizations within the company. *Data custodians* are responsible for the safekeeping of the data in the way data is stored and shared. They also take responsibility for regulation-related activities to ensure that data is stored and shared based on whatever regulation guidelines dictate in regulated industries or geographical/ political regulations that are prevalent in the region, such as the **General Data Protection Regulation** (**GDPR**) in Europe. Depending on the size of the organization, these roles could sometimes overlap as one role of data steward.

A data mesh focuses on decentralizing the data and creating data products around these localized data pods. This means that each of these data products will need a dedicated team to build and manage the product. While each product may have its own dedicated technical team, having a data governance team and an IT Ops team for every product might be overkill. In this case, we need the governance and IT Ops teams to be shared between all these product teams, creating multiple **virtual teams** (**v-teams**) that work closely toward ensuring the success of the data product. *Figure 2.9* shows typical shared and dedicated teams in an organization:

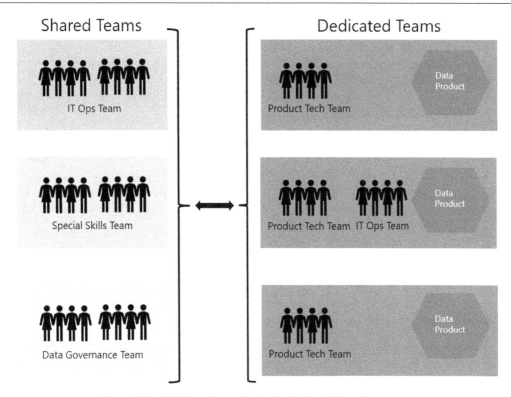

Figure 2.9 – Collaboration using dedicated and shared resources

The preceding diagram is an example of a team structure. Each product has its tech team. Some products might be larger and more strategic in nature and have a larger team and might include their own IT Ops team. All the other teams are shared resources. A central IT Ops team maintains all common infra and steps in to help any product team with its infra needs. Some companies maintain a special skills team that has experienced engineers specialized in skills such as **big data processing** or **machine learning** (**ML**) that can be shared across products. This way, each team does not have to invest in a full-time specialist whose skills are required occasionally. A data governance team works with the individual product teams to implement data governance for each product output.

In the last section of the chapter, we cover the topic of data governance. This is a fairly new topic for many companies. Though some aspects of data governance are implemented in companies in bits and pieces, bringing it to the center stage needs planning.

Data governance

Finally, the most important part of a modern data strategy is governance. Building a governance plan and documenting it can be a daunting task. It needs to be driven at the leadership level. A good place to start is to begin defining your business glossary and your data classification tags. These two alone can cover a huge portion of your data governance needs.

A **business glossary** is a standardized understanding of business terms that all employees can refer to and ensure that they are all talking in the same language. It helps remove ambiguity. By associating business glossary terms with data components, those consuming the data are able to understand the content. The term **average order value (AOV)** might mean different things to different people. But if you have a business glossary that defines what AOV means, then everyone can refer to it and have a common understanding.

Data classification is the process of classifying data into different sensitivity labels. This helps governance teams separate out sensitive data and manage it as per the required compliance guidelines. Microsoft standard data classification has the following classification tags: `https://learn.microsoft.com/en-us/azure/cloud-adoption-framework/scenarios/cloud-scale-analytics/govern-requirements`.

Data governance also includes managing access to data and ensuring that the right people and processes get access to data.

In summary, data governance is a large topic and can cover a lot of aspects of governance. It is important to start small and start with what is most critical to the business from a governance perspective.

Approaches to building your data mesh

Depending on the current stage of the analytics system, you could choose from two broad approaches to building your data mesh – a green-field approach or a surround approach.

If your business is at *Stage 1* or *2* of data analytics maturity and you currently don't have much data but see potential growth coming in the future, use the green-field approach where you start with a clean slate, describe your domains and products, and link them together in a data mesh. You then migrate all existing data from your current *analytical system* into this new data mesh, distributing the data to the domains and the products it belongs to:

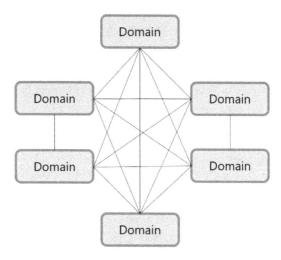

Figure 2.10 – Green-field data mesh implementation

If your business is at *Stage 3* or *Stage 4* of data maturity, then it will be difficult to start from scratch. Many stakeholders might be dependent on the analytics produced by the central analytics system. In this case, you should roll out the data mesh in two phases:

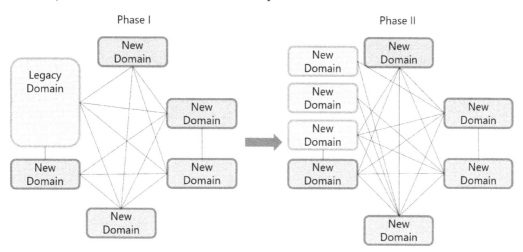

Figure 2.11 – Data mesh surround strategy

Figure 2.11 shows how companies can move from a centralized analytical system to a complete mesh by surrounding the legacy system with new domains for new projects and slowly breaking up the legacy into smaller domains over time.

Summary

In this chapter, we saw various elements of a data mesh strategy. We covered cultural, organizational, and technical changes that will need to be adopted to build a solid data strategy. Building a comprehensive, forward-looking data strategy will prove critical to building a collaborative data analytics system using a data mesh architecture. It is very important that a company spends a good amount of time and resources on building this strategy before moving forward with the implementation. Moving from a centralized data analytics structure to a decentralized, collaborative structure is a cultural change. Many companies employ a change management process by seeking help from external consulting companies to help employees adopt the change. Understand your current data maturity and select the appropriate strategy to implement a data mesh.

In the next chapter, we will understand how a data mesh architecture can be deployed using Microsoft Azure. Microsoft has built multiple guidance frameworks, such as the **Cloud Adoption Framework (CAF)** and the **Well-Architected Framework (WAF)**, to help companies adopt and migrate to the cloud. We will see how these frameworks can be leveraged to build a data mesh in Azure.

3

Deploying a Data Mesh Using the Azure Cloud-Scale Analytics Framework

In the previous chapter, we discussed how to build a **data mesh strategy**. Once a strategy is ready, it's time to implement it. The Microsoft Azure team has created a template for deploying a data mesh while using standardized methodology and best practices used by almost all of Microsoft's customers to create and manage their cloud infrastructure. It is called the **Cloud Adoption Framework (CAF)**. Based on the CAF, they have created the **Cloud-Scale Analytics (CSA)** framework, which provides the guidance and the required templates to roll out a data mesh in the Azure cloud.

In this chapter, we will dig deeper into the CAF and the CSA framework to understand how these frameworks can be mapped to a data mesh architecture. These frameworks are just guidelines (not written in stone) and you can choose to build your own methods to build a data mesh, but these frameworks can make the journey easier and also give you confidence as these frameworks are built based on Microsoft's experience and best practices.

The CAF is a very comprehensive framework that covers every cloud workload. It will not be possible to cover the entire CAF in this book. So, we will dig deeper into CSA as a sub-topic of the CAF, and I will provide online references about the CAF for you.

In this chapter, we're going to cover the following main topics:

- Introduction to Azure CSA
- Understanding landing zones
- Organizing resources
- Designing a cloud management structure
- CSA landing zones

- Automating landing zone deployment

- Organizing resources in a landing zone

- Network topologies

- Security and access control

- Streamlining deployment through DevOps

Introduction to Azure CSA

As big and small enterprises started moving their on-premises infrastructure to the cloud, Microsoft realized that there needed to be some standardization to how the cloud infrastructure should be set up on the cloud. To streamline the process of migrating workloads to the cloud or even building new greenfield infrastructure on the cloud, Microsoft created the CAF. The CAF provides the best practices, guidelines, documentation, and tools to help cloud technology experts quickly adopt the cloud. It helps you set up your basic foundational infrastructure in the cloud so that you can land your actual workload resources smoothly and ensure that they follow all the required security, network, and other best practices.

An in-depth coverage of the CAF is beyond the scope of this book. You can find more details about the CAF in the Microsoft documentation at `https://learn.microsoft.com/en-us/azure/cloud-adoption-framework/`.

Yet another framework created by Microsoft is the **Well-Architected Framework**. Once you have migrated or set up your system/solution in the **Azure cloud**, the Well-Architected Framework provides the guidelines to ensure that you continue to improve the performance, security, and scale of your solution. The Well-Architected Framework provides architectural excellence and best practices across five pillars:

- **Reliability**: The speed and consistency of recovering from failures

- **Security**: Protect all the resources, network, and data against threats

- **Cost optimization**: Proactively manage costs

- **Operational excellence**: Automate operations

- **Performance efficiency**: Scale the infrastructure and performance with the business

In-depth coverage of the Well-Architected Framework is beyond the scope of this book. You can find more details about the Azure Well-Architected Framework in the Microsoft documentation at `https://learn.microsoft.com/en-us/azure/well-architected/`.

The CAF provides good guidance for building applications on the cloud. However, there was not enough guidance for **data analytics**. So, when the data mesh concept became popular in 2018, Microsoft built new guidance based on the CAF and Well-Architected Framework. This is called CSA.

CSA can help you speed up your data mesh deployment. One of the core components of the CAF is **landing zones**. In the next section, we will learn what a landing zone is.

Understanding landing zones

The best way to describe the concept of a landing zone is with a real-life example. Let's assume that you have a product idea and want to build a business around it. Your product needs a manufacturing plant, a warehouse, and an office. You decide on a city to start your business and narrow down on a piece of land to set up your plant, warehouse, and office. Now, all you need to do is complete the purchase formalities and start building your business. You don't have to worry about electricity and water supply to your business. The city police and the legal system ensure that your business is safe. So, you can just run your business without having to worry about any of these basic requirements.

Similarly, an Azure landing zone provides the basic infrastructure for your analytical product. It ensures that all the **networking**, **security**, **policies**, and other basic infrastructure are set up based on best practice guidance provided by Microsoft so that you just have to bring your data, code, and expertise and start building your product.

The logical Azure landing zone translates to an Azure subscription, as shown in *Figure 3.1*:

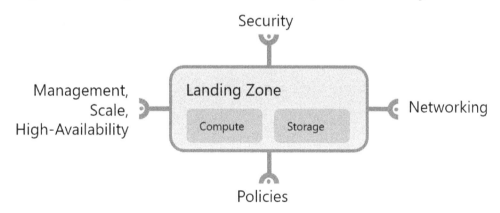

Figure 3.1 – Landing zone

An **Azure subscription** is a logical grouping of cloud resources that are managed together. A subscription also serves as a billing entity to separate the costs incurred by the included resources. To further group resources into smaller buckets, Azure has the concept of **resource groups**. For example, within a subscription, all the storage accounts could be grouped into one resource group because they have similar maintenance cycles and management needs. Sometimes, all the resources of a small project, irrespective of the type of resource, can be grouped into a resource group.

For more details on Azure landing zones, refer to `https://learn.microsoft.com/en-us/azure/cloud-adoption-framework/ready/landing-zone/`.

CSA derives from the CAF and Azure landing zones to create the data mesh landing zones. There are two landing zone definitions and templates provided by CSA to help you build your data mesh – data management landing zone and data landing zone.

Considering that the data mesh is a decentralized architecture, it is very critical to ensure that these landing zones are organized in a way that promotes the efficiency of management. Before we dive into the data mesh landing zones in depth, in the next section, we'll discuss more about how we organize these landing zones to implement consistent governance and operations.

Organizing resources

Microsoft Azure provides management levels to manage your cloud resources. These logical structures allow you to organize your resources in a hierarchy that matches your business organization and further provides an inheritance of the policies that you apply to them. *Figure 3.2* shows the hierarchy of management groups, subscriptions, resource groups, and, finally, the resources:

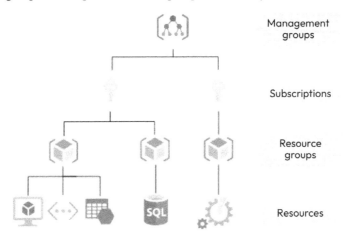

Figure 3.2 – Azure management levels

Let's understand the purpose of each of these entities in the hierarchy:

- **Management groups**: These are the highest level of management under the Azure tenant. They help you manage the access, policy, and compliance for all the subscriptions grouped under one management group.

- **Subscription**: A subscription groups a set of resources and associates a set of users to them. Subscriptions also have some quotas and limits to prevent over-use and manage costs.

- **Resource groups**: Resource groups are logical containers that group a set of resources that need to be managed together. If your subscription has only one web application project and one analytics project, you can group all the resources used by the web application into one resource group and all the data analytics project resources into another. This approach ensures that deleting the web application resource group won't affect the analytics application resources. Similarly, any policies applied to the analytics project resource group will apply to all the resources under the analytics application and not impact the web application.

- **Resources**: This is an instance of any of Azure's **Platform-as-a-Service (PaaS)** or **Infrastructure-as-a-Service (IaaS)** resources. This includes virtual machines, storage accounts, Azure Data Factory, Cosmos DB, and many others.

Now that we understand the hierarchy of an Azure cloud tenant, let's use these to build a cloud architecture that will map to the structure of an organization or an enterprise.

Designing a cloud management structure

As mentioned in the previous section, the **Azure management structure** should align with your business structure of how your divisions are internally organized and how you wish to percolate the policies down to each of these divisions. For example, almost all companies have a central **information technology (IT)** team that manages the global infrastructure of the company. This includes networks, firewalls, and identity. Most companies also have customer relationship management and enterprise resources planning systems such as SAP that need teams and management of their own. Other corporate systems are managed by different business teams.

Each of these divisions or teams needs different policies that typically do not overlap. For example, you won't want an employee from the sales division to manage the networks. Employees from the IT team have no reason to query the sales data. The life cycles of these infrastructure pieces and the corporate systems also differ from each other.

In conclusion, any given set of resources that you wish to separate at the policy level should be grouped under a separate management group. *Figure 3.3* shows an example of a typical hierarchy of management groups and subscriptions managed by an enterprise:

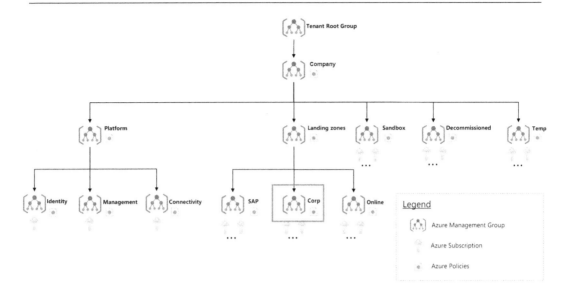

Figure 3.3 – Example of an Azure management architecture

Creating the structure of the management groups will involve important stakeholders from across the company. It is an important step toward optimizing infrastructure management across the company and is an important part of the CAF and CSA.

One of the core benefits of setting up this management group hierarchy is the ease of setting up policies. Let's understand how policies work and get inherited across this structure.

Hierarchical policies

Azure policies are rules defined in a JSON format file. These policies can be created using the **Azure portal**, **Azure PowerShell**, or **Azure Command-Line Interface** (`https://learn.microsoft.com/en-us/azure/governance/policy/overview`). These rules are then compared to the properties of resources to detect policy violations. This ensures that policies around networking and security can be applied uniformly across all resources to ensure the safety of the network and data. For example, there could be a company policy to ensure that all network traffic inside the company flows through **Azure Firewall** or a policy of white-listed IP addresses.

These policies should never change across the organization. However, manually applying these policies to every resource can be a time-consuming and error-prone task. This is where the management and subscription hierarchy described in the previous section helps.

Each management group inherits policies from its parent. Policies applied to one management group are applied to all the child management groups under it automatically. Any changes made to policies at one level trickle down to all child management groups, subscriptions, and eventually Azure resources.

Let's look at an example of a top-level policy. The company wants to restrict the Azure data center regions where their VMs can be created. There is a list of regions where a team or individual in the company should be allowed to create resources. All other regions are not permitted. Let's say these regions are East Japan, East US, and East Australia. The following code snippet shows a sample policy JSON definition to create such a rule:

```
1     az policy assignment create --scope \
2          "/providers/Microsoft.Management/managementGroups/
MyManagementGroup" \
3              --policy {PolicyName} -p "{ \"allowedLocations\": \
4                  { \"value\": [ \"australiaeast\", \"eastus\",
\"japaneast\" ] } }"
```

Valid scopes are management group, subscription, resource group, and resource:

- **Management group**: `/providers/Microsoft.Management/managementGroups/MyManagementGroup`

- **Subscription**: `/subscriptions/0b1f6471-1bf0-4dda-aec3-111122223333`

- **Resource group**: `/subscriptions/0b1f6471-1bf0-4dda-aec3-111122223333/resourceGroups/myGroup`

- **Resource**: `/subscriptions/0b1f6471-1bf0-4dda-aec3-111122223333/resourceGroups/myGroup/providers/Microsoft.Compute/virtualMachines/myVM`

For more details on Azure policies, refer to the Azure Policy documentation here: `https://learn.microsoft.com/en-us/azure/governance/policy/`.

Defining policies while starting at the highest level of the management groups is important as it reduces your efforts to manage the entire data mesh and also eliminates chances of error.

Once the policies have been defined at all levels of the management group hierarchy, we can start arranging the subscriptions. In the next section, we will learn how to create the subscriptions defined under CSA. This will help us build the data mesh.

Diving deeper into landing zones in CSA

CSA translates the data mesh concept to Microsoft Azure constructs. You must follow the design principles of these landing zones to ensure that there is no mismatch between what you wish to achieve through the data mesh and actual implementation.

CSA proposes two types of landing zones:

- Data management landing zone

- Data landing zone

The data management landing zone is central to CSA and the data mesh architecture. It is responsible for the governance of the analytical platform. The data landing zone hosts one or multiple data products. All the data landing zones are connected to the data management landing zone. It contains all the Azure services required to implement these data products. Each data landing zone could also be optionally connected to other data landing zones if they are sharing or receiving data from other data landing zones.

Depending on the complexity of your analytical requirements and how analytical work is being performed across your organization, you can choose to have one or more data landing zones. *Figure 3.4* shows a simple data mesh architecture with one data landing zone and one data management zone:

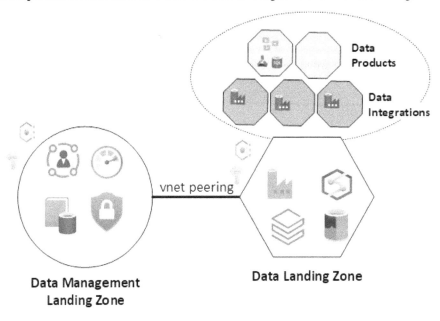

Figure 3.4 – A single data landing zone connected to the data management zone

If your organization has multiple projects under many departments with multiple teams, you can use a complex data mesh with multiple inter-connected data landing zones all connected to one data management zone to support the complexity and size of your organization:

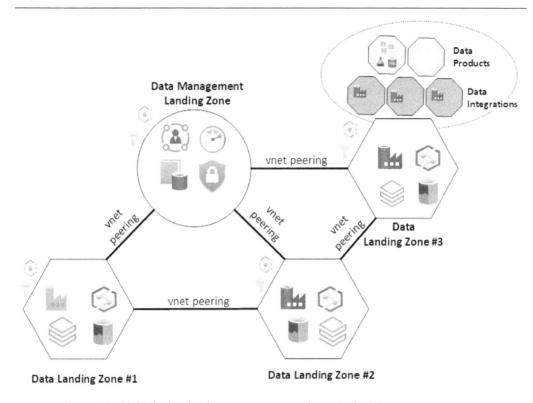

Figure 3.5 – Multiple data landing zones connected to a single data management zone

This interconnected network of data landing zones managed by a central data management landing zone will be your data mesh.

Let's dive a little deeper into what these landing zones are made of and what function they play in the data mesh.

Data management landing zone

The data management landing zone, also referred to as the **data management zone** (**DMZ**) is a separate subscription that is in conformation with the Azure landing zone standards. It serves the following purposes:

- Manages the networking for all the connected data landing zones
- Stores diagnostics data and monitors all the resources across the data landing zones
- Automates the deployment and management of all the landing zones
- Maintains common ingestion pipelines

- Maintains a common registry of virtual machine images

- Manages and maintains all the data governance components

The DMZ components depicted here are some of the common components that most organizations need and deploy. Some may not apply to your organization or some additional components may need to be added that are missing in this definition of a DMZ. The bottom line is that any common management component or any service that can serve all the data landing zones can be made part of this DMZ. *Figure 3.6* shows a block model of a DMZ:

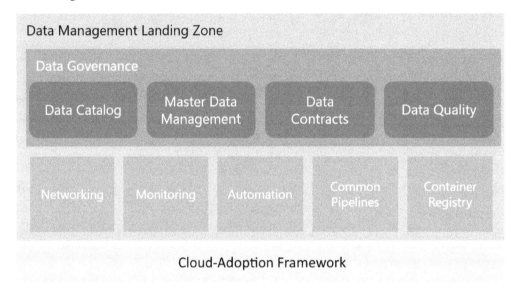

Figure 3.6 – Data management landing zone

The preceding block diagram, when translated into an Azure landing zone, will be a subscription with all the Azure resources required to complete the services networked together, as per the CAF guidelines. This can be seen in *Figure 3.7*:

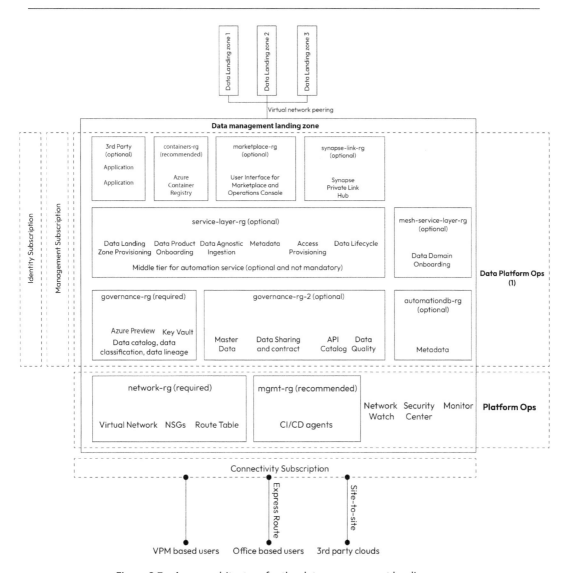

Figure 3.7 – Azure architecture for the data management landing zone

Observe that all the resources are bundled into boxes with a -rg prefix. These are Azure resource groups. As we saw in the *Organizing resources* section, resource groups are the third level of the Azure management structure under subscriptions. Resource groups have to manage resources that have a common maintenance cycle and need common access and policies under a subscription. Let's walk through the contents of some of the important resource groups in the DMZ architecture:

- **Network-rg**: This resource group clubs all the virtual networks that are needed to connect all the landing zones. The **network security groups** (**NSGs**) define traffic flow security rules between various Azure resources. The routing tables define how traffic flows between Azure, private networks, and internet resources.

- **Governance-rg**: This hosts the data governance components, such as **Purview**. If you are using a different data catalog software, then that will go into this resource group.

- **Mgmt-rg**: This resource group contains all the CI/CD Azure DevOps agents to be used for all the DevOps needed to automate the infrastructure's maintenance and deployment. Automation is a very important part of managing and maintaining a data mesh and will be discussed later in this chapter.

- **Container-rg**: A common container registry for all the standardized virtual machine and compute instance images can be maintained here.

Now, let's look at the structure of a data landing zone.

Data landing zone

Data landing zones are one or more subscriptions created to house one or more data products. They have the following functions:

- They host all the data products belonging to an organization of business domain

- They connect to the data management landing zone and help centralize the monitoring and governance data to the data management landing zone

- They group all the resources into resource groups for efficient management

- They provide common functionality required by all the products

- They host the local network and monitoring requirements (optional)

Figure 3.8 shows the block structure of a data landing zone:

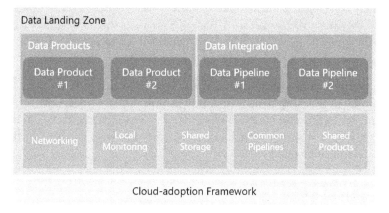

Figure 3.8 – Data landing zone

The preceding data landing zone block diagram (*Figure 3.7*) could be translated into an Azure landing zone architecture that might look like what's shown in *Figure 3.8*. This is an example of what a data landing zone could be like. In practice, it will contain services that are used by the individual data products or a set of services that have been approved by the enterprise:

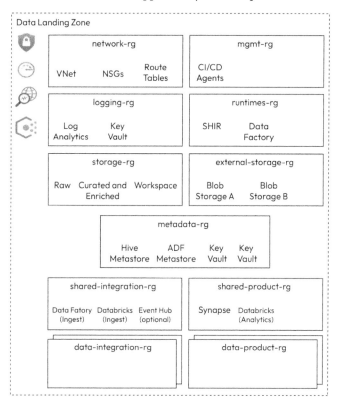

Figure 3.9 – Azure architecture for data landing zones

All data landing zones must be connected to the data management landing zone through VNet peering. The landing zone itself can be organized in many ways, depending on the number of data products and how they work with each other. Typically, products should be grouped into resource groups based on the products they belong to. There could be some resource groups that house the common or shared resources.

A data mesh architecture built using CSA is designed for scale. If each department gets a landing zone, you will soon have a lot of landing zones to manage. In large organizations, different teams across the globe can demand the creation of new landing zones to host their products. For the central IT team, it can become quite a challenge to maintain consistency and ensure that all the landing zones are being monitored and maintained.

In the next section, we will discuss the importance of templates and automation in building a data mesh architecture and how it helps make deployment and management easier.

Automating landing zone deployment

Decentralizing your data and analytics will mean multiple data landing zones. In large enterprises and global companies, this can mean many landing zones. Multiple groups and organizations will request a separate landing zone for their analytics projects. So, while data and analytics are being democratized, management of these disparate landing zones is becoming complex and challenging. Hence, it's critical to the success of a data mesh to automate the creation and management of these landing zones as much as possible.

This need for automating the deployment and management of infrastructure is common across any large cloud setup. Hence, Azure has many tools to help customers automate their cloud deployments. The collective term for this set of technologies is called **Infrastructure as Code (IaC)**.

IaC

The easiest and fastest way to create and manage infrastructure on the Azure cloud is through the Azure portal. It's a quick, user-friendly way to create Azure resources. However, if you have to create many resources every other day and modify resources based on some requirement changes, it can be very slow, cumbersome, and error-prone.

To automate the creation of Azure resources, Microsoft Azure provides a tool called **Azure Resource Manager (ARM)**. ARM is used by Microsoft Azure to create all the resources in the Azure cloud. The ARM has a JSON format template for every resource. The ARM template JSON defines the resource to be deployed. The ARM file contains the following:

- Parameters that can be substituted with different values and allow reuse of one template
- Variables containing values that can be reused within the template
- User-defined functions that can simplify and standardize your template

- Resources that you wish to deploy
- Output that's returned from the deployment of the resources

Deploying a single landing zone can involve a lot of resources. These will include multiple networking resources, storage resources, and other Azure services, as requested by the project team. This can make the ARM template very complex and long. To solve this problem, you can employ two techniques:

- Modularize the ARM templates into smaller pieces and link or nest them into each other
- Use parameters to define values that can be changed

This technique enables the reuse of these templates when similar resources are to be created in another landing zone. The following code snippet shows a sample of an ARM template for deploying a subscription.

Creating modular templates also helps maintain consistency while deploying different landing zones, especially the consistency of the core infrastructure requirements around networking, security, and policies. In *Chapter 6*, we will see how we can maintain these templates in a code repository, version them, and automate their maintenance and deployment through DevOps pipelines:

```
1"resources": [
2  {
3    "scope": "/",
4    "type": "Microsoft.Subscription/aliases",
5    "apiVersion": "2020-09-01",
6    "name": "[parameters('subscriptionAlias')]",
7    "properties": {
8    "workload": "[parameters('subscriptionWorkload')]",
9    "displayName": "[parameters('subscriptionDisplayName')]",
10    "billingScope": "[tenantResourceId('Microsoft.Billing/
billingAccounts/enrollmentAccounts',
11    parameters('billingAccount'), parameters('enrollmentAccount'))]"
12    }
13  }
14]
```

The parameters in the preceding code are stored in a separate file called the `parameters` file, as shown in the following code snippet. Parameter files help make the ARM templates more generalized and reusable:

```
1{
2  "$schema": "https://schema.management.azure.com/schemas/
3        2019-04-01/deploymentParameters.json#",
4  "contentVersion": "1.0.0.0",
5  "parameters": {
```

```
 6    "subscriptionWorkload": {
 7        "value": "Production"
 8    },
 9    "subscriptionDisplayName": {
10        "value": "salesanalyticslz"
11    },
12    "subscriptionAlias": {
13        "value": "salesfdomain"
14    },
15    "billingAccount": {
16        "value": "12345678-1234-1234-1234-123456789012"
17    },
18    "enrollmentAccount": {
19        "value": "12345678"
20    }
21  }
22}
```

A reference for Azure ARM templates for the DMZ and the data landing zone can be found at `https://github.com/Azure/data-product-analytics`.

Depending on how you plan your data mesh topology, the landing zones can also become quite complex, with multiple projects inside them. Multiple teams might be working on the same landing zone. In the next section, we will look at the best practices for organizing resources inside a landing zone.

Organizing resources in a landing zone

A landing zone is typically a subscription that needs to be governed by a common policy. However, creating one landing zone for every project in the company could lead to too many landing zones to manage. Hence, companies typically choose to make landing zones based on a business domain such as sales, marketing, finance, or HR or based on business zones such as North America, South America, Europe, and Asia. Then, within each landing zone, they allow multiple teams to create and manage their analytical projects.

Hence, inside a landing zone, the company needs to manage the resources efficiently in a way that each team is given access to only their resources. There might be some shared resources that might need separate management and common access to all.

This project level and shared resources management inside a subscription can be achieved through resource groups, as shown in *Figure 3.10*:

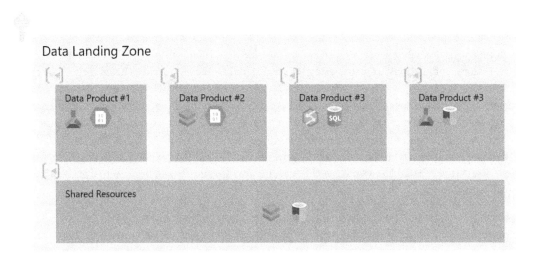

Figure 3.10 – Data landing zone resource groups

All the resources belonging to a product are added to a resource group created for that data product. These resources are the ones that are needed by the team and only the data product team may have access to these products. If, for any reason, the project ends, the IT team can simply delete the resource group and all the resources will be deleted. Any custom backup and maintenance policies can also be applied to these individual resource groups.

Depending on how you organize your landing zones, there could be some shared resources. For example, if you organized your data landing zones by departments, such as sales, marketing, and finance, there is a very high probability that these departments would have some shared data. Such data can be shared in an Azure data lake with granular access control; the data lake itself should be created in a shared resource group. Similarly, some departments might have a shared team of data scientists or data engineers working on common machine learning and data engineering solutions. The Databricks workspace for these common team members can also be added to the shared resource group. The shared resource group will have common life cycle policies and will ensure that shared data and shared resources are maintained separately and protected from accidental deletions.

So far, we have learned about the building blocks of a data mesh, known as landing zones, and how to structure them. The key concept of a data mesh is to link these landing zones together. That is what makes it a mesh. Depending on how to divide your landing zones, there can be multiple ways of linking them together using peer-to-peer networks. In the next section, we'll look at a few topologies that can be deployed to link these landing zones to create a data mesh.

Networking topologies

In a decentralized data environment, data can only be shared by linking the decentralized zones together. These connections are made using **Azure Virtual Network peering** (`https://learn.microsoft.com/en-us/azure/virtual-network/virtual-network-peering-overview`). The advantage of using Azure Virtual Network peering is that the latency of exchanging data between networked peers is the same as the latency of resources exchanging data within the private network. So, users from two different landing zones that are peered over an Azure Virtual Network see no difference in the speed of data transfer, so long as the two networks are in the same region. The Azure Virtual Network uses the high bandwidth Azure backbone network to connect the two peered zones.

The traffic between these peered networks is managed using forwarding rules that are configured when peering is enabled. These rules define how traffic is allowed to move between the two peered networks. For details on the options available, refer to `https://learn.microsoft.com/en-us/azure/virtual-network/virtual-network-manage-peering`. *Figure 3.11* shows a high-level block diagram of how landing zones are peered:

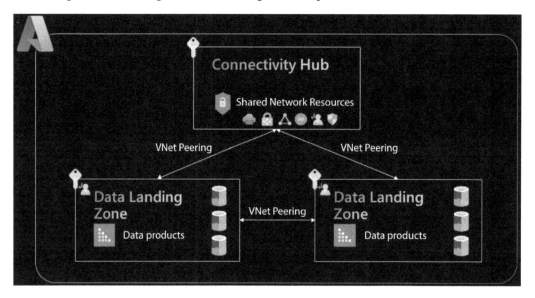

Figure 3.11 – Single-region connectivity

Every data mesh architecture must have a connectivity hub. Ideally, the connectivity hub can be inside the DMZ. However, many large enterprises deploy a third-party network management system. These systems manage the virtual networks, global connectivity, and IP ranges for enterprises. In such situations, the connectivity hub could be outside the DMZ.

For a medium- or small-sized organization, the networks are typically contained in a single Azure region.

Local VNet peering is employed to connect the connectivity hub (DMZ) to all the data landing zones. Each data landing zone is connected to other data landing zones based on the connectivity requirements.

For global organizations, this connectivity could span across Azure global regions. In such situations, regional landing zones can be locally peered and the landing zones across regions should be paired using global VNet peering. This ensures that even though the network traffic is crossing geographic regions, it's still routed via the **Azure backbone network** (`https://azure.microsoft.com/en-us/explore/global-infrastructure/global-network`):

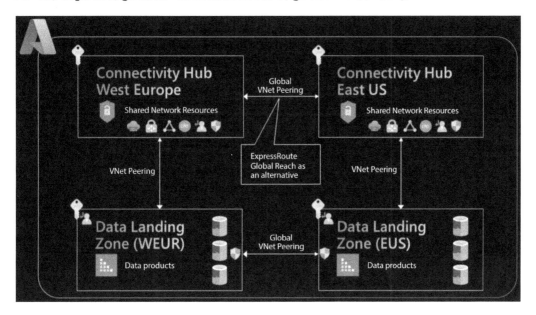

Figure 3.12 – Cross-region connectivity

This was a high-level description of how you should network the data mesh together. The networking setup will require setting up many inter-connected elements, such as **routing tables**, **gateways for on-premises connectivity**, **network address translation** (**NAT**) for outbound connectivity, and others. However, these are beyond the scope of this book. For more details on the Azure networking services, refer to `https://learn.microsoft.com/en-us/azure/networking/fundamentals/networking-overview`.

After connecting the various landing zones into a mesh, the next important aspect of a data mesh is security and access control. How do you ensure that these connected landing zones are accessing each other's data securely? We'll discuss this in more detail in the next section.

Security and access control

Once the various landing zones are all connected in a mesh, the next most critical element of a data mesh architecture is managing access and security.

There are two main layers to security and access control:

- **Authentication**
- **Authorization**

Authentication verifies the identity of a user (username and password) to provide or deny access to a given Azure service or resource. Authorization determines what the authenticated user can do with the resource, as well as the operations they are allowed to perform.

To implement standardized authentication and authorization across your data mesh, we need an identity provider. While multiple solutions or tools might be available to implement identity management, the best practice is to employ a single identity provider. The most popular authentication provider on Azure is **Azure Active Directory**. In August 2023, Microsoft renamed the Active Directory service to **Microsoft Entra ID** (`https://learn.microsoft.com/en-us/entra/fundamentals/new-name`). Microsoft is in the process of updating its documentation to replace Azure Active Directory with Microsoft Entra ID. Since this book was written during this name transition, Azure Active Directory will be used to refer to Microsoft Entra ID.

Azure Active Directory is a cloud-based identity and access management system that maintains a database of all resources and identities and helps the organization define the access policies for who should have access to which resource.

As shown in *Figure 3.13*, Azure Active Directory sits on top of the Azure architecture, even above the management groups, and hence it's pervasive throughout the entire cloud environment of the organization:

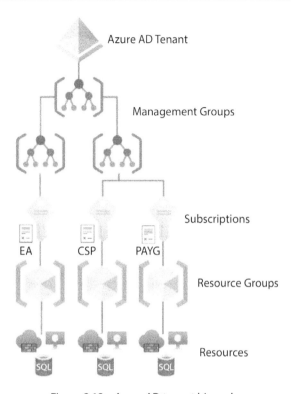

EA   CSP   PAYG

Azure AD Tenant

Management Groups

Subscriptions

Resource Groups

Resources

Figure 3.13 – Azure AD tenant hierarchy

We will dive deeper into how to design a secure data mesh in *Chapter 5*.

So far, we've focused on the physical building blocks of a data mesh, such as subscriptions, networking, and security. However, managing every block independently can be a very tedious and error-prone process. Any enterprise or company needs to automate these blocks into a streamlined process pipeline to make it repeatable and automated. In the next section, we will understand how DevOps helps put these blocks together to automate the deployment and management process of a data mesh.

Streamlining deployment through DevOps

Creating individual landing zones, networking them together, applying policies and security, and repeating this process for every landing zone can be a tedious and time-consuming process. Once the data mesh has been deployed, maintaining it by applying changes and fixes and tracking those changes can add another level of complexity.

DevOps is a set of tools and processes that help automate IT operations. If implemented early, they can help streamline the deployment and maintenance of a data mesh.

Let's define some key components of DevOps and understand how they are used to automate the data mesh deployment and maintenance:

- **Repo**: A repo (or repository) is a version control system that stores and tracks the artifacts of a process. These include ARM templates, JSON files, and code scripts. Azure supports two types of repos – Git repos and Azure DevOps repos (**Team Foundation Version Control (TFVC)**). Git is the default repo and is also the most popularly used. TFVC is a fully functional version control system compared to Git, so Microsoft's future investments are targeted toward Git.

- **Organization**: An Azure DevOps organization is a collection of related projects. An enterprise can create multiple organizations to group relevant projects together.

- **Project**: A project is like a workspace designed for the project team to collaborate on the project. It is connected to the repos, pipelines, plans, boards, and other components that constitute a project.

  Figure 3.14 shows the nested projects inside an organization's repo:

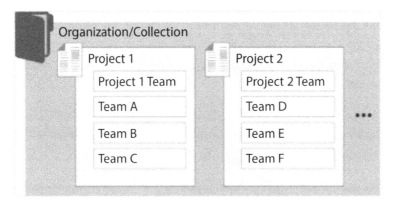

Figure 3.14 – Azure DevOps organization and projects

- **Pipeline**: A pipeline starts with a connection to the repo for the artifacts. It consists of the stages the pipeline is going to move through. In most cases, these are the dev, test, and production stages. However, depending on the individual process of each organization, it could be different. Some organizations go directly from dev to prod, while others might have more granular stages.

- **Tasks and scripts**: Tasks and scripts are steps that are taken to complete a stage.

  Figure 3.15 shows the relationship between pipelines, stages, steps, and agents running the scripts and tasks as jobs:

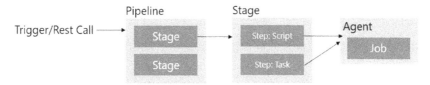

Figure 3.15 – Azure DevOps pipeline structure

- **Agents**: Agents are the runtime engine for DevOps. The tasks and scripts are submitted to an agent, who executes them. It's the computing infrastructure that executes the tasks and scripts as jobs. You have the choice to use the Microsoft-hosted agents if you want Microsoft to manage them or create self-hosted agents if you wish to control the configuration of these agents.

Once you've created the ARM templates and the necessary standardized scripts and bundled them into a DevOps pipeline, the pipelines can be triggered from an application or an automation script, depending on how you enable teams in the organization to request landing zones.

In *Chapter 6*, we will dive deeper into how to create these pipelines and how to trigger them.

Summary

In this chapter, we learned about the various components of the Azure cloud that map to data mesh concepts, broadly called landing zones. We learned about their functionality and how to organize them. Finally, we automated the deployment of these landing zones to ensure that managing a data mesh becomes more manageable through automation and reuse.

In the next chapter, we will learn how to govern and manage a data mesh using Microsoft services in combination with building a governance framework.

4

Building a Data Mesh Governance Framework Using Microsoft Azure Services

Distributed data and **federated governance** are key concepts of the **data mesh**. Data is dispersed across various domains or teams, allowing for scalability and agility. Federated governance ensures that each domain retains autonomy over its data while adhering to common principles and standards, driving collaboration and trust among the data product owners.

In the previous chapters, we looked at how to create a distributed network of **data landing zones** managed by a central **data management zone**. We saw how the data landing zone can be designed and built. As the mesh grows and more landing zones get added, the complexity of managing and maintaining these landing zones can grow exponentially. Having a solid, well-planned governance framework from the beginning will drastically reduce this management effort.

In this chapter, we will dive deeper into the governing aspects of the data mesh. We will cover both governance infrastructure and data governance.

In this chapter, we're going to cover the following main topics:

- Data mesh governance requirements
- Data catalog
- Metadata management
- Data quality
- Data observability

Data mesh governance requirements

One of the primary ideas behind a data mesh architecture is the concept of **data products**. Teams working on these data products need to be able to find good quality data, curate it, process it, and make the output available to anybody who can benefit from it and is authorized to use it. Similar to a software product, the team is also responsible for providing a **service-level agreement** (**SLA**) on their output so that the consumers of the data product know how reliable the output is.

For the various teams working on a data mesh to be able to work efficiently, we need good, streamlined governance of data and the underlying infrastructure.

Let's consider a sample workflow in a data mesh environment to understand the importance of governance.

A team of data scientists want to build a sales-forecast data product that applies a machine learning algorithm to enterprise sales data to provide a more accurate forecast. They are looking for good-quality sales data. In a world without data governance, they would have to first find the team that owns the enterprise sales data. Then, they would have to find a way to get access to it. They might have to seek permission from a higher manager. After they get permission to use the data, someone will have to grant them access. After jumping through all these hoops, they then inspect the data to see if it's the right data with the right quality. If not, then they have to go through the whole cycle again.

The preceding scenario can play out differently, depending on the size of the organization. In a small to medium-sized company, it might be easy for the data scientist to simply know who owns sales data and approach them for access, at which point they will either grant or deny it, depending on the company policy. But as the company grows, finding people and processes becomes more difficult. And a lot of time could get wasted in finding and getting access to quality data. This hinders the agility and speed of innovation for businesses to respond.

If we play out this workflow in a well-managed data mesh environment, it will start with a data catalog. The central data mesh governance function will have a data catalog that maintains a searchable metadata repository of all the data available across different data products. The data scientist would just log on to the enterprise data catalog that's stored as a part of data governance in the data management zone. At this point, they can search for the data they are looking for by typing in keywords such as `Sales` or `Sales FY22`.

If they have the required catalog access permissions, the relevant sales datasets will show up in their search results. They can see the structure of the data, look at the data contract, and see who the owner of the data is. Once they are satisfied with the dataset structure and its reliable source, they can initiate an access request from the catalog by clicking a button. This would trigger a workflow in the background, get the necessary approvals, and grant them access. Within minutes or hours, they will have access to the data they need and they can focus on building the ML model. If the data does not match the needs and quality, they can simply search for a different dataset in the data catalog.

There could be even more complex scenarios in regulated industries such as healthcare, **research and development (R&D)**, or pharma where portions of the data is extremely sensitive, and giving access to data might be more complex than just finding a dataset and getting access to it.

To catalog the data effectively and provide relevant access to the right users, we also need to classify the data. The company needs to understand the data they have and its level of sensitivity. Depending on the type of data in a dataset, the entire dataset can be classified as sensitive or non-sensitive. Certain industries and countries have regulations on how long a certain class of data can be stored before it should be destroyed. However, in some cases, data needs to be preserved for longer periods for auditing purposes. Hence, data classification becomes another important requirement of data mesh governance.

Data classification involves scanning the datasets, tables, and files and looking for patterns that can identify a certain data or field as a certain type. These could be dates, national identity numbers, credit card numbers, standardized patient record identifiers, birth dates, and many other such classes of information. Once such data types are classified in a dataset or a table, depending on the rules and policies of the organization, the entire dataset itself can be classified as highly sensitive, sensitive, or non-sensitive, depending on the labeling standards of the company.

Once the data has been discovered, it needs to be of good quality to be used meaningfully. Data catalogs will typically not show the actual data. They will only show you the structure/format, the owner, the lineage of its origin, and other such details. It's only after you get access to the data that will you be able to see the quality of the data. Maintaining quality data is also a big part of data governance. Cataloged data must be of a certain quality standard and anything that does not satisfy quality standards should be removed from the catalog.

Discovering quality data and getting access to it is just the beginning of building a good data product. The key principle of a data product is that it will be used by other data products or users. They may refer to it on a daily or weekly basis, depending on their requirements. And as a product, they expect certain guarantees of quality and availability of the data product. Inherently, this will depend on the quality and availability of the data that you have used to build the product. A mesh of such data products creates a lot of dependencies on each other. Any change to data availability, format, or structure can have a domino effect on downstream products. Some of these products could be business-critical and may not be able to afford downtime or low availability. Hence, the publisher of a data product or dataset must provide a contract for its quality and availability. These contracts need to be accessible to whoever is looking for data. These contracts also need to be maintained and updated from time to time.

The first contract is published when a new data product is launched. Subsequently, if there is any change to the frequency at which data is refreshed or a change to the format of fields or values, the contract must be updated immediately. The consuming product must also monitor the contract changes and ensure that their product is updated based on any changes to the contract.

It is evident that to run a data mesh that is agile, collaborative, and compliant with company and local policies, you will need data cataloging, data classification, data quality control, and data contract maintenance. In the following sections, we will dive deeper into each of these governance requirements and understand how to implement them.

Data catalog

A **data catalog** is a collection of metadata that contains information about all the data in the enterprise universe of data. This metadata contains a description of the data and its contents, owner, lineage, classification, and quality. It provides the ability to search this metadata repository so that users looking for data can find the data and check its validity, the source of data, and other attributes about the data that can help them understand its usefulness.

In short, a data catalog is an organized searchable inventory of the enterprise data. The data in the catalog is profiled, tagged, classified, and defined to help data consumers make informed decisions about using the data.

While this looks like a simple statement and solution, it can be extremely difficult and complex to implement as a custom solution. So, let's look at what goes into building a data catalog.

First, we need to list all the data sources and data repositories in the enterprise. This will include legacy systems, **enterprise resource planning** (**ERP**) and **customer relationship management** (**CRM**) systems such as Dynamics 365, SAP, or Salesforce, functional databases from **human resources** (**HR**), finance, and other departments (Oracle, MySQL, SQL Server, PostgreSQL, or other types), blob storage, NoSQL databases, data lakes, and analytical data stores such as data warehouses and delta lakes.

Once all the data sources and databases have been identified, you need to connect to these data sources using some kind of connector and read the data structures, schemas, and all the other data definitions that each source provides. Then, you must bring this information back to your data catalog and format it in a way that can be stored and indexed for a search. This process is called **scanning**.

The problem can become even more complex if we want to classify the contents of the data source. The scanning process will also need to sample the data columns, run some regular expressions on them to recognize the format of the data, and conclude a classification for each column of data.

As you can see, building a data catalog on your own can be a daunting task. Hence, a product or a service such as **Microsoft Purview** will simplify most of the heavy lifting and allow you to focus on building a catalog.

Microsoft Purview provides a unified data governance solution to help manage and govern your on-premises, multi-cloud, and **Software-as-a-Service** (**SaaS**) data. *Figure 4.1* shows a high-level block of Microsoft Purview's components:

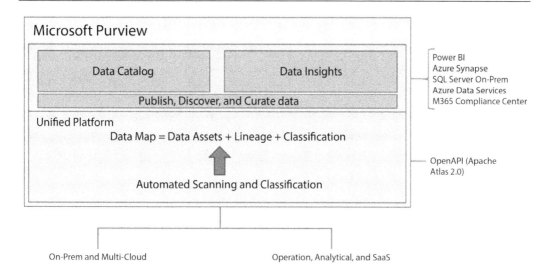

Figure 4.1 – Microsoft Purview components

Let's briefly go through each of these components to understand how Microsoft Purview works.

Data sources

At the bottom of *Figure 4.1*, you will see the data sources that Microsoft Purview can scan. These are broadly categorized into on-premises and multi-cloud and operational, analytical, and SaaS. On-premises sources can be your legacy SQL Server or Oracle databases. Multi-cloud can be all your cloud sources across Azure, Amazon Web Services, and Google Cloud Platform. Operational databases can be your sales, HR, finance, and other databases used by different operational teams, including SAP. Analytical systems consist of your SQL data warehouses, Databricks databases, lakehouses, and other analytical storages. SaaS systems could include Salesforce, Tableau, Snowflake, and others.

Scanning and classification

Microsoft Purview provides connectors to 40+ data sources. It connects to these data sources and scans them for all the metadata that it can extract from the various schema and data definitions it can find on the data source. It also has an option for advanced scanning where it dives deeper into the data to extract more accurate intelligence about the data in terms of its storage pattern.

Data map

A **data map** is a hierarchy of data sources to be scanned using a certain capacity unit required to run the scan itself. A data map is the foundation of a **Purview catalog**. The scans can be scheduled on a daily, weekly, or monthly basis or triggered by changes to the data source. The data map scan ensures that all the metadata that's collected as part of the data map is kept up to date. A data map is the foundation of all the higher-level services that Microsoft Purview provides, such as the data catalog and insights.

Data catalog

The **data catalog** is a collection of metadata collected by the data map and stored in a searchable repository.

Data insights

Data insights are a collection of reports and dashboards generated by Microsoft Purview that show the health of the data estate. It visually represents data relating to how much of the data has been curated, tagged, owned, and classified. It shows the health of glossary items and governance gaps.

Unified experience

The data catalog and the data insights are surfaced to enterprise users in the form of a **search and insights user interface**. **Search** provides an internet search-like interface where users can search for keywords and the data catalog will bring back the results. This allows the users to filter the data based on certain filter fields. **Insights User Experience** is a dashboard that brings all the insights into one pane. Users can then click and drill down into the insights.

While Microsoft Purview has all the required components for you to build a data catalog, rolling out Microsoft Purview still needs a lot of organizational planning.

In the following subsections, we will look at the different steps and phases that you need to consider to successfully roll out a data catalog using Microsoft Purview.

Phase 1 – plan

Identify all the sources of data in the organization. Build a document that lists all these sources, along with information that answers questions such as, *Where is the data?* (on-premises or the cloud), *What is the type of this data?* (SQL database, data lake, Amazon S3), *Who owns the data?, and Who should have access to it?* Most importantly, document the access requirements, such as connection strings and authentication methods. Azure provides a service to securely store connection strings and secrets called **Azure Key Vault** (`https://azure.microsoft.com/en-us/products/key-vault/`). Consider creating a separate Azure Key Vault to store connection secrets.

Define the roles and responsibilities to govern and manage the data catalog. In *Chapter 2*, we had a section called *The analytics team*, where we described the need for a governance team. That is the team – as well as its roles – that you need to define further at this stage. Microsoft Purview has a set of pre-defined roles that allow you to perform a certain set of activities. So it's advised that you align with these Microsoft Purview roles. However, if need be, you can also design custom roles. Information about Microsoft Purview roles can be found here: `https://learn.microsoft.com/en-us/azure/purview/catalog-permissions#roles`.

Understand how Microsoft Purview billing works and make budgets for it. Get approvals from stakeholders if required.

Phase 2 – build

Deploy Microsoft Purview in the data management landing zone of your data mesh. Since Microsoft Purview will be governing all the data sources across your data mesh and also the source systems outside of the data mesh, the best centralized place to manage this is the data management landing zone.

One very important aspect of deploying Microsoft Purview is **networking**. Multiple components in Purview get accessed by users who need access to other systems. Hence, ensure that all the required **private networks** and **private endpoints** are deployed. For best practices on Microsoft Purview networking, please refer to `https://learn.microsoft.com/en-us/purview/concept-best-practices-network`:

Next, you must build the data map. A **data map** is the foundational component of the Microsoft Purview catalog. A data map is a logical representation of your organization's entire analytical and data landscape. It maps various data sources and stores them in a hierarchical organization. This hierarchical map allows Microsoft Purview to enable a lot of critical governance features, such as data classification, access control, metadata scans, and many others. Hence, it is very important to get the data map right.

Small companies limited to one location can design the data map as a collection of departments and teams, as shown in *Figure 4.2*. However, I still recommend adding a level for geo-location on top to accommodate for future expansion:

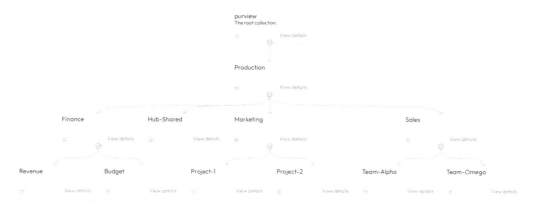

Figure 4.2 – Example of a data map for a small to medium-sized organization

Large global enterprises can add a layer of geography to their hierarchy, as shown in *Figure 4.3*. But these are just examples. You can create your own data map based on your organizational requirements and how various teams function. You could split the leaf nodes further into *raw* and *processed* zones, as an example. This will give more granular governance of these data zones:

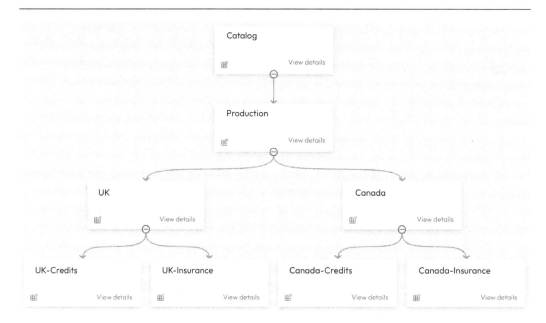

Figure 4.3 – Sample data map for a large global organization

Phase 3 – onboard

Once the data map has been finalized, it's time to onboard your first landing zone to the Microsoft Purview catalog. Start by deciding the collection where the landing zone's data sources must go to. Then, you can start creating the connections to these data sources.

Microsoft Purview provides more than 40+ connectors to various data sources. Once the connections are ready, run some initial scans and verify whether the assets are showing up in the catalog. Match the scanned and ingested numbers.

Once the initial scan tests have been verified, plan the schedule for each scan and finish onboarding all the data sources. In parallel, let the governance team start building the glossary and start labeling the data assets. This will require a virtual data governance team consisting of the central data governance team and members of the team that own the data source. The data source team knows the data and the central team knows the governance process. Together, they will build the labels and glossary for the data.

Phase 4 – repeat

Once the first landing zone has been onboarded, learn from that experience and fine-tune the scan rules, optimize the glossary and the classification, and start onboarding more landing zones.

After planning the data catalog, we need to be able to plan for the metadata that will drive the catalog.

Collecting and managing metadata

In the previous section, we looked at how data can be cataloged using Microsoft Purview. The built-in Microsoft Purview scanners scan and ingest basic technical metadata from data sources. This includes file types, column names, column types, and basic out-of-the-box classifications. However, this initial technical metadata is extracted from the data source purely based on the definitions available in the data source itself. Some data sources, such as **Microsoft SQL Server**, maintain significant amounts of data relating to the schema and its relationships. But others, such as CSV files stored in blob storage, do not have any information other than a column header. Hence, after the initial scan and ingest cycle, the governance team needs to get to work editing and enhancing the metadata to make the data assets more meaningful.

The real advantage of cataloging data and making it searchable is to make data more meaningful to the users. Users searching for data should be able to see how the data has been defined and classified. Sometimes, the column names of various tables are cryptic and difficult to understand and a tagged standardized business term should be able to explain what that column means. They should also be able to see the source of the data, the transformations that have been applied to it, and other such information to be able to decide whether the data is useful to them.

Let's look at the various steps of managing the metadata of the cataloged assets.

Step 1 – ensure accuracy and completeness

Look at the asset page and ensure that the information that's displayed is complete (*Figure 4.4*):

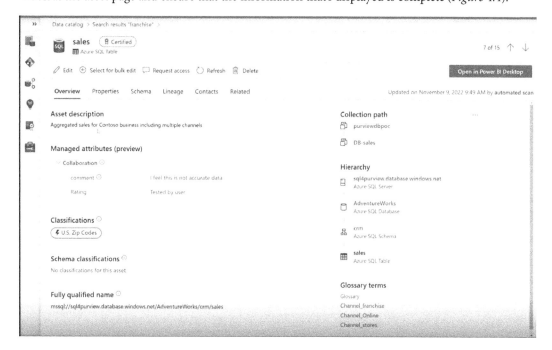

Figure 4.4 – Data asset information

If the asset page contains inaccuracies, then it needs to be edited and corrected. This can be done in two ways – you can edit the individual asset to make modifications or use the bulk-edit option to edit multiple assets. If you see a one-off discrepancy in the asset definition or a column definition, then you can fix this by editing the asset individually. But if you have a situation where a common column across multiple assets needs a custom definition, then you can use the bulk-edit option to apply the same column definition to all the associated assets at once. For more details on bulk editing, please refer to `https://learn.microsoft.com/en-us/azure/purview/how-to-bulk-edit-assets`.

Step 2 – verify data classification

Data classification is important for effective data governance. By classifying data based on sensitivity, criticality, and regulatory requirements, the company can establish clear guidelines on handling, access control, and compliance. Data classifications can be seen on the asset page. If you see something misclassified or if some column should have been classified and is not, then it's time to fine-tune the classification rules.

Microsoft Purview has over 200 built-in data classifiers. You can pick which rules to apply to a dataset at the time of creating the scans. Look at the scan ruleset you've selected. By default, all the rules will be selected. This can be an overkill. So, only pick those that apply. For example, if you know that the dataset contains US-based financial data, then there is no use in selecting the Canadian or Australian bank account number, as shown in *Figure 4.5*. For a complete list of supported classification rules, please refer to `https://learn.microsoft.com/en-us/purview/supported-classifications`:

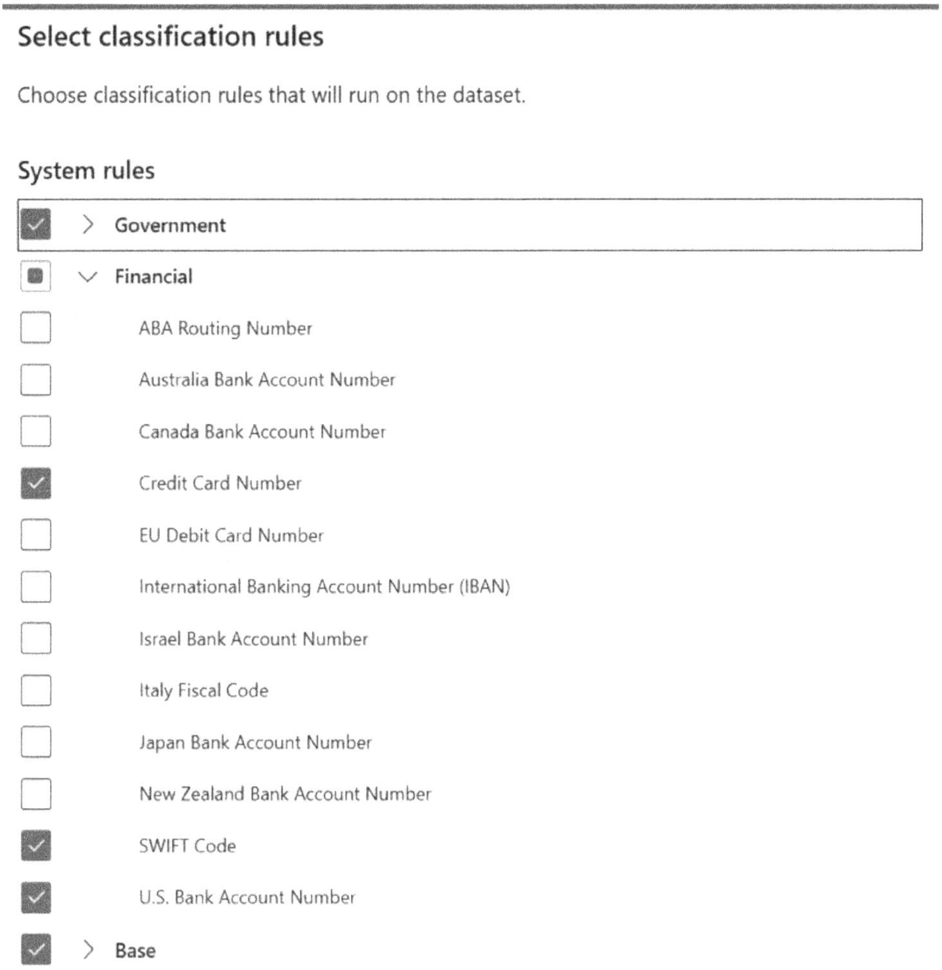

Select classification rules

Choose classification rules that will run on the dataset.

System rules

☑	>	Government
▣	⌄	Financial
☐		ABA Routing Number
☐		Australia Bank Account Number
☐		Canada Bank Account Number
☑		Credit Card Number
☐		EU Debit Card Number
☐		International Banking Account Number (IBAN)
☐		Israel Bank Account Number
☐		Italy Fiscal Code
☐		Japan Bank Account Number
☐		New Zealand Bank Account Number
☑		SWIFT Code
☑		U.S. Bank Account Number
☑	>	Base

Figure 4.5 – Selecting scan classification rules

If the data contains some fields that are specific to your company or industry that need to be classified, then you can create custom scan rules. To learn how to create custom classifications, go to `https://learn.microsoft.com/en-us/azure/purview/create-a-custom-classification-and-classification-rule#steps-to-create-a-custom-classification`.

Step 3 – add a business glossary

To further enhance the friendliness of the catalog and help employees and users understand the data better, the company must standardize a **business glossary**. This is a very important task for the governance team and should involve all relevant business stakeholders to build a good-quality standardized business glossary. Here are some tips on making an effective business glossary:

- Create a well-defined hierarchy of glossary terms that includes the business domain.

- Glossary terms in Microsoft Purview are case-sensitive. So, make sure you consider that and do not create duplicates.

- Always search the glossary term before creating a new one. Microsoft Purview provides a search glossary term feature.

- Use the business term approval workflow to ensure that new business terms are checked by a data governor before they are added to the repository. For details on how to enable an approval workflow, please refer to `https://learn.microsoft.com/en-us/azure/purview/how-to-workflow-business-terms-approval`.

Step 4 – add lineage information

Lineage is a part of catalog metadata that tracks the data over time. It shows where the data originated, and how it was transformed before it reached its final destination. Lineage is used by data engineers and data scientists to decide the quality and trust aspect of the data. It is also used for debugging data pipelines or data analytics. If a dashboard is showing incorrect information, then the data that's used to create the dashboard can be traced back to its origin and the team can investigate the reason. You can find the lineage of a data asset by navigating to the **Lineage** tab of the asset page, as shown in the following figure:

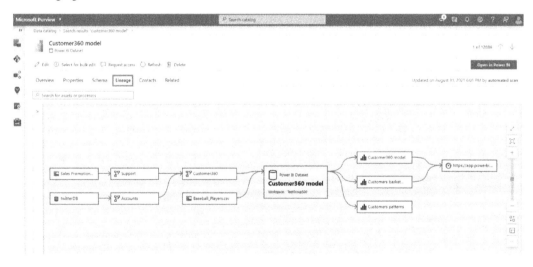

Figure 4.6 – Sample lineage in Microsoft Purview

Microsoft Purview extracts data lineage from a subset of data sources it supports. You can check out the Microsoft Purview documentation to see whether lineage information is supported or not. The list of supported data sources can be found here: `https://learn.microsoft.com/en-us/azure/purview/microsoft-purview-connector-overview#microsoft-purview-data-map-available-data-sources`.

If lineage extraction is not supported for a data source, you can manually define the lineage in Microsoft Purview using a friendly user interface. To learn how to manually define lineage, please refer to `https://learn.microsoft.com/en-us/azure/purview/catalog-lineage-user-guide#manual-lineage`.

Having a well-defined classification, glossary, and lineage will help the data users find the trusted data they are looking for faster. But once they find it, the next thing they will need to ensure is the quality of the data. In the next section, we'll understand what it takes to monitor and maintain the quality of the data in the data mesh.

Monitoring and managing data quality

The data mesh is all about converting analytics in data products, bringing the application development paradigm to data, and operationalizing data and analytics just like DevOps in the application world. One of the key aspects of application development is **quality assurance** (**QA**). The same principles will also apply to data products. Data products are designed to be consumed by other data products or end users. These data products and end users will rely on the quality and availability of this data. Bad data can have a domino effect in a data mesh, with multiple products failing to deliver because of the unacceptable quality of one dataset.

Data quality management is an important aspect of data governance. It is an involved process and begins with defining the data quality standards. To define data quality standards, a company can form its own standards through a cross-organization standards committee or borrow a framework from standard organizations such as ISO and others. Irrespective of what standards you choose, the first step is to identify the data quality dimensions. Various papers and articles define different numbers and types of dimensions across which data quality should be measured. The most common dimensions are as follows:

- **Completeness**: This is the minimum amount of data required to process the entity that the data represents. For entities such as a customer's address, a few optional address lines might be missing, but it may not stop an application from processing the data. The customer's name, email ID, city, and postal code might be enough information. Meanwhile, for another entity, such as a product or financial data, it might be necessary to have all the fields populated for downstream applications to process the data. Product details or financial numbers are not optional entries.

- **Accuracy**: The accuracy of data compares the data to a verifiable source. The verifiable source can be a third-party standard or some verified master data in the company itself.

- **Consistency**: This ensures that data, once presented, is consistent. It could be about consistency over a certain period, consistency concerning the source, or consistency in terms of a transaction across different tables. This is one of the difficult dimensions to measure.

- **Validity**: This is similar to accuracy but applies to other aspects of the data, such as the data format. Examples of this include postal codes that need to be in a certain format or date formats and their values.

- **Uniqueness**: This ensures that the data is present only once in a dataset or across datasets. With numbers, this is usually about the same ID and value combination; with names and strings, this can be challenging. Names of people could be written in short forms or initials and two different records might be the same people. Such records need to be detected and corrected or removed.

- **Timeliness**: This is about the difference between an event and the time the data is captured. In real-time and mission-critical systems, this can be a big factor.

There are other dimensions we can consider, such as precision, integrity, and others. These can be included if the business data demands these dimensions. It's a decision of the standards committee.

Once the data quality standards have been defined, it's time to implement them and ensure that data cataloged across the data mesh follows these quality standards. Data quality management can be implemented in one of the following ways:

- **Invest in a data quality tool**: Microsoft Purview has a data quality feature that is currently in a *private preview*. If you need a proven, tested data quality management product, you could also look at some Microsoft partner products, such as Profisee (https://profisee.com/), that integrate with Microsoft Purview.

- **Build your own data quality framework**: This can be a very involved and time-consuming project. Consider this solution only if you think your data quality requirements are unique. There are multiple open frameworks available to build data quality frameworks. One of the most popular data quality open frameworks is **Great Expectations** (https://greatexpectations.io/). Great Expectations allows you to build unit tests against your data, known as **expectations**. These tests are then executed against your transformed data to ensure that they meet expectations before you use them. This framework is also very useful for building data contracts.

Whatever the implementation method, having a solid data quality tool is critical to the efficiency of your data mesh.

With that, we have covered some of the important aspects of data governance. Other finer aspects also belong to data management, such as *data contracts* and *access management*, but we will cover those separately as larger topics.

In the next section, we'll look at data observability as a concept.

Implementing data observability

A data mesh is about converting data into a product and applying the application management and monitoring concepts to data. While application observability has evolved and matured over time, today, we have mature monitoring and observability tools and products. However, **data observability** is a relatively new concept since data as a product is a new concept. Data observability is the ability of an organization to know the health and performance of its data. It is a combination of all the governance aspects covered so far in this chapter and some monitoring. It is important to tie all these governance aspects into a monitoring system that will help maintain the health, performance, and quality of your data. *Figure 4.7* shows how the various monitoring aspects become a part of the data observability framework:

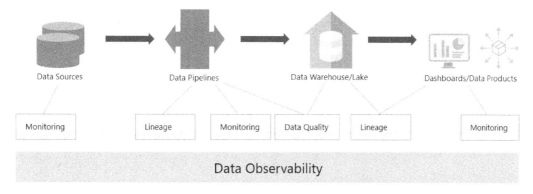

Figure 4.7 – Data observability

Some monitoring aspects can be automated. For example, data quality alerts can be triggered by running automated unit tests against data whenever it gets transformed or just before it gets consumed. Other monitoring aspects have to be manual, such as checking lineage accuracies or metadata accuracies.

The important difference between data observability and other governance aspects described in this chapter is that data observability should be able to find the root cause analysis in case of a situation where inconsistent or poor-quality data was supplied or consumed. Using lineage, you should be able to track the source and transformations that have been performed on the data. Using data quality alerts, you should be able to find the tests that have been executed on each transformation. Using monitors, you should be able to alert slow-running pipelines. Finally, by using combinations of these tools, you should be able to pinpoint what went wrong and fix it.

Data observability is not a one-time implementation and setup. It needs to be set up, modified, and improved over time. As you start investigating data quality and downtime issues, you will discover the need to fine-tune your data pipeline monitoring or your data quality expressions. The **cloud-scale analytics** (**CSA**) framework defines a maturity model that can be used as guidance on how data observability should mature over time. You can find this data observability maturity model here: https://learn.microsoft.com/en-us/azure/cloud-adoption-framework/scenarios/cloud-scale-analytics/manage-observability#data-observability-maturity-model.

Data is core to a data mesh and hence managing the data quality and standards is critical to a data mesh. Setting up a solid data governance framework will set you up for a successful data mesh implementation.

Summary

In this chapter, we covered all the important aspects of data mesh governance, starting from infrastructure to data. Governance is critical to a data mesh as federated governance is its key feature. Building a good governance framework from the beginning is critical to the success of a data mesh in an enterprise.

Another very important aspect of a data mesh is its **security architecture**. As the number of landing zones increases and more data products get added, more people start interacting with the data mesh. Security management becomes critical as the data mesh grows.

In the next chapter, we will dive deeper into the security architecture of the data mesh.

Security Architecture for Data Meshes

The big promise of **data meshes** is to decouple producers and consumers, create data products, and allow the producers and consumers to share and consume the output of a product however they want. In the era of centralized data analytics, access control was governed centrally and was more focused on the consumption of the data stored in a central data repository because the serving and consuming layers were one and the same. In the data mesh world, this concept needs to change. Data is owned by the data product team. They are responsible for managing access to it. Additionally, they know which data is sensitive and which is not. While data product owners decide the parameters for access to their data, some security standards need to be maintained based on the company's policies. In this chapter, we will look at how security principles apply to distributed data ownership.

In this chapter, we're going to cover the following main topics:

- Understanding the security requirements of data mesh architecture
- Understanding authentication and authorization in Azure
- Managing data access
- Managing data privacy

Understanding the security requirements of data mesh architecture

In a centralized analytics platform, data access and security are managed centrally. The business decides the policies of who should access data and what data should be private. IT departments implement these policies. This has been the traditional setup in most companies, and there is enough evidence that the business goals are not completely met by IT, resulting in a constant conflict between IT and business. The developers, data engineers, and data scientists get caught in the cross-fire. Enabling a new project is also difficult in such an environment, hindering innovation. Some companies solve this problem by merging a portion of the IT team and the business team under common management, creating concepts such as **business IT** or **shadow IT**. Data meshes take a different approach.

A data mesh splits the boundaries of the exchange of data into multiple data products. This provides a unique opportunity to partially distribute the responsibility of data security. Each data product team can be made responsible for how their data should be accessed and what privacy policies should be applied. But a federation of responsibilities can have its challenges. Hence, it's important to completely understand the security requirements of this distributed architecture. *Figure 5.1* shows how the various data protection elements span across security and privacy.

Figure 5.1 – Data protection

Let us investigate the security requirements in each layer:

- **Network security**: Data meshes have multiple data landing zones with multiple products. None of the resources used in these products should be exposed to the internet unless it's designed to be a public-facing service. In a data mesh environment, data moves from one product to another. The products must have access to each other, but only if they are authorized to do so. This means that connectivity should be allowed only between the resources of products that have been specifically allowed to communicate with each other.

  A data mesh is an architectural pattern implemented on top of a standardized enterprise cloud infrastructure. Hence, all the other security best practices that apply to an Azure cloud deployment under the **Cloud-Adoption Framework** and the **Azure Well-Architected** guide are also data mesh requirements.

- **Data access security**: Data access security is critical to a data mesh. Many data products will be dependent on other data products for their source data. These dependencies and exchanges are what make it a mesh. However, not everyone can have access to everything. This means every time the data of a data product are accessed, you need to first authenticate whether a user is a valid user in the enterprise system; secondly, you need to know if they are authorized to access the data.

  If a data product or data product team does not have access to the required data from another data product, then they need to request access. In a centralized analytics system, this request would go to the central IT team, and they, in turn, will decide if access should be granted based on predefined policies. However, in the case of a data mesh, the ownership of the data lies with the data product team. The request for access should go to an authorized person from the data product team.

We not only need strong access management; we also need an efficient way to request, grant, and deny access. This is critical to providing a nimble, agile environment for developers, engineers, and scientists to build data products faster.

- **Data privacy**: Data privacy is different from data security. Data security is about preventing unauthorized access to data and the policies and methods surrounding this access. It also protects the system from hackers and malicious users who could steal data. Data privacy, on the other hand, is about collecting, retaining, and recycling personal and sensitive data. There could be a few overlaps between security and privacy. Sometimes, you have sensitive data that needs to be provided to the user, but that also needs to be modified to protect its privacy requirements, for example, if a data engineer wants to see how many users have a certain type of credit card. This can be found by looking at the first two numbers of a credit card. However, the entire credit card number cannot be shown, as it's both a privacy and a security concern. In such cases, the remaining 12 digits of the credit card can be masked or obfuscated. So, certain requirements, such as data masking or obfuscation, can be considered both security and privacy requirements.

The data privacy requirements of a data mesh can vary greatly depending on the vertical business of the enterprise. A consumer goods company might have to worry about customer data, credit card numbers, and pricing as important information that must be safeguarded. A manufacturing company might have intellectual property, and the IoT data might be treated as sensitive data. A healthcare company's patient data, drug formulas, and a host of other information might be treated as sensitive. Above all, the local country laws such as the **General Data Protection Regulation** (**GDPR**) in Europe, the **California Consumer Privacy Act** (**CCPA**) in the USA, the **Digital Personal Data Protection Act** in India, and the **Personal Data Protection Act** (**PDPA**) in Singapore must be adhered to.

Almost every country has its own law for personal data protection and privacy; the ones that don't are in the process of creating one. There might also be industry regulations such as **Health Insurance Portability and Accountability** (**HIPAA**). Banks and financial institutions may have local regulations, such as the **European Union Financial Services regulation**, the **Reserve Bank of India** guidelines in India, or the **Australian Prudential Regulation Authority for Financial Services** (**ARPA**), that govern financial systems.

In summary, data privacy covers the following aspects:

- How is data classified so everyone understands the sensitivity of the data?
- How is data shared?
- For how long are data stored and archived, and when are they deleted?
- What are the regulatory restrictions, as per local data privacy laws?

When considering all these external and internal requirements governing data privacy, it is the owners of the data who represent the best team to decide the privacy requirements. In a data mesh, the data products are separated into resource groups and subscriptions, and these are assigned to different teams. With all the experience and expertise, it's easy for this team to document their requirements and build the data product with privacy baked in. These requirements can then be applied to their resource groups or subscriptions as policies.

Now that we have understood the high-level security and privacy requirements of a data mesh, let's discuss the implementation of these requirements with Microsoft Azure.

Understanding authentication and authorization in Azure

Authentication means validating a user by using credentials to ensure that they are a valid user on the enterprise system. **Authorization** validates their rights to access a particular resource or perform certain operations on it.

There are various methods of authentication, starting with simple usernames and passwords to more sophisticated authentication mechanisms such as token-based, multi-factor, certificate-based, and other security techniques. A username and password represent the simplest and most insecure way of authenticating users. For more secure methods of authentication, there are various frameworks and platforms available, and these are called providers. While there are many authentication providers available that can be used on the Azure cloud, the best practice is to use only one provider for the entire enterprise. The enterprise-class authentication provider in Azure is **Microsoft Entra ID** — referred as Azure Active Directory throughout the book (`https://learn.microsoft.com/en-us/entra/identity/`).

Microsoft Entra ID is Azure's identity provider; it helps with managing access to internal and external resources. Let's dive deeper into the authentication and authorization requirements of a data mesh and how **Azure Active Directory** can be used to implement it.

In a data mesh, there can be multiple types of access requirements:

- Data engineers and data scientists accessing data to perform exploratory analysis
- Data pipelines or automated jobs that move and transform data from a source to a target
- A data product reading the output of another data product

The first requirement can be simply implemented by giving users with valid Active Directory IDs access to certain resources in a data product. The second and third requirements are applications for trying to access the resources of a data product. In Azure Active Directory, this can be implemented in two ways:

- **Service principal**: A service principal is the identity of an application in an Active Directory. You can create and register a service principal using the **Azure portal**, **Azure Command-Line Interface (CLI)**, or **Azure PowerShell** (`https://learn.microsoft.com/en-us/azure/active-directory/develop/howto-create-service-principal-portal`). Once registered, it will create a service principal with an application ID, object ID, and an authentication key. You can then use the application ID and authentication key to add this service principal to a resource group or a resource and assign a role or a policy to it that decides what kind of access the service principal has.

As a best practice, the authentication key or the certificate should also be stored in an **Azure Key Vault** so that they do not have to be hardcoded. The service can access the key vault and retrieve the key when required (`https://learn.microsoft.com/en-us/azure/key-vault/general/authentication`).

Service principals are very important to enterprise access management and security. They abstract access away from developers and engineers. This is important because if any developers or engineers leave the company or change roles, the pipelines still need to be executed securely. If they use a service principal, then they will continue running independently of the team changes.

Service principals use a secret key or a certificate for authentication. One of the challenges of maintaining service principals is the secure storage of these keys, and the keys need to be recycled from time to time to improve security. Storing and recycling keys and certificates can be a management overhead. This problem is solved by managed identity.

- **Managed identity**: Managed identity is a built-in service principal identity managed by Azure. This means that as a developer, you don't have to manage the secrets and certificates associated with the identity. No separate key vault is required, and the recycling of keys and certificates is also internally managed.

  There are two types of managed identities: **system-assigned managed identity** and **user-assigned managed identity**. System-assigned managed identity is created by Azure AD and is tied to a resource. If the resource is deleted, then the managed identity is also deleted. A user-assigned managed identity is created externally by a user as a separate Azure resource and is assigned to one or more resources. The lifecycles of the resource and identity can be managed separately.

  Managed identity is the preferred way to define application identities for access management unless the Azure resource under consideration does not support managed identities, in which case, you can create service principals. For more details on managed identity, refer to this link: `https://learn.microsoft.com/en-us/entra/identity/managed-identities-azure-resources/overview`.

So far, so good. We have the provision to define an identity for users and for programs to access resources. Now, consider a situation with a large enterprise with thousands of employees. If we try to assign individual access to each of these users and the programs from different resources that they need access to, it will be a complex access management mesh to manage. If an individual changes roles, then that person's access will have to be changed for all the resources in the previous role and be re-assigned to the new resources in the new role. This could be a management nightmare for IT operations.

In order to solve this issue, Azure Active Directory uses the concept of security groups (*Figure 5.2*). A **security group** is a set of user identities and/or service principals bounded together. These groups can then be granted access to the resources they should have access to. If a person changes roles, they can simply be moved from one security group to another. No other changes are needed. If, due to some policy changes, access to a resource is revoked for a security group, then the changes are made to the security group, and they apply to all the users in the group:

Individual Access   Security Groups

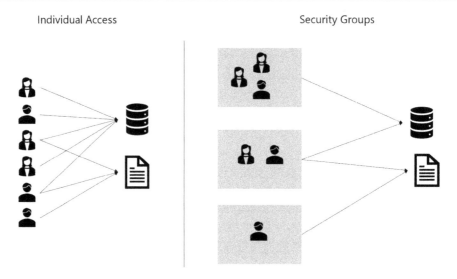

Figure 5.2 – Azure Active Directory security groups

A person or a service principal can be a member of multiple security groups. Security groups can also be nested. This means one security group can belong to another security group. These features make Azure security groups a very powerful tool for managing access rights in a data mesh. A good design is important to simplify the access management in a data mesh; hence, enough effort and time must be put into designing security groups:

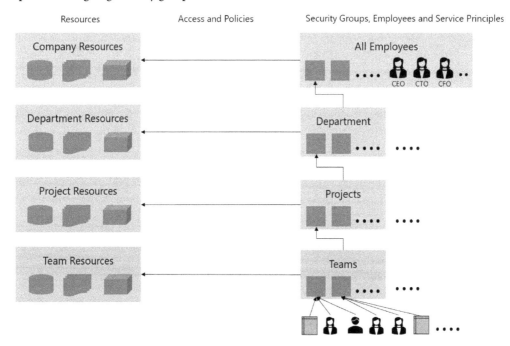

Figure 5.3 – Security groups hierarchy

Here are some tips on how to design a good security group structure for your organization (*Figure 5.3*):

1. Create a naming convention for the group. For example, `CompanyName_Department_Team_Role`.

2. Create one group called `All_Employees`. This group will have the very high-level rights that every employee in the organization has. For example, access to the company portal.

3. Create one group for every department.

4. Create one group for every project in the company.

5. Create groups for all the teams in that department.

6. Create additional subgroups if the team is further divided into roles and nest them into the team's security group.

7. Add employees and service principals to the lowest level of the groups they belong to.

Now, you can start boxing these groups into each other. All the department groups should belong to `All_Employees`, along with any other users that don't belong to a department, such as the CxOs.

All the teams that belong to a project should be added to that project's group. The projects group should be added to a department group.

Once you have this nested hierarchy of groups, you can now start assigning access to resources at every level. The access levels given to a subgroup or a team represent only the resources that they manage under that project. A department group does not have access to these resources, but because the team is part of a department, they have access to all the department resources, too.

Let us understand this more with a simple example. Assume the following groups:

-   `USSalesPrinter`: A local security group that has access to a specific printer on the sales floor

-   `USSales` and `AsiaSales`: Two security groups that have employees from the US sales and Asia sales departments, respectively

-   `GlobalSales`: A universal sales group that has access to all the sales applications and documents

To set the access in the most efficient way, and by using nested security groups, the groups will be organized as follows:

-   The `USSales` group will be added to the `USSalesPrinter` group

-   `USSales` and `AsiaSales` will be added to `GlobalSales`

In this way, all the sales employees have access to the sales apps and resources, but only `USSales` employees have access to `USSalesPrinter`.

After the security group hierarchy is created and you have all the employees and resources assigned to their appropriate groups, you can start granting them authorization to different resources.

Authorization is the process of granting or denying a set of actions that can be performed on a resource based on a set of permissions. The actions performed can be operational or managerial in nature. A data scientist working with a dataset in a data lake will need read-write operational access for the dataset or an entire section of the data lake. A project admin will not perform read-write operations on the data lake but will need permissions to back up the data or change the archiving policy on the data lake.

Let us look at a few key terms for implementing authorization:

- **Resource**: A resource is an entity managed by Azure. Virtual machines, storage, networks, and Azure Data Factory workspaces are some examples of resources.

- **Role**: A role is a set of permissions that can be assigned to people or programs regarding their requirements. For example, an **Administrator** role can perform read, write, and delete operations on a resource, but a **Reader** role can only read from the resource.

- **Scope**: A role has a scope that defines the level at which the permissions are applied. The scope can cover a **Management Group**, **Subscription**, or **Resource groups**.

Assigning built-in roles consistently at these scopes allows you to build a robust access management system and reduces the need to tweak roles for each user or security group. Azure Active Directory also allows custom roles to be built. However, custom roles should be avoided as far as possible. Custom roles don't apply to other similar resources and become specific to one instance. Too many custom roles will increase the management effort.

Roles in Azure can be assigned using the Azure portal. **Management Groups**, **Subscriptions**, **Resource groups**, and **Resources** have an **Access control** (**IAM**) section on the left. Clicking on this will take you to the **Access control** blade where you can assign roles to security groups, users, and other resources. For details on how to assign roles, refer to https://learn.microsoft.com/en-us/azure/role-based-access-control/role-assignments-portal:

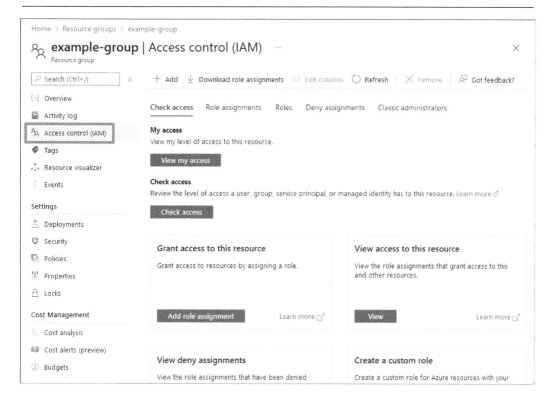

Figure 5.4 – Assigning roles through the Azure portal

However, using the Azure portal to assign roles is not preferred. One of the requirements of a data mesh is to automate infrastructure management by implementing Infrastructure-as-Code. Hence, you should create parameterized scripts to assign roles using the command-line interface or PowerShell script, as shown in the following:

```
1# Grant access to individual user at a Subscription Level
2 function GrantAccessAtSubscription ($userID, $roleDef, $subScope) {
3    New-AzRoleAssignment -SignInName $userID `
4    -RoleDefinitionName $roleDef `
5    -Scope $subScope
6 }
7
8# Grant access to a security group at a Subscription Level
9 function GrantGroupAccessAtSubscription ($groupID, $roleDef,
$subScope) {
10    New-AzRoleAssignment -ObjectID $groupID `
11    -RoleDefinitionName $roleDef `
12    -Scope $subScope
13 }
```

```
14
15# Remove access of a security group at a Subscription Level
16 function RemoveGroupAccessAtSubscription ($groupID, $roleDef,
$subScope) {
17    Remove-AzRoleAssignment -ObjectId $groupId `
18    -RoleDefinitionName $roleDef `
19    -Scope $subScope
20}
```

These parameterized functions with which to manage access can be called from a workflow or a data mesh management portal for requesting access. PowerShell scripts can be executed in Azure in many different ways. They can be included in Azure run books as part of Azure Automation. They can also be executed using Azure functions.

Here are some reference materials for executing PowerShell scripts:

- `https://learn.microsoft.com/en-us/azure/automation/learn/automation-tutorial-runbook-textual`

- `https://learn.microsoft.com/en-us/azure/azure-functions/functions-reference-powershell?tabs=portal`

Infrastructure-as-Code helps in building self-service tools, which, in turn, help in accelerating the deployment of landing zones and managing team changes.

Each Azure service comes with its own built-in roles. **Azure Data Lake** comes with three built-in roles: **Reader**, **Contributor**, and **Owner**. The **Reader** role allows users to only read the blobs and lists. The **Contributor** role allows the user to read, write, and modify the blobs and lists but does not allow them to change access or manage the storage account itself. The **Owner** role allows the user to read, write, and modify the contents of the data lake, as well as change access. There are more fine-grained roles, too, such as **Storage Account Backup contributor**, **Storage Account Blob data reader**, and many others. Similarly, **Microsoft Purview** has a comprehensive set of built-in roles, such as **Reader**, **Curator**, different types of **Admins**, **Policy Author**, and others. These built-in roles have been thought through by the product teams and will almost always suffice the needs of any organization.

Azure also provides custom roles, where IT teams can define their own custom role and the combination of operations it can perform. However, it is not advisable to use these custom roles, primarily because they will only apply to that instance of the service. If you create new instances, these custom roles will have to be copied to those instances. This can become a security management challenge.

Let us summarize high-level guidance regarding access control over resources:

- Create a nested design for security groups similar to the one provided in *Figure 5.3*

- Assign more generic access rights to the management groups and subscription levels to reduce the number of role assignments at the lower levels

- Use built-in roles and avoid custom roles
- Use PowerShell script or CLI functions to assign, revoke, or change role assignments

So far, we have covered access to resources. In a data mesh, access to actual data stored inside a database or a data store is equally critical.

In the next section, let's discuss how we can manage data access.

Managing data access

Data can be stored in many different ways and in many different storage mediums. The two most popular data stores on Azure are **SQL Database** and **Azure Data Lake Gen2**.

Certain resources, such as a data lake or SQL databases, provide more granular access to the data contained inside these stores. Let's cover some aspects of data-level access management, as this is key to providing granular access in a data mesh.

In this section, let's see how we can control access to data stored in these two data stores.

SQL Database

Assuming that the peripheral network security of a database is in place, you should focus on the data security aspect of a data mesh. Authentication in **Azure SQL Database** can be set up in two ways: **SQL Authentication** and **Azure Active Directory authentication**. Assuming you have enabled Azure Active Directory for your Azure tenant, it is recommended that you implement Azure Active Directory-based authentication for SQL Database, too. This will help centralize the authentication mechanism and avoid a situation of managing two separate authentication systems. It also brings all the advantages of Azure Active Directory, such as not storing passwords, single sign-on, token-based authentication, and others, to Azure SQL Database.

All the benefits of Azure Active Directory authentication apply to SQL Database, too. You can create security groups and assign them specific SQL roles such as db_accessadmin, db_datareader, db_datawriter, and many others, as listed here: https://learn.microsoft.com/en-us/sql/relational-databases/security/authentication-access/database-level-roles?view=sql-server-ver16#fixed-database-roles.

Azure SQL Database also provides a feature called **Conditional Access**. This feature gathers signals from multiple Microsoft Security services, such as **Azure Active Directory**, **Microsoft Defender**, and **Microsoft Endpoint Manager**, and then applies company-level policies to these signals to either grant or deny access. If your organization has these security services set up, then **Conditional Access** is highly recommended. This is especially important if your data mesh is being accessed by vendors and contract employees.

Once you have set up all the required security groups and assigned them various roles, it is time to go more granular and focus on row- and column-level security. Azure SQL Database and **Data Warehouse** provide the row-level security feature. It can be enabled through SQL commands. The following code snippet shows an example of a statement that allows users to select only columns from the `Sales` table that have their name in the `SalesRep` column:

```
CREATE SECURITY POLICY SalesFilter
ADD FILTER PREDICATE (SalesR = USER_NAME()) ON Sales
WITH (STATE = ON);
```

For more details on how to implement row-level security, refer to the following link: `https://learn.microsoft.com/en-us/sql/relational-databases/security/row-level-security?view=azuresqldb-current`

Similarly, you can also implement column-level security by executing a `GRANT SELECT` command and limiting the number of columns that can be selected by a certain role. For example, if we have a table called `Customer` that has `CustomerID`, `FirstName`, `LastName`, and `SSN` columns and we don't want a set of users from `Project XYZ` to access `SSN`, then the following code snippet shows an example of a `GRANT` command that can implement this security requirement:

```
GRANT SELECT ON dbo.Customer (CustomerID, FirstName, LastName) TO
ProjectXYZTeam;
```

Another feature in **SQL Server** that can be used to hide sensitive data is views. Views are virtual tables created out of a query. So, for the same requirement for the `Customer` table mentioned in the preceding example, we could create a view and grant the `Project XYZ` team access to that view, as shown in the following:

```
1 CREATE VIEW Customer_woSSN
2 AS
3 SELECT CustomerID, FirstName, LastName FROM dbo.Customer
4 GRANT SELECT ON dbo.Customer_woSSN TO ProjectXYZ
```

You could also add a `where` clause to the select statement and restrict the rows too.

The choice of using row- and column-level security or views to restrict access to information depends on the scenario. For more generic restrictions that apply to most of the people in the organization, such as for social security numbers and credit cards, which can only be seen by the finance team and no other employee, views can be an easy way to implement this. However, if more granular access is required, where only a select set of people have access to different columns in different tables, then row- and column-level security is more suitable.

Data lakes

Other than databases, the next popular storage of choice is a data lake. As more analytical data gets pushed into data lakes, the technologies to process and analyze semi-structured data are also gaining traction. One such popular technology is **Delta Lake**. Delta Lake builds on top of data lake storage to provide features such as ACID transactions (`https://en.wikipedia.org/wiki/ACID`) and time travel. With technologies such as Delta Lake (`https://delta.io/`) gaining popularity, data lakes are exploding in size. Azure Data Lake Gen2 offers granular access to the files and folder hierarchy stored within it. It uses a combination of **role-based access control** (**RBAC**) and a model called **access control lists** (**ACLs**).

We have already looked at RBAC previously when assigning access rights to resources through Azure Active Directory roles and permissions. In a data lake, RBAC is only applied to the storage accounts and containers. That RBAC policy then applies to all the data under that storage or container. It provides very broad access control over all of the data in storage or in a container. Optionally, you can apply more fine-grained access control to the folders and files stored inside the data lake by using ACLs.

An ACL is a model based on the POSIX standards (`https://pubs.opengroup.org/onlinepubs/9699919799.2018edition/`). It's a sequence of three letters that represent permissions. The letters are R for read, W for write, and X for execute. So, RWX represents the permission to read, write, and execute, whereas --X represents the permission to only execute. Read and write permissions are self-explanatory.

What is an execution permission? An execute permission only applies to folders, and it means that anyone with this permission can list the files stored under this folder. So, --X means that the user with this permission can list the files stored in the folder but will not be able to read or write to them. *Table 5.1* depicts the POSIX standard ACL permissions.

Permission type	File	Directory
Read (R)	Can read the contents of a file	Requires read and execute to list the contents of the directory
Write (W)	Can write or append to a file	Requires write and execute to create child items in a directory
Execute (X)	Does not mean anything in the context of Data Lake Gen2 storage	Required to traverse the child items of a directory

Table 5.1 – Access control list permissions

ACLs come in two types: access ACLs and default ACLs. **Access ACLs** control access to an object, and they apply to folders and files. **Default ACLs** apply to all child items created under a folder. They apply only to folders.

So, let's look at an example of how this will work. A company's data mesh has a data product (**A**) and a data lake. The data lake contains **raw**, **developer**, and **curated** zones, with files stored in folders named after the dates when the files landed:

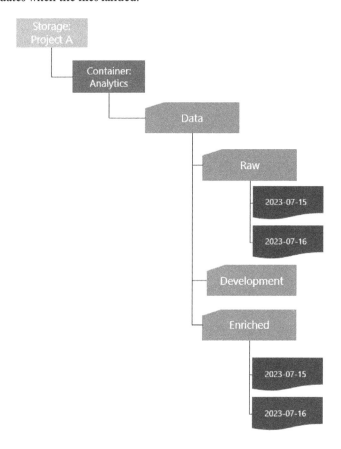

Figure 5.5 – Sample data lake hierarchy

Take a look at *Figure 5.6*; **Data Product A** has a data lake with **Raw**, **Development**, and **Enriched** zones:

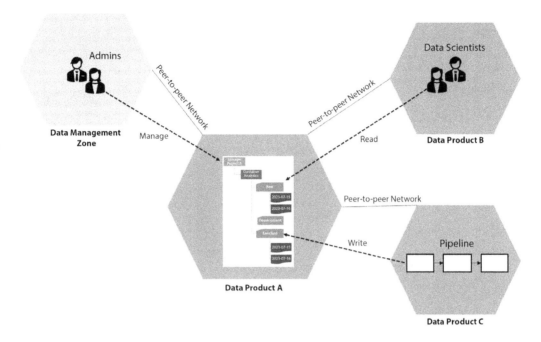

Figure 5.6 – Sample access requirements

The **Admins** team from the **Data Management Zone** must be able to access the storage account for deployment, backup, archival, and networking management.

Data Scientists from **Data Product B** are building a product and want to explore the raw data from the **Data Product A** data lake.

A pipeline for **Data Product C** provides some enriched data to **Data Product A**:

Users	Storage_ Project_A	Container_ Analytics	\ Data	\Data\ Raw	\Data\ Enriched
DMZ_Admins	RBAC: Storage Account Contributor	NA	NA	NA	NA
Product_B_ Data_ Scientists	NA	NA	--X	R--	---
Product_C_ Pipeline_ Service_ Principle	NA	NA	--X	---	-WX

Table 5.2 – Example of RBAC and ACL

An important point to note is that a user needs a minimum of the execute permission to be able to perform any further operations.

ACLs also provide a set of additional features, such as default and mask ACLs.

A new technique called **attribute-based access control** (**ABAC**) has recently been added to Active Directory access management. ABAC uses attributes-based logic to grant or deny access to resources. A combination of RBAC, ABAC, and ACLs can provide more granular access at all levels of the data lake.

Data lake access management is a very lengthy topic. In this section, we have covered what is relevant to a data mesh. For more details on data lake access management, RBACs, and ACLs, refer to this link: `https://learn.microsoft.com/en-us/azure/storage/blobs/data-lake-storage-access-control-model`.

Data lake structure

The folder hierarchy in a data lake is critical to maintaining efficient access control. The highest level of the folder should be the most abstract. It should become more specific as you go down the hierarchy. The last folder should usually be a timestamp of when the data was collected.

Data lakes, unlike relational databases, usually get a dump of raw data from a source. The source can either be a structured system, such as SAP, or a semi-structured source, such as web-page data or IoT. Once it lands in the data lake, it needs to be processed and cleaned to make it more usable. The clean version is then used by data scientists and data engineers to produce curated datasets by merging data together and adding calculated fields or aggregates. These different zones through which data moves have multiple nomenclatures. Some companies name them **Raw**, **Processed**, and **History** or **Bronze**, **Silver**, and **Gold**; this is popularly called **medallion architecture**.

This categorization of raw, clean, and processed data should be the highest folder level in your hierarchy. It is also recommended as best practice to bring this abstraction to the container level. So, there is a container for raw, clean, and processed. The next level should be the country or the zone, followed by department, projects, subprojects, and finally, a folder with a date stamp of when the data was stored.

Depending on the company's size and its current operating systems, you can also introduce a layer for source systems. Some companies also introduce a version folder at some level.

In short, there are many ways of building a folder structure for a data lake. Enough deliberation and time must be spent on designing this structure, as it plays a key role in access management. *Figure 5.7* shows a sample of what a typical data lake folder hierarchy might look like:

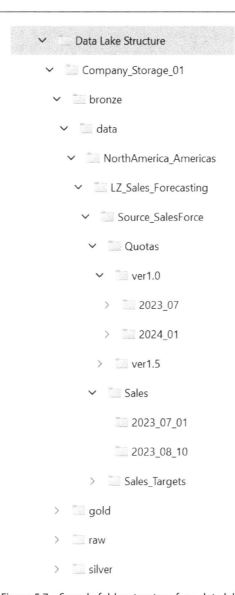

Figure 5.7 – Sample folder structure for a data lake

In this section, we have covered data access control; this decides who has access to the data and who does not. In the next section, let's look at data privacy. Data privacy goes into a deeper level: the individual components of data that may have private information, such as names, phone numbers, and national numbers, which might all have to be conditionally protected.

Managing data privacy

In the *Understanding the security requirements of a data mesh architecture* section, we learned that data security and data privacy are related topics and have an overlap. If you have implemented all aspects of data security, then you have covered most of data privacy, too. There are only two more topics that we should cover to complete the data security and privacy topic: **data masking** and **data retention**.

Once again, we will consider the two dominant data stores—SQL Database and Azure Data Lake Gen2.

Data masking

Often, data engineers and data scientists have a requirement to query sensitive **personally identifiable information (PII)** as a part of their experiment or pipeline. While this data should flow through the system, it should not be visible to the human eye to prevent any malicious use or data leak. Sometimes, sensitive data, such as social security numbers, can even be part of a table relationship and, hence, part of join operations.

For such requirements, a technique must be used to partially hide sensitive data in a way that is recognizable for tests but not identifiable. Various techniques are used to achieve this; obfuscation, static masking, anonymization, and tokenization are some examples.

SQL Database has had a feature called **dynamic data masking** since SQL Server version 2016. It is also available in the Cloud SKUs of Azure SQL Databases. Dynamic data masking allows you to create a central policy to define data masks. Various options are available for masking. The default mask detects the data type and masks accordingly. **String data** is masked xxxx. For example, a credit card number could be masked as xxxx xxxx xxxx x445. **Numeric data** types are masked with 0s. SQL Database also has some out-of-the-box masks for email addresses, dates, and times.

Data masks can be defined using SQL, as shown in the following. The phone number is masked with the default function, and the email address with an email function:

```
1-- table with masked columns
2CREATE TABLE Data.Customer (
3    CustomerID INT IDENTITY(1, 1) NOT NULL PRIMARY KEY CLUSTERED,
4    FirstName VARCHAR(100) MASKED WITH (FUNCTION = 'partial(1,
"xxxxx", 1)') NULL,
5    LastName VARCHAR(100) NOT NULL,
6    Phone VARCHAR(12) MASKED WITH (FUNCTION = 'default()') NULL,
7    Email VARCHAR(100) MASKED WITH (FUNCTION = 'email()') NOT NULL,
8    DiscountCode SMALLINT MASKED WITH (FUNCTION = 'random(1, 100)')
NULL
9);
```

You can also use the CLI to enable and set data masks, as shown in the following. It sets a mask on `Column01` as a default number mask, from the sixth digit to the fourteenth digit:

```
1Set-AzSqlDatabaseDataMaskingPolicy
2     -ResourceGroupName "ResourceGroup01"
3     -ServerName "Server01"
4     -DatabaseName "Database01"
5     -PrivilegedUsers "public"
6     -DataMaskingState "Enabled"
7
8New-AzSqlDatabaseDataMaskingRule
9     -ResourceGroupName "ResourceGroup01"
10     -ServerName "Server01"
11     -DatabaseName "Database01"
12     -SchemaName "Schema01"
13     -TableName "Table01"
14     -ColumnName "Column01"
15     -MaskingFunction "Number" -NumberFrom 6 -NumberTo 14
```

Once masking policy and masking formulas are set on the required columns, you can provide very granular access to unmask the data to only a set of employees in the company who are authorized to see the data. The following is some example code to provide access to unmask and revoke access if required:

```
1GRANT UNMASK TO AutorizedUsers;
2EXECUTE AS USER = 'AutorizedUsers';
3SELECT * FROM Data.Customer;
4REVERT;
5
6-- Removing the UNMASK permission
7REVOKE UNMASK TO AutorizedUsers;
```

For more information on dynamic data masking in Azure SQL Database, refer to this link: https://learn.microsoft.com/en-us/sql/relational-databases/security/dynamic-data-masking?view=azuresqldb-current.

Other modern databases, such as PostgreSQL and MySQL, have different techniques to mask data.

Relational database systems have strong support for masking because they store their data in rows and columns, and hence, it is easier to implement masking by applying formulas to an entire column. But how do you apply data masking to semi-structured data stored in a data lake?

Unfortunately, data lakes don't have a simple solution, such as relational databases (i.e., Azure SQL Database). However, there are a few techniques that can be employed to manage data masking on data stored in Azure data lakes.

This is PII data that is sensitive and needs to be masked using a transformation pipeline and moved to another location in the data lake (it's like a copy of the original data that is masked). We can now provide separate access to different team members with access to masked or unmasked data based on their authorization.

Imagine a data folder hierarchy in a data lake, as depicted in *Figure 5.8*:

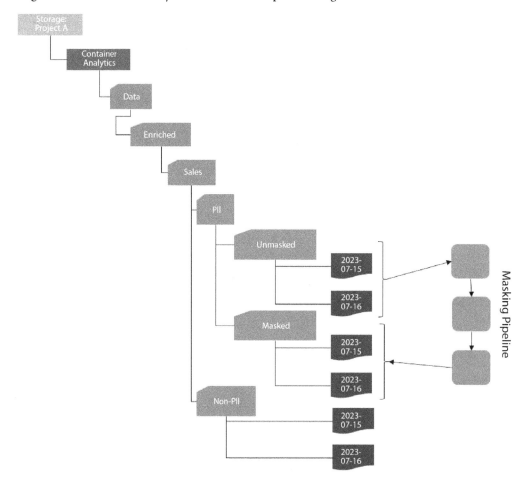

Figure 5.8 – Masking data in a data lake

We have split the **Sales** folder further into **PII** and **Non-PII**. The **PII** folder is further split into **Masked** and **Unmasked**. Original source data lands in the **Unmasked** folder. As the files in the **Unmasked** folder are copied, modified, or deleted, a data-masking pipeline is triggered automatically. A step-by-step walk-through of setting up an **Azure Data Factory** pipeline trigger on a file change or a file drop can be found here: https://learn.microsoft.com/en-us/azure/data-factory/how-to-create-event-trigger?tabs=data-factory. The data masking pipeline uses some popular data masking formulas to hide part of the sensitive columns and copy the data to the **Masked** folder.

These two separate **Masked** and **Unmasked** folders can now be given access to different security groups based on who is authorized or not authorized to see the data.

This technique can be a bit of a management overhead in terms of maintaining the pipeline and ensuring that it gets triggered every time the data in the **Unmasked** folder changes to ensure that the **Unmasked** and **Masked** folders are always kept consistent.

If you are using Delta Lake storage, you can use third-party frameworks, such as Immuta (`https://www.immuta.com/`) and others, to implement and manage data masking in Delta Lake. These solutions integrate with your data lake storage and provide a layer of protection that includes data masking.

Data retention

Different country laws mandate how long personal data can be stored by companies. Some countries leave that choice to the consumers. Consumers can decide if a company can save their data or not. The **General Data Protection Regulation** (**GDPR**) in Europe does not mandate a specific period for which the data should be retained by a company, but it says that data should not be kept longer than it's needed. As an example, employees' personal data should only be kept as long as they are with a company. In most cases, companies get approval from customers, employees, and partners, to store their data, as per the company's retention policy. If another party does not agree, then the data must be immediately destroyed after use.

For a data mesh, the central data catalog can play a very critical role in managing data retention. Microsoft Purview supports sensitivity labels from Microsoft Office to label business data. You can turn on automatic labels. Standard sensitivity labels include personal, public, general, confidential, and highly confidential. These labels can vary from company to company. In the case of military and government organizations, there might be an even higher level of label called "secret."

Labeling documents for sensitivity has been around for more than a decade now. Microsoft Purview allows you to leverage the existing labels you have already defined and apply them to the data. You can define new sensitivity labels through the Microsoft Purview compliance portal. Once new labels are defined, you can enable the labeling of data in Microsoft Purview. You can also define a labeling policy in the Microsoft Purview compliance portal. In the policy, you can define the scope of the labels. Purview will automatically classify and label the data.

For more details on sensitivity labeling in Microsoft Purview, refer to this link: `https://learn.microsoft.com/en-us/microsoft-365/compliance/sensitivity-labels?view=o365-worldwide`.

Summary

In summary, with the right combination of data access security, masking, and retention policies, you will be able to build a good data privacy framework for your data mesh. The most important aspect is that while the decisions on access and privacy are decentralized to each data product, the policies and tools must be central and standardized.

In the next chapter, we will see how resource manager templates and DevOps can be used to create the building blocks of data mesh automation.

6

Automating Deployment through Azure Resource Manager and Azure DevOps

Federation is about providing autonomy to each data product owner to make their own decisions about the storage, computing, and sharing of data. However, this autonomy cannot come at a risk to the security and compliance standards of the company. So, how do we ensure that all the landing zones and resources inside those zones are configured as per the enterprise security and privacy policy? How do we ensure that the networking for these landing zones is standardized? The answer to these questions is **automation**. Building standard deployment templates, maintaining and versioning them, and deploying them through a standardized pipeline is the solution to ensure that even the most complex data mesh is maintained as per enterprise standards with no room for human error.

The networking, security, and actual deployment aspects of various services are beyond the scope of this book. What this book will cover are the techniques and technologies available for automating the deployments. We will add Microsoft Azure documentation references where deeper understanding is required.

In this chapter, we're going to cover the following main topics:

- Azure Resource Manager templates for landing zones
- Source code control for ARM templates
- Azure DevOps pipelines for deploying infrastructure
- Automation using Azure DevOps pipelines and ARM templates

Azure Resource Manager templates for landing zones

If you have never built landing zones before using **Azure Resource Manager** (**ARM**) templates, then I suggest you first start with the landing zone templates provided by the **Azure Cloud Adoption Framework** (*Chapter 3*). This will cover all the core requirements, such as networking, security, resource organization, and monitoring, of a landing zone. You can start with the ready deployment template that you can find here: `https://learn.microsoft.com/en-us/azure/cloud-adoption-framework/ready/landing-zone/implementation-options#environment-development-approaches`.

In a data mesh, product teams typically request a landing zone. These requests can come through a central portal or an email with a completed requirements template attached. Irrespective of the mechanism to submit a requirement for a landing zone, you should have a complete list of the services required to build a landing zone before you start building the automation templates.

As mentioned at the beginning of this section, for your first landing zone, you can start with the templates provided by Microsoft Azure as part of the **Cloud Adoption Framework** (**CAF**). You will need to modify this template based on the requirements you get for the landing zone.

You can also find more specific landing zone templates for the cloud-scale analytics here: `https://github.com/Azure/data-landing-zone`.

As your data mesh grows and you gain more experience with building ARM templates, you will have your own set of templates to start with and will not need the ready templates from Microsoft.

Let us look at the different ways of structuring a template. These structures help manage the complexity and scale the deployment of the landing zones.

Understanding the ARM template structure

Depending on the landing zone team's requirements, there are two approaches to structuring your templates. If the team is experimenting with some data and is unsure of their future resource needs, you can start small with a simple template that incorporates all the elements of the data landing zone and the required resources into one template. As the team's requirements grow, you add more resources and other elements to the template. But at some point, a single template will become very complex to manage a large number of resources. Additionally, ARM templates have certain quotas and limitations. For example, only 256 parameters are allowed on one template, or the template size cannot exceed 4 MB. These are hard limits, and changing and restructuring after hitting these limits can be very inefficient. Instead, it's important to keep these limits in mind, and as you approach them, start to restructure your template architecture to avoid hitting these limits and quotas (see `https://learn.microsoft.com/en-us/azure/azure-resource-manager/management/azure-subscription-service-limits`).

In another approach, a product team might request a landing zone with very clear requirements. Or it might be a situation where an existing project is being migrated from some other location to the data mesh. Both these scenarios will have researched their requirements and provided very clearly documented services and capacities that they need. In such a situation, the approach should be to plan and structure the template in a more modular way. Let us look at ways of building modular templates that help with two things: manage complexity and avoid hitting the limits and quotas of an ARM template. The three specific techniques to structure an ARM template are the following:

- Monolithic

- Nested

- Linked

The simplest format is to have one **monolithic template** with all the subscriptions, resource groups, and resources defined in one ARM template. This is ideal for small landing zones that will not grow much in the near future. Sandbox environments, temporary workspaces, and small projects with pre-defined requirements are ideal candidates for a monolithic template.

If a monolithic template starts to grow with multiple teams across different resource groups using the landing zone, then the data mesh operations team can consider building a **nested template**. A nested template breaks the larger template into smaller pieces and then makes a reference to these small pieces inside larger templates. All the references are resolved at runtime into a large monolithic template. A nested template will help organize the monolithic template into smaller modules. These modules can be maintained and tested independently but executed as one single template. Nested templates also make the template more readable (*Figure 6.1*).

A nested template, however, will not decrease the size of the template. It cannot be used to solve the 4 MB template size limit requirement for growing templates. To manage template size, you can use the third template structure called linked template.

One important concept in nested templates is **scope**. The ARM template deploys resources. But where are these resources deployed? How does the ARM template know where to deploy? This is defined by a *scope*. The scope can be a tenant, management group, subscription, or resource group (see `https://learn.microsoft.com/en-us/azure/azure-resource-manager/templates/deploy-to-resource-group`).

There are other intricacies to how scopes work, especially with functions. So, it is important to understand scopes. For more details on how scopes work, refer to this link: `https://learn.microsoft.com/en-us/azure/azure-resource-manager/templates/scope-functions?tabs=azure-powershell#function-resolution-in-scopes`.

A **linked template** is similar to a nested template in terms of the modularization of the templates. The reference to these modularized templates is in the form of a link. The execution of these templates is done independently as opposed to the nested template. This feature solves the 4 MB size limitation.

Figure 6.1 shows how monolithic, nested, and linked ARM templates are organized:

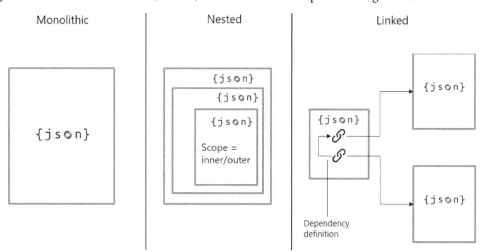

Figure 6.1 – Azure Resource Manager template structures

Linked templates don't need a scope definition because the scope is always resolved by the external template scope. In contrast, linked templates have a concept of dependency. If you wish the separate templates to execute in a particular sequence irrespective of the sequence in which they are defined, then you need to add a dependsOn attribute to the definition. It takes a template resource ID as a parameter and ensures that the template referenced under dependsOn is executed before the template that contains the definition. For more details on linked templates and dependencies, refer to this link: https://learn.microsoft.com/en-us/azure/azure-resource-manager/ templates/linked-templates?tabs=azure-powershell#linked-template.

One of the big differences between nested and linked templates is that nested templates allow you to deploy resources across different scopes of tenants, subscriptions, and resource groups. Each template maintains its own scope. While linked templates derive their scope from the parent template. Hence, linked templates allow you to deploy resources across different tenant, subscription, or resource group scopes.

All three ARM template structures—monolithic, nested, and linked—are not an either/or option. They can and, in most cases, should be used in combination. The usual pattern observed with customers is as follows:

1.   Start with a small template.

2.   If the template starts to grow, then change the design to a nested template.

3.   After the template reaches the 4 MB limit, change the nested references to linked references.

At each stage, ensure that the entire template and its parts are tested thoroughly.

Like any development work that involves coding, testing, and deployment, ARM template development also needs testing every time changes are made to the template. Depending on the size and the number of templates, testing can become a daunting task for the data mesh operations team. From a data mesh governance standpoint, there are two important features that need to be implemented to support the smooth testing and deployment of ARM templates:

- Version management
- Continuous integration and deployment

In the next two sections, let's look at implementing these two aspects.

Source code control for ARM templates

Source code control is a system of storing code and system artifacts in a central repository. This central repository is used by the team to do the following:

- Track modifications
- Maintain different versions of the same code
- Collaborate
- Audit changes
- Automate deployment

Microsoft Azure provides two options to create a centralized code repository: Git and **Team Foundation Version Control** (**TFVC**). Which one of these two options is best for you? TFVC is a mature source code management system with a rich set of features, as Microsoft has been working on TFVC for many years. GitHub is a more recent acquisition of Microsoft and implements source code with a different architecture. TFVC is centralized. Git is distributed.

One of the important concepts in source code control is branching. **Branching** involves copying the source code and tagging it as a separate version. From the time a repository is branched, all the changes to the two repositories are tracked separately. Git branching is scoped at the repository level. TFVC implements branching at the path level. Such differences can be the deciding factor for choosing between the two repositories.

While Git is new and is lacking features available in TFVC, it is still a recommended repository from Microsoft. Many features, such as work-item tracking, project reporting, CI/CD pipelines, and others, were either missing or less developed in Git. However, Microsoft's future investments are going towards Git. As a result, GitHub has been catching up on its missing/lacking features, and this trend will continue. So, unless there are some hard reasons to use TFVC, you should go for Git.

You can learn about all the differences between TFVC and Git here: `https://learn.microsoft.com/en-us/azure/devops/repos/tfvc/comparison-git-tfvc?view=azure-devops`.

Once the source repository decision has been made, it is time to start building deployment pipelines using Azure DevOps. In the next section, let's look into the components of a pipeline, specifically the ones required to deploy data mesh landing zones.

Azure DevOps pipelines for deploying infrastructure

In *Chapter 3*, in the *Streamlining deployment through DevOps* section, we learned that DevOps pipelines are made of stages. Each stage is made of steps. These steps can be a task or a script that is executed by an agent. In this section, let's understand how to construct a DevOps pipeline for infrastructure deployments.

The first step is to create an **Azure Pipeline** service instance if you don't already have one. This can be done by going to the Azure Pipelines landing page here: `https://azure.microsoft.com/en-us/products/devops/pipelines/`.

Click on **Start free** or **Start free with GitHub** based on your repository decision in the previous section:

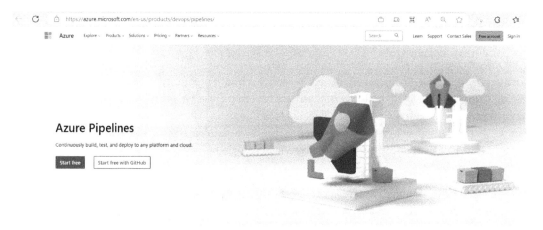

Figure 6.2 – Azure Pipelines

As a part of the setup process, you will be asked to create an organization and a project (see `https://learn.microsoft.com/en-us/azure/devops/organizations/accounts/create-organization`). Once a project is created and you open the project on the Azure DevOps portal, you will need to create a service connection to your Azure subscription. This creates a **service principal** in your Azure subscription that is used to execute DevOps pipelines. For details on how to create a service connection, refer to this link: `https://learn.microsoft.com/en-us/azure/devops/pipelines/library/connect-to-azure?view=azure-devops`.

Open the project, go to the **Pipelines** section, and create a new pipeline. In this pipeline, you have three options to deploy an ARM template:

- **ARM template deployment task**: This is the easiest way to deploy a landing zone. It picks up the ARM template from the repository you provide and deploys it. As part of the task, you provide parameters such as deployment scope, the actual management group/subscription/ resource group where it needs to be deployed, and the Azure location. This method works well if you have a simple landing zone template that is checked into the repository. Sandboxes or experimental landing zones can be deployed using the ARM template deployment task.

- **PowerShell script task**: Most of the deployments are not simple. Complex projects have complex needs. They have parameters that change over time; hence, simply taking an ARM template from a repository and deploying it may not work. In these cases, you need a script that will execute any additional functionality, such as reading parameters from a file and then deploying the ARM template. Scripting acts like a glue between two tasks.

- **Copy and deploy tasks**: The third method of deployment is to copy the ARM template to a staging location and then deploy it. One of the scenarios of using this method is when you have the exact same landing zone configurations to be deployed to multiple locations.

Detailed step-by-step instructions on how to build a pipeline using the preceding tasks can be found here: `https://learn.microsoft.com/en-us/azure/azure-resource-manager/ templates/add-template-to-azure-pipelines#select-your-option`.

We have learned about ARM templates and how to use ARM templates with DevOps pipelines. Now, let's look at how to automate the creation and management of landing zones.

The key feature of a data mesh is to allow teams to manage and maintain their data products in their own landing zone based on their requirements. It's about shifting the responsibility of the data product to the individual teams rather than a central analytics team. This allows for more autonomy in technology decisions and increases the speed of innovation. A team that wants to build a product is no longer dependent on a central analytics team to define how they should go about implementing the projects and mandate the tools they need to use. These teams can decide what tools they want to use and in what capacity and configuration as long as they comply with the company policies.

Data mesh provides teams with the freedom to build their own framework for their data product, but this cannot come at the risk of violating the company policies on security, networking, and access. This means that while the teams are free to pick their technology, the deployment of these technologies must comply with the company's security and standards. The landing zones that get deployed for each team or department can have different development tools and components but must follow the same networking, security, and policies. The core infrastructure pieces of a landing zone must be templatized and kept consistent for all the landing zones that get created.

Azure Resource Manager templates represent a tool to achieve this consistency. The data mesh IT Ops team can create a template for networking and security. The template is versioned and maintained in a Git Repo. This base infrastructure template can then be linked or nested along with other project-specific templates and deployed on demand. This process ensures that the same infrastructure template is used for all the landing zones. If there are any changes to company security policies, the changes can be made to this one common infrastructure template, and all the deployment pipelines can be re-run to ensure that the changes are effective across all current and future landing zones. In the next section, let's understand what a base template should contain.

Base data product templates

Data workloads are broadly divided into a few types of workloads, mostly big data processing, advanced analytics, machine learning and data science, business intelligence, and real-time analytics. Microsoft Azure provides a set of standardized architectures for these data workloads. These are a combination of various Azure services. Based on these guiding architectures, your company can come up with its own standardized architectures for these workloads. In order to simplify deployment tasks and not have to build templates from scratch every time a landing zone request comes in, a set of base templates that follow these standardized architectures can be created. The set of tools best suited for each workload is also fairly well defined, with just a few exceptions where there are overlaps. Azure Synapse can be a tool used for big data processing, advanced analytics, and machine learning. Similarly, Azure Databricks can be used for various workloads. Azure machine learning is specifically used for machine learning and deep learning projects.

In *Chapters 14–17* of this book, we will discuss some of these standard architectures and the landing zones for these workloads.

Once the data mesh Ops team creates these base templates, they can be used as the starting point for building a landing zone. Minor changes to the templates can be automated through code, too. Major changes might involve the Ops team creating a modified version of the base template.

For the next step, in order to decide the size of the deployment, it is important to note that Azure services come in different sizes. These sizes define the computing, memory, and storage allocated to these services and directly impact the performance and cost of these services. The data product teams will need to provide the sizes of these services as part of the requirement. One way to make it easy for these teams to decide the size is to provide them with standardized sizes. Just like walking into a clothing store, you can see "S," "M," "L," "XL," and "XXL" sizes, and you generally know what size of clothing will work best for you. The IT Ops team can provide a chart of such standardized service deployment sizes called T-shirt sizes.

T-shirt sizing

Azure resources can be deployed with different capacities. These capacities come at different costs. When a team requests a landing zone, they might have a budget to work within, or a team might need a landing zone for some initial experimentation and might want to keep the costs to a minimum. These teams might ask the data mesh Ops team to provide them with a ballpark cost for a landing zone with a certain capacity. A recommended practice in the industry is to define landing zones of varying capacity in the order from small (S), medium (M), and large (L) to extra-large (XL) and extra-extra-large (XXL) sizes. This size chart can then be provided to teams when they request a landing zone to help them make a decision on what sizes cost, how much, and which one is appropriate for their requirements.

Landing zone requests

A standardized request form should be created by the data mesh IT Ops team. This request form should be filled in by the team requesting the landing zone and submitted to the IT Ops teams. It should include the following:

- The name of the team
- A brief description of the project
- Business justification stakeholder names
- A table of required services with their T-shirt sizes
- Business criticality:
  - Availability requirements
  - Disaster recovery requirements
- Data life cycle requirements
- High-level architecture (if applicable)

These are sample entries of a request form. Depending on your business requirements, you could add or remove these entities. In a manual process, this form is typically a Microsoft Excel template.

Landing zone approval

The request form is submitted to the stakeholders and the other authorizing members who need to approve the requirement. The process could involve budget teams or a senior executive, such as a chief data officer who approves projects in the company. If the requirement is rejected because of any reason, an email is sent to the requesting team stating the reasons. If the requirement needs to be changed, then the team modifies the requirement, and the approval workflow is restarted over email.

If the requirement is approved, then an email is sent to the requesting team and to the data mesh Ops team.

Landing zone deployment

Upon receiving the approval email, the data mesh Ops team prepares the necessary deployment templates from the Git Repo, prepares the pipelines, and deploys the landing zone. The deployment pipeline should also typically have a verification step. Once verified, an email should be sent to the requesting team, along with instructions on how to access and use the landing zone.

The steps defined here are a manual method of requesting and deploying landing zones. The only automated parts are the ARM templates and the pipelines.

Self-service portal

In smaller companies, having a manual process to request and deploy a landing zone could be efficient. Additionally, if a company thoroughly designs and plans its initial data mesh deployment in a way that new landing zones will not be needed in the near future, a manual request and deployment process will work well. However, in large corporations with an ever-changing landscape of data products, it might be more practical to have a self-service portal to request landing zones. All the components discussed here can be put behind a portal and automated using workflows and scripts.

A self-service portal is a central portal that hosts a landing zone request form. The form has all the fields mentioned in the **Landing zone request** section. The request form can also be in the form of a wizard UI. After filling in the initial inputs, it also presents the requesting team with a set of standard landing templates. The requester can select a template and finally submit their request.

Figure 6.3 shows how a landing zone request flows through the data mesh portal:

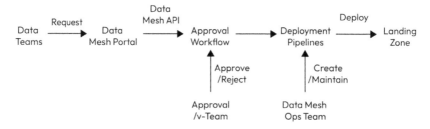

Figure 6.3 – Request and deployment automation

The portal backend is a set of APIs that call workflows and other APIs to manage the portal interactions. Upon getting a request, the Portal calls an API to trigger the approval workflow. The approval workflow will validate the entries. It will create an email with the details of the request, find the approval email address, and send an email to the concerned team for approval. The approval team will have a link to the approval UI of the portal where they can accept or deny the request. If accepted, a new deployment workflow is triggered that will pull the required templates from the Git repo and execute the DevOps pipeline that will deploy the landing zone. These workflows can be DevOps pipelines or GitHub actions, depending on how you wish to implement your deployment pipelines. The DevOps trigger will receive a success or failure message. If successful, the trigger function will spawn another function that will notify the requesting teams and all the stakeholders in the request that the landing zone has been created.

In our experience, a self-service portal has been an extremely valuable part of a data mesh; hence, irrespective of the size of the company or the complexity of the data mesh, we recommend that a self-service portal be built.

The initial version of the self-service portal can be a simple request form with simple workflows in the backend. However, with time, the self-service portal can start hosting other aspects of the data mesh. A few common functionalities or features of a data mesh self-service portal can be the following:

- A common data catalog UI that can consolidate multiple data-cataloging tools into one interface.

- A catalog of standardized pipelines for pulling data from legacy systems outside of the mesh.

- Access management.

- Documentation of the data mesh. This will include manuals on how to interact with the mesh, best practices, guidelines, and other useful information.

- A data products browser.

- A high-level data mesh health dashboard.

- Customizable landing zone templates.

This list of features is just an example set. Once you release an initial version of the portal to your teams and once they start using the data mesh, you will start getting feedback on what other processes can be simplified through the portal.

The portal becomes an entry point into the data mesh. It also serves as an excellent tool to market the data mesh in large organizations that need to convince and onboard diverse teams across the company. It converts the data mesh from an architecture to a product.

Just like any product, the data mesh portal should also have a product roadmap that is owned by the data mesh Ops team. The data mesh Ops team should continuously take feedback from users to improve the product and, at the same time, lookout for industry trends or popular services being used by different teams and incorporate those into their templates. Over time, the portal will grow in terms of the number of features and the variety of landing zone templates.

Customized templates

Often, the product teams requesting landing zones may not find a template that meets their exact requirements. Certain services might not be needed, or some tools that they use might be missing. In such scenarios, the self-service portal should allow requesters to customize the template and submit the request. A customized template will follow a different workflow path:

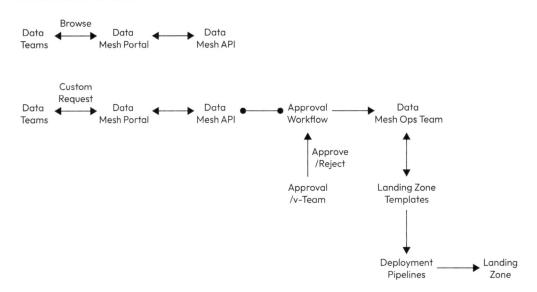

Figure 6.4 – Customized landing zone templates workflow

The team first browses the data mesh portal for suitable templates. They find the one that is the closest to their requirements. Once they select the template, they will be presented with another UI to customize the template. By using this UI, they can add their customization requirements. This could be either removing resources or adding new resources to the landing zone. After completing their customization requirements, the modifications and the selected template will be submitted for approval. After getting approved, they will be submitted to the data mesh Ops team. The data mesh Ops team will manually edit the template by forking a version of the original template, testing it, and making any pipeline modifications if required. The customized landing zone will then be deployed, and the requesting team will be notified.

This modified template will be added to the repository of templates for anyone else with similar requirements. This process helps grow the repository over time. As more and more templates are available, the need for manual customization keeps reducing, driving higher automation.

The data mesh Ops team should also continuously innovate the customization process. If they observe that some of the manual modifications can be done through code, then such functionality should be added to the data mesh portal.

An important point to note is to start small and grow the automation over time. A data mesh portal is key to this strategy.

Summary

In this chapter, we covered the techniques and technologies used for automating the deployment and management of data mesh landing zones. We saw how to standardize the deployments using the ARM templates and then how to automate the deployment and testing of the deployments using Azure DevOps.

The deployment of a landing zone starts with a request coming from a data product team. We saw that this request can be submitted in multiple ways. They can send an email for the details. Or fill out a form (typically a Microsoft Excel template). Or the data mesh team hosts a centralized portal where teams can fill out this form and submit a request. The last option of submitting a request through a central portal is the most convenient way. This central portal can also serve many other purposes and make it very easy for the data product teams, and data mesh IT Ops teams to work together efficiently.

In the next chapter, we will focus on this central data mesh portal. We will discuss how to get started with building this portal, how to gather requirements, and how to build it. We will also see a list of the most common features that companies incorporate into this centralized portal.

7

Building a Self-Service Portal for Common Data Mesh Operations

In *Chapter 6*, we briefly looked at a self-service portal for requesting **landing zones**. It highlighted the need for automating the deployment and maintenance of landing zones. However, a **central data mesh portal** can be more than just requesting for landing zones. In fact, in some situations, a landing zone request feature may not even be required. The data mesh portal can serve many other purposes, hosting pipeline templates, data catalog search, requesting access, and monitoring dashboards. It can become the face of your data mesh and create a pull for teams to collaborate on.

In this chapter, we will learn how to build a data mesh portal, as well as all the typical functionality it must implement, and the components and the architecture required for building it.

In this chapter, we will cover the following topics:

- Why do we need a self-service portal?
- Gathering requirements for the self-service portal
- Requesting landing zone or data products
- Building a data catalog
- Hosting common data pipeline templates
- Other common features of a self-service portal
- Architecting the self-service portal

Why do we need a self-service portal?

Having a self-service portal to manage a data mesh is not mandatory. That's right! You don't have to have a self-service portal. There can be multiple reasons for not having one, such as the following:

- Small and medium-sized enterprises that can easily define their landing zones upfront and won't need additional landing zones or new project resource groups don't need a self-service portal

- Small companies that can simply create a landing zone based on an email sent by one of their departments don't need a self-service portal

- Even large or medium-sized companies that have a well-defined business and don't need the agility of creating landing zones or pipelines on the fly don't need a self-service portal

However, having one will definitely have benefits irrespective of whether you need one or not. So, if you have the resources to build one, you should.

A portal for your data mesh has several advantages:

- It enforces automation

- It standardizes processes

- It ensures security and compliance

- It promotes reusability

- It drives agility

Let's look at how these benefits are achieved:

- **Automation**: Because a portal is programmed, you are forced to automate all the data mesh jobs. Doing anything manually outside of the portal is counter-intuitive and a waste of an investment made on the portal. Hence, you are forced to think about automating every little process and job that you execute to set up and maintain the data mesh. The portal becomes the driving factor for automation.

- **Process standardization**: The portal is a piece of software. All aspects of the **software development life cycle** come into play. The team must create templates, pipelines, and jobs for all the activities. These artifacts need to be checked into a version control system such as Git and maintained.

- **Compliance**: This plays into the previous point. Because the company has to follow certain network and security policies and because everything is deployed through a template, there can be a base template created for network and security that is used by all the landing zones. Since everything is checked into a Git library and versioned, teams can conduct periodic reviews to ensure that all policies are being upheld.

- **Reusability**: If a team requests a landing zone that is very similar to a previously created landing zone, then the ARM template used for the already deployed landing zone can be checked out and branched to create a new version for the new landing zone. Similarly, other artifacts such as pipelines can be reused. Reading data from a SQL Server database and copying it to a data lake is a very common activity. Why re-create this pipeline every time? Simply build a pipeline template and let teams replace the source and the destination.

- **Agility**: Because of reusability, teams can very quickly configure their landing zone and request a deployment. In many cases, human intervention will only be limited to approval. The pipeline will do the rest. Deployment of landing zones can go from days to hours.

The portal becomes an entry point into the data mesh. It also serves as an excellent tool to market the data mesh in large organizations that need to convince and onboard diverse teams across the company. It converts the data mesh from an architecture to a product.

Before we start building the portal, let us look at how to gather the requirements for the portal. This is a critical step as the portal must serve business and technical teams across the company and hence, the requirements should come from them.

Gathering requirements for the self-service portal

A data mesh portal should be treated like a product. It's the entry into the mesh. The first part of building any product is gathering requirements. This is the most critical part of product development.

You need a lot of brainstorming around the requirement-gathering activity. Depending on the size of your company and the complexity of your data platform, this might mean a few day-long meetings with all the stakeholders or weeks of meetings and interviews with stakeholders, data scientists, engineers, and business analysts.

Here are a few pieces of criteria that will drive the development of the portal:

- The size of your company
- The complexity of the **data estate**
- The nature of the data and analytics projects
- The size of the data mesh operations team
- The available full-stack resources to build the portal

Now, let us look at some of the most common requirements that are a bit obvious and also the most commonly implemented across most companies.

Requesting a data product zone

One of the most common functionalities provided by the data mesh portal is the ability to request a new data product zone. This could be a new subscription or a new resource group within an existing subscription. However, this is not a required functionality for all data mesh. Whether you need a form or a wizard-based interface to request a data product zone completely depends on your initial data mesh design and architecture discussion.

In the *Designing a cloud management structure* section in *Chapter 3*, we discussed the various factors for deciding landing zone creation and growth. If you did that exercise well and have a strategy in place, then it will now be an easy decision if you need a landing zone request functionality or not.

Also, nothing stops you from building one later if needed. But should the effort be spent now is the important decision.

So, for the sake of this book, let's assume that you will need a landing zone request functionality. We will discuss how to build this functionality in detail in the *Requesting landing zones or data products* section.

Browse and reuse pipeline

It starts with first analyzing your data estate. Get your IT operations team and any other teams involved with managing the infrastructure into a room and start creating a list of all the data systems in the company. This includes data sources, data lakes, databases, file stores, dashboards, pipelines, and integration services. Spill everything on the table. Once you have all the artifacts on the table, bucket them into two buckets. The artifacts in the first bucket should be the ones that are used by multiple teams. These typically are enterprise source systems and certain pipelines that pull data from common sources. The artifacts in the second bucket are those that are specific to a single team. Their functionality and data are designed for use by a single product or team.

This exercise will help figure out the common data sources that people pull data out of. These could be enterprise systems such as SAP or legacy applications with on-premises SQL Servers or Oracle servers. Some data products might also be very popular with multiple teams depending on the kind of data they provide.

Once you have these pipelines sorted out, you will have an estimate of how many of these pipelines can be hosted on the common data management zone and provided access through the portal.

Data discovery

This is a critical requirement of a data mesh. Depending on the data cataloging tools you pick, you will need to decide whether this functionality should be hosted on the data mesh portal. If you pick **Microsoft Purview** as your primary and only data catalog, then the **Microsoft Purview Search** portal can become your go-to data discovery tool. You could provide a link to it from the portal but you will not need to build a new UI for data discovery. You could also have a situation where you already have a data catalog tool such as erwin Data Catalog (`https://www.erwin.com/products/erwin-data-catalog/`) implemented for your enterprise. Or, your data scientists are using **Databricks Unity Catalog** search through Databricks workspaces (`https://learn.microsoft.com/en-us/azure/databricks/data-governance/unity-catalog/`).

Many customers use a combination of different vendors for data catalogs. Some tools such as Databricks Unity Catalog specialize in cataloging data across Databricks workspaces. They provide detailed metadata that Microsoft Purview may not have access to.

In situations like these where multiple data catalog products are involved, you could have a strategy to consolidate all of them under one umbrella catalog. This umbrella catalog is a custom catalog that imports the metadata from all these other catalogs mentioned previously using their individual API. The imported metadata is stored in a document database (such as **Cosmos DB**).

In the *Data catalog* section of this chapter, we will learn how to build this custom catalog and search it through the data mesh portal.

Access management

After discovering data, teams will need access to the data that they have found interesting. Requesting access to data typically involves a workflow. This workflow can be initiated from the data mesh portal depending on your decision on the data discovery feature. Microsoft Purview also has a data access request feature (`https://learn.microsoft.com/en-us/purview/how-to-request-access`) that can be leveraged if you plan to make the Microsoft Purview search your primary data discovery tool. Otherwise, you need to plan a way for scientists and engineers to request access to data through the data mesh portal.

The preceding are some of the most common functionalities and features provided by a data mesh portal. But it's not limited to just these features. Conducting interviews with the teams and holding brainstorming meetings will bring additional features to the table.

In the next set of sections, we will learn how to design and architect these features into the portal.

Requesting landing zones or data products

As discussed in the previous section, this functionality may not be included as part of the portal depending on the data mesh design that you have adopted and the needs of the company. If new projects are rare and experimentation is also not a requirement for your company, then most of the landing zone creation work can be done upfront using pipelines and ARM templates. But if your industry is competitive with a constant need for innovating analytics to keep yourself ahead of the curve, then there will be a need for creating landing zones on the fly. In this case, requesting landing zones needs to be an important feature on the portal.

In order to build a frictionless functionality to request landing zones, it's critical that your backend infrastructure and automation to create landing zones are in order. Assuming that a new data product request is a new landing zone, the following needs to be ready before you can start building this functionality on the portal:

- **Base ARM template for a landing zone**: An ARM template for creating an Azure subscription that has all the network and security policies applied.

- **A list of standardized Azure services**: A list of commonly used and approved services on Azure. Certain regulated organizations might have limitations on the kind of technology they can use or might have stringent security approvals before clearing an Azure service for use. They also might have a mandate of using only those services that are generally available (not in preview) and fully supported by Microsoft.

- **Base ARM templates for the preceding services**: A base ARM template for each of these services is complete with standardized and approved deployment parameters. In *Chapter 6*, we discussed the T-shirt sizing of the resources. The ARM templates need to be parameterized accordingly so that the parameters determining the sizes can be substituted.

- **Parameterized pipelines**: Parameterized pipelines that can be configured at run time to deploy the landing zone and the resources within.

- **Workflows for approvals and deployments**: A standardized process needs to be documented for deploying new landing zones.

Figure 7.1 shows a sample workflow for requesting and approving a landing zone.

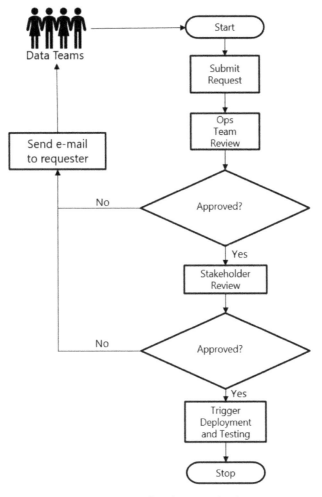

Figure 7.1 – Sample workflow for a new landing zone

The actual workflow will be completely dependent on your company's requirements and processes. Workflows can be built using Azure Logic Apps (https://learn.microsoft.com/en-us/azure/logic-apps/logic-apps-overview).

Also, the preceding functional readiness is based on a new landing zone deployment. If your company has decided to have a fixed number of landing zones and create new data products only as resource groups, then the requirements will change. ARM templates will be resource group based.

ARM templates are just one of the ways to deploy infrastructure as code in Azure. There are other technologies, such as **Terraform** or **Bicep**, that you can choose to use.

Terraform is an infrastructure-as-code software tool by **HashiCorp**. It supports multiple cloud providers and hence is the preferred tool of companies that have a multi-cloud strategy (`https://developer.hashicorp.com/terraform?product_intent=terraform`). Bicep is a tool from Azure that uses a declarative syntax to define infrastructure as opposed to the JSON format used by ARM. There are a few other differences between Bicep and JSON. To learn more about Bicep, refer to the following link: `https://learn.microsoft.com/en-us/azure/azure-resource-manager/bicep/overview?tabs=bicep`.

Once you have all the preceding infrastructure ready, you can start thinking about the user experience you wish to build on the portal to deploy landing zones. While building this experience, you must keep all personas in mind, such as the following:

- **Beginners**: For people who are new to technologies in general, you could have a guided approach. A wizard that begins by asking basic questions such as "What do you wish to do with this landing zone?" and provides options such as "machine learning," "big data analytics," and "IoT." Also, as they choose the answers to these questions, build a requirements document for them by adding the relevant technologies.

- **Intermediate**: You can offer them ready-made templates of required T-shirt sizes that they can pick from depending on their workload.

- **Advanced**: They will be directly taken to a menu of different services. They can pick and choose the services they need. They can fine-tune their requirements by directly tweaking the service parameters.

The end result of any of the preceding approaches is a requirements document in JSON format. This requirements document is then moved along the workflow until it gets approved by all and is ready for deployment.

At the time of deployment, as a final step, the workflow should read the JSON file and supply them as parameters to the DevOps pipeline. The DevOps pipeline should then be triggered to configure the ARM templates and deploy the landing zone.

The user experience and the entire request-to-deployment flow completely depend on how the workflow, DevOps pipeline, and ARM templates have been designed. Parts of the ARM templates might have to be built using the API to dynamically link other service templates as chosen by the requester. The DevOps pipeline must parameterize and run this template code. Without this coding and linking, some manual intervention will be required to stitch the ARM template together before the pipeline is run.

Having said that, one of the best ways to approach this functionality is to keep it manual in the beginning. You can create a request form and once the form is submitted, an operations team can take over and build the template and run the DevOps pipelines. Keeping the process manual will help you understand all the requirements. As you run the manual process, you can start automating the obvious repeatable tasks. For complex tasks, you can re-design the **user interface** (**UI**) to possibly get more information and then automate it eventually.

It's perfectly OK to start simple and manual and automate your way out of it. In fact, it would be the recommended approach.

Once the landing zone is deployed, it should be tested to ensure the deployment is done correctly. This again can be manual or automated or both.

This documentation from Microsoft provides good guidance on setting up automation through Bicep/Terraform and DevOps: `https://learn.microsoft.com/en-us/azure/cloud-adoption-framework/ready/considerations/development-strategy-development-lifecycle`.

Once the landing zone is deployed and tested, the last step of the workflow is to send an email to the requesting team with details on how to access and configure their landing zone.

Data catalog

Ideally, if you have chosen Microsoft Purview as your data catalog tool, then the search portal of Microsoft Purview should be your data catalog, in which case you should simply point to the Microsoft Purview Catalog Search landing page from the portal.

However, sometimes companies want to abstract the data catalog to a higher level. This is primarily done for two reasons:

- **Microsoft Purview Catalog Search** is very advanced and some users might want a simpler search tool
- Microsoft Purview may not be the only catalog tool being used

To build a catalog of your own that consolidates other catalogs, you need to do the following:

- Extract metadata from all your other third-party catalogs
- Design a metadata schema that encapsulates information from other catalogs
- Select the right storage for your custom metadata
- Select the right search technology to index and search the metadata
- Design a UI that meets the requirements of the data mesh users

The first step is to ensure that all the third-party catalogs you are using have an API to extract/export metadata. You need to test these APIs and ensure that you are getting all the metadata that you need. In case of any gaps, you should work with that catalog vendor to provide you with alternatives or get the roadmap for data export functionality.

Once you have the data export documented and tested for all the catalog solutions, you should start designing **data catalog metadata**. The data catalog metadata will have a fixed portion and a dynamic portion. The fixed portion of the catalog will consist of all the attributes that are common to any data. These include the following:

- Name
- Source
- Source type
- Description
- Hierarchy
- Data classification (list)
- Schema classification (list)
- Associated glossary terms (list)
- Creation date and time
- Last modified date and time
- Owner
- Steward
- Data experts (list)
- Status (approved, curated)
- Version

The dynamic part of the data catalog schema is attributes that may or may not exist for a given source. Examples of these are as follows:

- Schema
- Lineage

Images, text documents, and audio files will not have a schema. But you might want to extract other attributes that are common to all or most of the images in the folder. Examples are average size and average resolution.

Similarly, not all sources provide lineage information of where their source is and the transformations that they have been through.

All these attributes will be bundled into a JSON schema.

Now, you need to think of a storage system to store and search these schemas. The most ideal store is Azure Cosmos DB. Azure Cosmos DB is a fully managed NoSQL, multi-model data store that provides scale and low latency. For more details on Cosmos DB, refer to `https://learn.microsoft.com/en-us/azure/cosmos-db/introduction`.

After ensuring data export from third-party catalogs, designing the schema, and finalizing the catalog store, you need separate pipelines that pull data from the catalogs into the custom catalog store (Azure Cosmos DB) as shown in *Figure 7.2*.

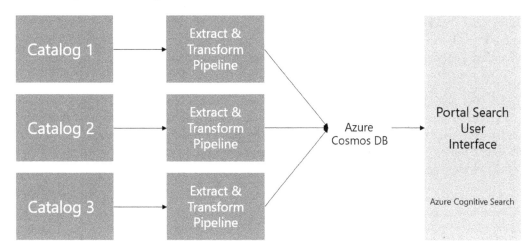

Figure 7.2 – Pipelines for consolidating multiple catalogs to the portal search

For searching the data catalog, you need a good keyword and entity search engine. Azure provides an out-of-the-box search service called **Azure Cognitive Search**. It's very simple to configure and use. Cosmos DB is one of the preferred data sources for Azure Cognitive Search and they are a very common combination for an industry-standard search solution.

For more details on using Azure Cognitive Search and Azure Cosmos DB together to build a search engine, refer to `https://learn.microsoft.com/en-us/azure/search/search-howto-index-cosmosdb`.

Start with a simple keyword search UI and add filters and sort functionality in subsequent versions. It is extremely important to take feedback from the different technical and non-technical users. Based on their feedback, you can enhance the search experience. It is very important to ensure that the search provides value to its users; that is the only way to ensure adoption. A powerful search functionality can help accelerate the adoption of the data mesh. If people are able to find relevant data easily, they will adopt the data mesh faster.

Now, let's look at how to host the pipeline templates that can be used by any team that wants to pull data from the source they have found on the catalog. These templates help save effort as the teams don't need to build these from scratch.

Hosting common data pipeline templates

After exploring the data mesh and finding the right data for their project, the next step for data product teams is to access that data directly or move that data to their data product landing zone. Small or medium-sized data kept in databases or data lakes can sometimes be directly accessed into a Python workbook by using a connection string and reading the data into a data frame. But for large datasets and data coming from on-premise legacy systems or **enterprise resource planning** (**ERP**) and **customer relationship management** (**CRM**) systems hosted outside the data mesh, you need pipelines.

In Azure, these pipelines are typically built using **Azure Data Factory**. While sources for these pipelines are common across data products, the type of storage where this data is deposited is also quite standard. It's either a data lake or an SQL database that is typically used to store this data. If each data product team starts building pipelines to get data into the mesh or copying data from popular data products, a lot of duplicated pipelines get created all across the data mesh. This can be a waste of effort and time.

Instead of each team building their own pipeline, we can create parameterized templates for commonly used pipelines and surface them on the data mesh portal. Data product teams can browse these templates, and find pipelines that suit their needs and reuse them. They can substitute the destination (or the source and the destination) connection strings with their own and deploy the pipeline.

For deployment, they have two choices. They can deploy it in the data management zone or deploy it in their own data landing zone. The typical best practice is that if you are getting data from external sources such as ERPs and CRMs, then the pipeline should be hosted in the data management zone. That way, the central operations team can manage the connectivity to the source systems. If the pipelines are copying data from one data product to another, then the pipeline should be hosted in the destination data product's landing zone so the team that needs the data can maintain it.

Now, let's look at a few concepts of how to create parameterized Azure Data Factory pipelines.

Azure Data Factory

Azure Data Factory is a fully-managed data integration platform on Microsoft Azure. It has more than 90 connectors that can be used to connect to source and target systems to flow data from source to destination. The list is growing as new connectors get added. For an updated list of connectors, refer to the following link: `https://learn.microsoft.com/de-de/azure/data-factory/connector-overview`. In the process of transferring the data, the data can be cleaned and or transformed using various methods and activities provided by Azure Data Factory.

An Azure Data Factory pipeline consists of activities and datasets. The activities interact with the datasets. The datasets are attached to sources or destinations.

To learn about Azure Data Factory, refer to the following link: `https://learn.microsoft.com/en-us/azure/data-factory/introduction`.

In order to build, save, and run parameterized pipelines, you need to prepare a few artifacts. Let's look at each of those one by one and then build an architecture for hosting, browsing, and running pipelines on the data mesh portal.

Azure Data Factory instance

You need an instance of Azure Data Factory to build your common pipelines. This instance needs to be the data management zone on the same virtual network as the data mesh portal artifacts. Appropriate access levels should be set for these Data Factory instances.

This instance should be ideally created through a data mesh automation script, or should already be part of the data management zone. In *Chapter 3*, the *Data management landing zone* section mentions that you could have analytical and data engineering tools deployed to the data management zone at the time of initial setup. In case you did not include the Azure Data Factory instance in your original data management landing zone, then you could deploy one now. Just remember to modify the ARM template for the data management zone for this change.

For details on how to deploy an Azure Data Factory instance using CLI, refer to the following link: `https://learn.microsoft.com/en-us/azure/data-factory/quickstart-create-data-factory-azure-cli`.

To create Azure Data Factory using the ARM template, refer to the following link: `https://learn.microsoft.com/en-us/azure/data-factory/quickstart-create-data-factory-resource-manager-template`.

Integration runtime

The Azure Data Factory pipelines eventually get instantiated and executed. Like many Azure resources, this pipeline too needs memory and compute to run the pipeline. These resources are set up in the form of an **integration runtime**. You can have an Azure-hosted integration runtime that is managed by Azure, or you could have a self-hosted integration runtime that you can install on a **virtual machine** (**VM**) and manage on your own. For this section, we will consider an Azure-hosted integration runtime.

Creating linked services

Creating a pipeline involves first creating some linked services that connect to the source and the target. So, if you are copying data from a SQL Server database to an Azure Data Lake location, then you need one linked service to connect to the SQL Server database and one linked service to connect to the Azure Data Lake location.

Create a sequence of activities

In most cases where you are simply copying data from one location to another, all you need is one **Copy activity**. It is the most commonly used activity for copying data. The Copy activity has a source, a sink, and a transformation map that maps source columns to sink columns.

For more information on Copy activity, refer to the following link: `https://learn.microsoft.com/en-us/azure/data-factory/copy-activity-overview`.

Parameterize the pipeline

This is the most important part of the process of making pipelines reusable. You have to carefully select what you wish to parameterize depending on how reusable this pipeline should be. If you parameterize everything, then configuring the pipeline will become a big project and it will lose its convenience, but parameterizing only one to two parts of the pipeline will make the pipeline too specific and not very useful to the users.

Azure Data Factory allows users to define pipeline parameters and pipeline variables. **Pipeline parameters** are defined at the pipeline level and are passed in at the time of pipeline run. They cannot be modified during the pipeline execution. **Pipeline variables** are defined inside the pipeline and the values can be changed by the activities in the pipeline. For example, the folder location of copying files to an Azure Data Lake can be a pipeline parameter. However, the filenames can be generated at runtime based on source filenames. Hence, filenames can be a pipeline variable.

For more details on how to use pipeline parameters, refer to the following link: `https://learn.microsoft.com/en-us/azure/data-factory/how-to-expression-language-functions`.

Continuous integration/continuous development

The pipeline development team can use a combination of Visual Studio with the Azure Data Factory SDK or the Azure Data Factory Studio to build pipelines. Starting from **Azure Data Factory V2**, the web-based Azure Data Factory Studio development environment is the preferred form of development. Azure Data Factory V2 has Git integration and hence from the **Data Factory Studio** itself you can publish to and pull artifacts from a Git repository.

Alternatively, you can also use the Azure Data Factory SDK. This is a code-first approach to building and maintaining Azure Data Factory pipelines. Every artifact of the pipeline is generated using code. While it can be complex and time consuming, for complex pipelines that need finer control, developers prefer to use the SDK with Visual Studio.

For details on how to use the SDK to build an Azure Data Factory pipeline, refer to the following link: `https://learn.microsoft.com/en-us/azure/data-factory/quickstart-create-data-factory-dot-net`.

Figure 7.3 shows a high-level architecture of hosting and browsing data pipelines.

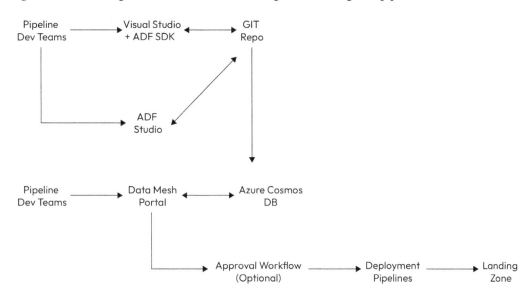

Figure 7.3 – Developing and browsing ADF pipelines

Data mesh portal integration

The Git Repo associated with the pipelines can be accessed using the Git API. The list of pipelines can be periodically updated in a Cosmos DB database acting as a metadata store. The data mesh portal can list the pipelines on the portal for the users to browse and pick. Once the users find the pipeline they want, they can supply the parameters as per their requirements and choose to deploy the pipeline in their landing zone or the data management zone, depending on the pipeline. An optional workflow can be activated for approvals. Once approved, the deployment is done through DevOps pipelines.

This was the high-level process of creating a browsable repository of parameterized pipelines. Once again, you should start small here. Ideally, companies start with common pipelines such as getting data from **systems applications and products (SAP)** or on-premises systems. These pipelines require less parameterization and customization and almost always are deployed in the data management zone. As your data mesh and the number of data mesh portal users grow, you can add more commonly used pipelines based on user feedback.

The data mesh features discussed thus far are the most common and the most important features of a data mesh portal. There are a few additional/optional features that can be added depending on the requirements of a company. Let us discuss some of these less common features of a data mesh portal.

Other common features of a self-service portal

We discussed some of the most common functionalities that companies build on their data mesh portal. Depending on the requirements of the users and how the company is structured, additional features can be added to the portal. Here are some examples of these features:

- **Data mesh explorer**: A UI that allows users to explore the data mesh. It allows them to see how the mesh is structured, which landing zones are connected to each other and which are not, and what projects run under each landing zone.
- **Data mesh health dashboard**: A high-level color-coded dashboard showing the health of all the data landing zones. This is a dashboard used by users to immediately check the health of their landing zones when something is not working and before they raise a support request with the operations team.

    There may be other features you might want to add depending on the feedback from the users.

- **Data contracts management**: As we will see in *Chapter 8*, if you are maintaining data contracts in a separate store, then the data mesh portal is an ideal location to surface these contracts for users to browse, search, and view them. Contracts can also be created from the portal.

This concludes an exhaustive list of features that can be implemented in a data mesh. Let us now architect the data mesh portal.

Architecting the self-service portal

Architecting the data mesh portal is like architecting any web portal. You need to treat your employees as customers of the portal and build a responsive, user-friendly portal that will become an important tool for making their work easier.

From a high-level architecture perspective, a simple **N-tier architecture** will be sufficient to take care of the scale required for the data mesh portal.

Let's walk through some of the core components of the N-tier architecture and possible options to build on the Azure cloud.

Active Directory and Domain Name System (DNS)

As a standard practice, all access to the portal needs to be integrated with Active Directory and a DNS to resolve the URL to a specific app gateway IP address. You also need to decide on the URL for the service. Depending on how the company intranet is designed, you can have the data mesh as a subdomain (`https://learn.microsoft.com/en-us/azure/dns/delegate-subdomain`), for example, `datameshportal.company.com` or a path such as `company.com/datameshportal`.

Application Gateway

Putting internal applications behind an application gateway is a standard practice across most companies. **Azure Application Gateway** will provide scale and security to your application with its built-in features for SSL termination, web application firewall, and load balancer.

For more details on Application Gateway, refer to the following link: `https://learn.microsoft.com/en-us/azure/application-gateway/overview`.

Azure App Service

Azure App Service will provide you with all the required services you need to build the web frontend, the backend, and the workflows all bundled into one scalable service. Azure App Service comes with multiple plan options depending on your requirements. They have the **shared compute** option, where your app gets hosted in VMs shared by other apps from other Azure customers; the **dedicated compute** gets you dedicated VM resources for your App Service plan, but the network is shared; and the **isolated compute** plan provides complete isolation of compute and network.

Dedicated compute is what I would recommend for the data mesh portal. You can use an existing App Service plan that your company already has or get a new service plan. Dedicated compute is available in a choice of tiers: Basic, Standard, Premium, Premium V2, and Premium V3. The VM specifications are improving along these tiers. For details on the Premium pricing, refer to the following link: `https://learn.microsoft.com/en-us/azure/app-service/overview-hosting-plans#premium-v3-pricing-tier`.

Do note that if you choose the dedicated App Service plan, it cannot be changed to another plan later.

The choice of operating system (Windows or Linux) also impacts pricing.

However, my observation has been that a Standard S2 or S3 plan is usually sufficient to support the data mesh portal workload.

Figure 7.4 shows the data mesh portal architecture.

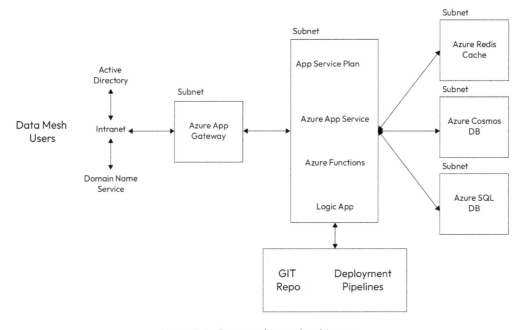

Figure 7.4 – Data mesh portal architecture

Azure Cosmos DB

Cosmos DB is the NoSQL document database that can store your catalog metadata along with any data-mesh-related metadata. One instance of Cosmos DB can host multiple databases and containers.

Git Repo and Azure DevOps pipelines

These are used to store artifacts such as ARM templates and Azure Data Factory templates. DevOps pipelines will be used to deploy the landing zones and other resources.

Network and security

All different components will be in their own subnet with private endpoints. Network security group rules that ensure communication between these subnets are limited to these subnets and no other network.

Azure Cache for Redis (optional)

This is an optional component. In my experience, it plays a huge role in making the portal responsive as you don't have to keep running queries against the database. Frequently used data or even the user's session can be stored in the Azure Cache for Redis.

Azure SQL DB (optional)

This is another optional store you can choose to have to store any relational models required for implementing your data mesh functionality.

Summary

This concludes our chapter on building a data mesh portal. We looked at the requirements of a portal and how to gather the requirements, the various important and optional features of a data mesh portal, and finally, how to architect the portal.

This also is the end of *Part 1* of the book. In this part, we discussed all aspects of designing and deploying a data mesh. In *Part 2*, we will discuss some practical challenges faced while deploying a data mesh and how to overcome or avoid them.

Part 2:
Practical Challenges of Implementing a Data Mesh

Even after mapping the theory to a practical architecture, there still are several challenges and some big gaps to fill. These are typically systems that are critical to the success of the data mesh but have no out-of-the-box solution, and hence, need to be built or bought. In this part of the book, we will discuss some of these big rocks, such as data contracts, master data management, data quality, data mesh monitoring, and others. We will understand the requirements of each and learn how to build these capabilities in your data mesh.

- *Chapter 8, How to Design, Build, and Manage Data Contracts*

- *Chapter 9, Data Quality Management*

- *Chapter 10, Master Data Management*

- *Chapter 11, Monitoring and Data Observability*

- *Chapter 12, Monitoring Data Mesh Costs and Building a Cross-Charging Model*

- *Chapter 13, Understanding Data-Sharing Topologies in a Data Mesh*

8

How to Design, Build, and Manage Data Contracts

Data contracts are a very important requirement for collaboration across the **data mesh**. However, they are a very new concept in the industry and there are no out-of-the-box solutions or products available to build and maintain data contracts. As a result, it becomes one of the most challenging parts of data mesh design and implementation. It's one of those situations where you know what it is but you don't know where to start.

In this chapter, we will discuss how you can design, plan, and implement data contracts for your data mesh.

In this chapter, we will cover the following questions:

- What are data contracts?
- What is the content of a data contract?
- Who creates and owns a data contract?
- Who consumes the data contract?
- How do we store data and access contracts?
- How do we link data contracts to data consumption or pipelines?

What are data contracts?

While building multi-tiered applications that integrate with multiple other external systems, the most common mode of communication is the **application programming interface** (**API**). These APIs are interfaces to the functionality of the application. APIs have the following elements bundled into a contract:

- The protocol used
- The URL of the API
- The request format
- The response format
- Any special security information

Various standards for APIs exist. **Simple Object Access Protocol** (**SOAP**), **representational state transfer** (**REST**), **GraphQL**, and **WebSocket** are some of the examples.

Once these APIs are built, they keep changing over time. New functionality, new data elements, and several other reasons can force teams to change, deprecate, and build new APIs.

In a small project, these changes are easy to manage. It's a small team that communicates very effectively because the API builder and consumer are probably sitting across the desk in the same office.

In large projects, however, the project is divided into modules and sub-modules. Different teams are working on these modules spread across the globe. They rely on each other's APIs for their part of the application to work. However, if the team that owns the API changes the API format without notifying the teams that are consuming the API, the system will stop working. This results in lost hours of work and delays in project delivery. It also generates a lot of back-and-forth communication to either roll back the changes or fix the application to use the new API format. Often new APIs have to be tested for integration before consuming teams can completely switch to the new version. This means the APIs also need to be versioned.

To avoid this situation, the world of application development has a solution. A commonly used technology called API management helps to develop, manage, test, and version the APIs. The API development team can publish one version of the API that has been tested and is ready to be used. As soon as they create a new version, they can publish another version of the API. Teams consuming the API are not impacted by the new version as they continue to use the old version. They can discover the new version and migrate their application to the new version. Once all the API consumers have migrated to the new version, the API dev team can deprecate the old version.

Tools such as Swagger (`https://swagger.io`) allow development teams to develop and publish their APIs along with documentation. This helps their users explore the APIs and understand the API parameters, usage, and version before they can use it.

One of the core principles of a data mesh is to treat data like a product. Similar to the APIs above, the data output of one product is being consumed by other data products. This builds dependency. If the format of source data changes, it can have a domino effect on all the downstream data products, so concepts of API management need to be brought to data if teams are to effectively collaborate across data products.

Data is different from APIs. APIs only expose the use of a coded functionality. They don't expose the underlying code itself. Data on the other hand has to be used with its content, and the content can be **structured**, **semi-structured**, or **unstructured**. Data can also be sensitive, such as **personally identifiable data** (**PII**) or trade secrets.

Hence, data needs a more holistic approach to standardizing its generation and use.

Data catalogs solve some of these challenges by cataloging all the data in the data mesh under a standardized metadata schema. **Data stewards** and data owners can then apply labels and business terms to the metadata. They can update information such as who owns the data and who is an expert on this data. You can also augment information such as data lineage. **Data lineage** informs the user where the data is originating and what processing has been done on the data.

Even after providing all this information about the data, once data is discovered in the catalog, the users typically have many questions before they start building their data product with this newly discovered data:

- At what frequency is this data updated?

- Is new data always appended to existing data?

- Is the data maintained on a sliding time window?

- What is the availability guarantee for this data?

- What if the owners change the schema? Will they notify me?

A similar set of questions is also applicable to the data owners who publish the data:

- Who will use this data?

- How can I let the users know about the sensitivity of the data?

- We refresh this data every night at 9 p.m. How can I let everyone know this without people having to flood my email inbox?

- How can I assure people that this data is reliable and always available? How do I tell people that this data is for experimental purposes only?

One solution to answer all these questions is to build a *data contract*.

A data contract is a definition of how two parties (the producer and the consumer) must exchange data. It defines the structure, format, service level agreement, sensitivity, and any other information that could be important for the producer or the consumer of the data.

The primary purposes of a data contract are as follows:

- **Data ownership**: The data contract documents details about who owns the data. This helps the data consumers make an informed decision about using the data.

- **Maintain compatibility**: The structure and rules of the data are defined and guarantees that they will be adhered to are provided, hence ensuring that the data produced and the consuming pipeline are always compatible with each other.

- **Enforce consistency**: The contract binds the producers and consumers to follow the rules of engagement, hence any discrepancy can be referred to in the contract.

- **Data versioning**: Schema changes are forced to be managed more systematically. Any changes to the schema are treated just like software changes. Change documents are made and communicated, the contract is checked out, changes are made, and the version is updated and checked back in. Any data pipelines executing this data as a source or target can continue to use the old schema version. The consumers are notified of the new data contract. The consumer now has an opportunity to test the new data on their data pipelines. After the tests are successful, the production data pipelines can switch to the new version of the data.

- **Documentation**: Unlike code, data does not have built-in documentation. Data contracts help to document data. Though most of the documentation can be done as part of the data catalog, any documentation feature not supported by the catalog can be added to the contract.

- **Preventing errors and failures**: Any data pipeline or any piece of code that depends on data that has a data contract can first check the version of the contract. If the contract version matches the one they are supposed to use, the pipeline or code will continue executing. If the version does not match, the pipeline or code can abort and log errors. By ensuring that data contracts are being checked by the pipelines and programs that consume the data, production failures can be averted and concerned teams can be notified of any changes to the contract that don't match the current version on the consumer's end.

Now that we have understood the importance of a data contract, let us look at the contents of a data contract.

What are the contents of a data contract?

The contents of a data contract will depend on a company's requirements. The content can be segmented into a few buckets:

- **Identification**: This is a way to uniquely identify a contract and associate it with the data it represents. Ideally, this should be a string formed by combining the department, the project, and the store that the data belongs to.

- **Basic information**: This bucket has the obvious attributes that any user would want to know about the data, such as its name, description, and version, and the owners.

- **Schema**: Schema defines the structure of the data. For *structured* data, this can be the table schema. For *semi-structured* data, this could be a JSON document with the schema explained. If it is an *unstructured* document, such as an image, it could be the image details such as image size, resolution, or image format. A schema definition can be provided as part of the contract. This helps users to ensure that the schema matches with what they had previously, and if not, then what has changed.

- **Data quality**: Data quality rules involve date formats, currency formats, and fields that should never be null or empty. Data quality is a topic in itself. A lot of information can go into data quality.

- **Service-level agreement** (**SLA**): The SLA should typically include data accuracy SLA and timelines SLA. Data accuracy SLA can be very elaborate. It could be a set of rules that are used to ensure that data is accurate, for example, range checks of a person's age, valid date checks, and certain business values that cannot go out of a certain range. Depending on the business, data accuracy could be even more complex. Timeliness SLA defines the age of the data included in the dataset. It provides a guarantee that the data collected is no older than a few hours/days from the time of the collection.

- **Security**: Security elements describe how the data is stored and secured in its original location. It also describes who can have access to it. If employees below a certain level cannot have access to this data, then that should be mentioned. *What kind of authentication is required to access this data?* Restrictions such as "only service principals access this data." This kind of information should be in the **Security** section of the data contract.

- **Privacy**: First and foremost, this should include the privacy label for the overall dataset. The typical labels used are **high business impact** (**HBI**), **medium business impact** (**MBI**), or **low business impact** (**LBI**). If the data contains any specific column that is masked and needs special permissions for access, then that should be mentioned here.

What actually goes into your data contract also depends on your choice of data catalog. If you have **Microsoft Purview** as your data catalog, then a lot of these data contract elements are already covered as part of the data catalog. Elements such as name, description, owner, privacy tags, and others will be covered as metadata in Microsoft Purview. Elements of data quality will also eventually arrive in Microsoft Purview. At the time of writing this book, data quality was in private preview. Certain attributes such as version and availability are missing from data catalogs and need to be provided. They are critical information for data consumers. Hence, an additional data contract document will be required.

If you have chosen not to use Microsoft Purview, then a more comprehensive data contract schema will be required that covers all the aspects that we have discussed.

The most common attributes in a data contract are as follows:

- Document ID

- Data ID

- Name

- Description

- Owners

- Version

- Last updated

- Update frequency

- Maintenance cycle

- Availability

- Security

- Privacy tags

The general trend is that if you have a data catalog service deployed, then the data contract can be short and simple, but if there is no data catalog service deployed, then the data contract must be elaborate and lengthy.

Once you finalize the attributes, you should build a JSON schema for the data contract, as shown in the following code snippet:

```
1{
2"UID": "1246573435",
3"DataID": "sales:forecast:weeklysales:fy22",
4"dataProductName": "Data product name",
5"dataProductDescription": "This is a test data product",
6"dataProductOwner":[
7    "xyz@companye.com",
8    "byx@companye.com"
9],
10"schema":{
11  "schemaURL": "http://url"
12 },
13"dataProductVersion": "1.01",
14"maintainanceCycle": {
15  "frequency": "Weekly",
16  "dayOfTheWeek": "Saturday",
17  "time": "9:00 PM"
```

```
18   },
19"SLA": "98.5%",
20"udateFrequency": {
21   "frequency": "Daily",
22   "time": "9:30 PM"
23   },
24"sensitivity": "HBI",
25"privancy": "L3",
26"security": {
27   "minEmpLevel": "L4",
28   "needSecApproval": "Yes"
29   }
30}
```

Who should be responsible for making and maintaining this data contract? Let us discuss this in the next section.

Who creates and owns a data contract?

This should be a short discussion because the answer is fairly obvious. The data owners create and maintain the data contract because the data owners are the only ones who know everything about their data. They know how to check the quality of data and they know the availability of their sources to justify the service-level contract.

While the data contract is created by the owners, the responsibility of keeping it up to date is divided between the data owners and the pipeline builders/developers. Typically, any data made available at a storage location is brought there by some program or pipeline. Every time this program or pipeline runs, as a last step, it should update the contract fields such as **Last updated**. Similarly, every time data owners see a change in the source systems or need to change the data format or structure, they should communicate this to the developers. The developers should then develop a new schema and update the **Schema** and the **Version** fields in the contract.

A new schema should be posted at a new location with a new URL. The URL typically should include the version number.

Change is an inevitability in a technology solution, which means that data formats and schemas will change over time. What is important is that these changes have to be maintained as different versions and must be traceable. This is especially true for regulated industries. This requirement leads to the important discussion of storage. How and where should a contract be stored in a way that can be versioned and tracked?

In the next section, let's discuss how contracts are referred to and used.

Who consumes the data contract?

The data contract is consumed by *data teams* who are looking for data to build their data products and by the pipeline managers who are consuming data based on the contract.

The users typically look at the contract to ensure that the data has the quality and reliability they need for their project. Once they decide to use this data, they typically build the code to consume this data. This could be a pipeline that pulls data from this source and lands it in their landing zone or it could be direct access to this data source through memory data frames, such as Python code running in a notebook. Irrespective of this, they should first confirm that the data contract has not changed and that the schema and the version are still valid. *Figure 8.1* is a simple version of how a contract can be maintained and consumed:

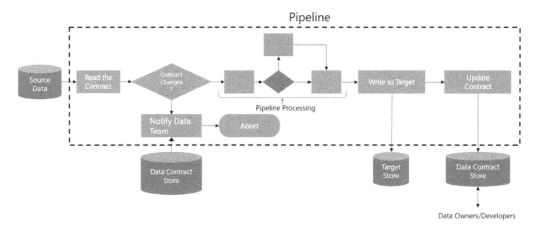

Figure 8.1 – Maintaining data contracts

In reality, it might be more complex than that. Depending on how you have implemented the data catalog, some parameters might be in the catalog and some in the custom data contract. Depending on the storage mechanism used, the pipeline might have to call multiple APIs from Microsoft Purview and the custom contract storage to update or fetch the contract.

In the next two sections, we will see how the storage of and access to contracts can be simplified in such a way that the implementation complexity is hidden from the contract producers and the consumers.

How do we store data and access contracts?

We cannot help but observe that a lot of the content of a data contract is also part of a typical data catalog such as Microsoft Purview. *Would it make sense to maintain the contract information as added attributes in Microsoft Purview?* While that might look like a tempting option and hence eliminate the need for additional storage, some features such as data versioning are yet not available in Microsoft Purview. While the Microsoft Purview product team might eventually bring this feature to Microsoft Purview, you need this feature now.

Considering this situation, you have two options:

- Spread the information across different data catalogs including Microsoft Purview and maintain the missing attributes as JSON files in a separate store
- Implement a data contract as a completely separate system decoupled from the catalog

The choice between these two depends on your roadmap. If you think you will eventually switch the data contract completely to Microsoft Purview, then go with the first option. If you wish to develop a data contract as an independent system with a rich set of features, then go with the second option.

In the *What are the contents of a data contract?* section, we saw that the data contracts are ideally stored as JSON files. The JSON format provides the necessary structure to be programmatically read from some code and the flexibility to change the structure if our data contract needs to change. While JSON is the preferred document format, you can choose to store it in any other format that is convenient to you. For example, if you implement your data mesh with a lot of upfront planning and design and you have a solid data contract format, you can even choose to store it in a relational database. It will give you a lot of programmability. Therefore, if your company has never dealt with a document database and doesn't wish to spend time learning about it, then a relational database can be a good choice.

Another obvious store for a JSON document is a NoSQL store like Azure Cosmos DB, which can also be a great way of storing data contracts.

One challenge with maintaining data contracts in databases is that there is no out-of-the-box ability to do change tracking as new versions of the data contract are introduced. With a relational database, you can build a system with the updates-as-inserts operation and ensure that all changes maintain a new record with a timestamp. Updated-as-inserts is a technique where you covert database updates as inserts with a timestamp. The inserted record has the same ID as the existing record but with a different time stamp. With Cosmos DB, you can enable Synapse Link. Synapse Link is a feature that enables analytics on Cosmos DB data. Along with analytics, it enables properties such as analytical time-to-live, hence enabling time travel operations. For more details on Synapse Link and time travel on Cosmos DB, refer to `https://learn.microsoft.com/en-us/azure/cosmos-db/synapse-link-time-travel?tabs=scala`.

An alternative and often preferred option is to store data contracts in a Git Repo and manage them as documents. This has a few benefits:

- It offers the ability to version the documents.
- Data owners can check out contracts, make changes, and check them back in.
- It has built-in traceability if you wish to see how a contract has changed.
- It also provides a URL for every contract. This greatly simplifies accessibility.

The last advantage of being able to access the document through a URL is a very important one.

You can add the data contract URL as a custom attribute to the data asset in Microsoft Purview. When users search the data catalog, they can see the contract URL as part of the search details. Clicking on it will take them to the GitHub site where they can read the actual contract.

Depending on how you plan to maintain and store your contract, you can choose to build an API that gets people and pipelines access to the contracts. These APIs could query an Azure Cosmos DB database or call a Git Repo through the Git API, read the document, and provide information as a parameter. The API abstracts the data contract implementation.

In the next section, we will see how to link data contracts with pipelines.

How do we link data contracts to data consumption or pipelines?

Hosting contracts in a central repository that data owners and data consumers can access and maintain is just one-half of the solution. Sticking to these contracts and ensuring that data pipelines are not failing because they are using the wrong version of the data completes the end-to-end data contract implementation. We also need to ensure that this consistency check is done in an automated fashion so that the pipelines or programs are aware of the consistency and take the necessary actions if they observe a mismatch.

The first step in this process is to ensure that you have programmatic access to the data contracts. Other than providing read-and-write access to the data contract, you also have to allow users to browse and search the contract with keywords.

As mentioned in the *What are the contents of a data contract?* section, certain attributes in the data catalog might overlap with the attributes that we are storing in the data contract and some attributes and features might be missing from the data catalog, such as data versioning. We have two options:

- Integrate all the attributes along with custom attributes such as version into a single Cosmos DB database

- Maintain the contract database as a completely separate system independent of the data catalog

The choice between these two will also depend on your decision on the data catalog implementation. In *Chapter 7*, in the *Data catalog* section, we discussed the approach of abstracting the data catalog into a Cosmos DB database and surfacing it onto the data mesh portal. If you go with this approach, then the first option works really well. The data contract can be a document URL of the data catalog metadata. Storing and searching all this data under one Cosmos DB database will be convenient and maintenance will be easier.

Let's build this solution step by step.

Catalog and contract document design

Design a JSON document that incorporates the catalog data along with the contract data. In Cosmos DB, there are two ways to model a document relationship. One is to embed the data contract inside the data catalog asset document. This method is preferred when the two documents typically have changes happening together. In our case, this will not be the situation. Data contracts will be independently updated and at a different frequency than that of the data assets. We should therefore go for the second method called **Referencing**, where you link two documents together, so the data catalog asset entry has a link to the data contract document. These two documents can be updated independently.

Your final data contract plus data catalog asset JSON will look like the following code snippet:

```
1 {
2   "//comment": "Data Asset",
3   "id": "1",
4   "Name": "Data Asset 1",
5   "Source": "Server=myServer; Database=myDatabase",
6   "SourceType": "Azure SQL Server",
7   "Other Fields": "<Values>",
8
9   "Data Contract":
10    [
11      {"contractID": 1}
12    ]
13 }
14
15
16 {
17   "//comment": "Data Contract",
18   "contractID": "1"
19   "DataID": "1"
20   "dataProductName": "Data product name",
21   "dataProductDescription": "This is a test data product",
22   "dataProductOwner":[
23        "xyz@companye.com",
24        "byx@companye.com"
25   ],
26   "schema":{
27     "schemaURL": "http://url"
28   },
29   "dataProductVersion": "1.01",
30   "maintainanceCycle": {
31     "frequency": "Weekly",
32     "dayOfTheWeek": "Saturday",
```

```
33    "time": "9:00 PM"
34    },
35   "SLA": "98.5%",
36   "udateFrequency": {
37     "frequency": "Daily",
38     "time": "9:30 PM"
39    },
40   "sensitivity": "HBI",
41   "privacy": "L3",
42   "security": {
43     "minEmpLevel": "L4",
44     "needSecApproval": "Yes"
45    }
46 }
```

Do note that creating a reference-based data model is an option with an assumption that data contracts will be more frequently updated than data catalog assets. If for any reason you think that the update frequency is not that different and it is better to have a faster read response, then you can embed the data contract into the data asset. Overall, this database is not going to be millions of records, so performance may not be a big issue either way.

Set up Cosmos DB

Set up a Cosmos DB instance with one database and two collections if you are using the reference data model or one collection if you are using the embed data model. Do enable Synapse Link at the instance and database level so that we can conduct time travel operations on the data contract.

For details on setting up Cosmos DB, refer to `https://learn.microsoft.com/en-us/azure/cosmos-db/nosql/`.

Write the integration code

Depending on your setup, you will need to write code that extracts information from Microsoft Purview and other legacy catalogs into Cosmos DB. This is done by calling the APIs of these systems and writing the data to the Cosmos DB database. You will also have to write a batch updater that can do bulk operations, especially for the first time you have to populate the Cosmos DB database. A user interface (form) will be required to enter data that needs to be entered manually.

Details on Purview API can be found at `https://learn.microsoft.com/en-us/purview/tutorial-using-rest-apis`.

Searching contracts and data assets

After the Cosmos DB has been set up and populated with data, you now need to surface this data on the data mesh portal in the form of a search interface. Users can search the database with keywords and find data assets and contracts. From there, they can choose to view, edit, or even delete the contracts or data assets if they are no longer applicable.

To implement this, Microsoft has a service called **Azure Cognitive Search**. This service allows you to plug in data sources and quickly build a search index with some simple configuration. Using its API, you can then build a very sophisticated search engine and interface to query the index and fetch results. As the documents change, you can re-index the search with a simple API call:

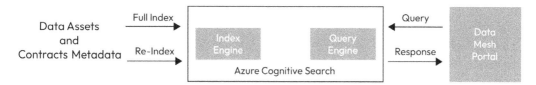

Figure 8.2 – Using Azure Cognitive Search

For more details on using Azure Cognitive Search with Cosmos DB, refer to `https://learn.microsoft.com/en-us/azure/search/search-howto-index-cosmosdb`.

Put the pieces together

Once the database, the search, and the backend integration are ready, start gluing them together on the data mesh portal and the data pipelines. Changing existing data pipelines to update the contracts programmatically can be a tedious task and will need to be done systematically ensuring that the contract updating pipelines are in sync with the contract consuming pipelines. The design for the data contract search is shown in *Figure 8.3*:

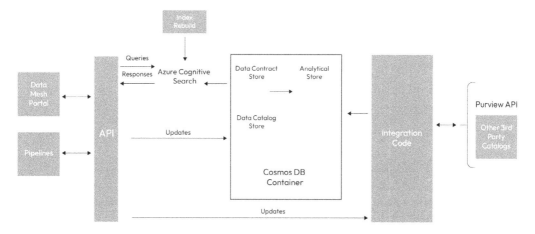

Figure 8.3 – The architecture for data contracts and data catalog

This concludes the chapter on data contracts. Due to the lack of a complete solution for data contracts, it is one of the more difficult parts of the data mesh in terms of implementation. It is not difficult because it is complex, but it is difficult because not much information is available on this topic, hence you have to just go with your instincts on how to design and implement it. Not only does it involve building and stitching the technical pieces together, but it also involves a cultural change. It is the discipline of ensuring that data contracts are maintained accurately and referenced by all consumers.

Summary

In this chapter, we first learned what data contracts are and how they are an important element for transforming data into data products. We looked at the contents of a data contract and understood the concept of having a standalone data contract system as well as a hybrid system where some components are maintained in a data catalog and some in a custom contract. These contract documents can then be stored in a data store such as Azure Cosmos DB or even an SQL database. We learned about the components required to build, write, and read these contracts through an API and also to search them through the data mesh portal.

In the next chapter, we will look at the next important feature of a data mesh, which is data quality management.

Data Quality Management

Data in a data mesh is being shared across different data products. These data products either deliver some key analytics or forecasts for the company or they are part of a chain of products that eventually deliver important analytics that drive the company's top-line and bottom-line performance. Hence, data quality must be maintained throughout the entire data mesh so that the interlinked data products keep delivering accurate and timely analytics. Poor data quality can lead to errors, misinterpretation and misguided decisions, and potentially reputational damage to the organization.

In this chapter, we will discuss how to manage and maintain high-quality data that your data consumers can rely on. The quality of your data will drive your data consumption. Users will leave good ratings on the **Data Catalog** for your data and that will further drive the popularity of your data.

In this chapter, we will cover the following:

- Why is data quality important?
- How is data quality defined?
- How to manage data quality
- Data quality management systems
- Build versus buy
- Popular data quality frameworks and tools

Why is data quality important?

In the previous chapter, we discussed how the data is distributed across the data mesh inside each data product. The responsibility of maintaining the data quality and availability is with the data owners. We also discussed how data products could be built using data from other data products. This could create a chain of dependency between different products. Failure of one data product to provide data in a timely manner could have a domino effect on the rest of the data product chain.

We drew a parallel between **API management** and **data contracts**. It's important that data schemas are versioned and provide all the relevant information to its consumers so that they can make an informed decision about using the data. This is just like how APIs are managed and maintained.

Data contracts ensure that data is available when it says it's going to be available and is of the same schema version written in the contract. But what about the data itself? Is the data inside of the right quality? Can it be relied on? Data availability will ensure that the critical KPI or forecast is delivered on time. *But is the KPI or the forecast derived from accurate data?* Having accurate analytics at the right time is going to help the business grow and beat the competition.

It has to be both accurate *and* timely. It cannot be either or. Having the wrong analytics at the right time is like having no analytics at all. Hence, it's critical to get the right data in the right format to the right people at the right time. This is the backbone of a reliable analytics system.

Data quality has a role to play in both accuracy and timeliness.

Let us say that some market data from the US is being used to build some prediction models in Europe. The data pipeline skipped converting the date format from MM/DD/YYYY to DD/MM/YYYY. Depending on the range of dates, the dates might pass as valid dates with the date and month switched and provide completely wrong results. Or, the invalid dates might force the system to error out, resulting in delays. Either way, it's bad for business. Despite adhering to the data schema version and availability promises, the end result and the company's performance were still impacted.

Certain elements of the data quality, such as formats, data lengths, nulls, and zeros, are easy to detect by simply sampling the data. But complex data accuracy, such as ensuring that the data from the source systems actually matches the data in the pipeline, can be complex.

Managing data quality is an ongoing process of continuously monitoring old and new data to ensure that the data does not drift on its data quality parameters. Hence, it's very important to put a formal **data quality management system** (**DQMS**) in place. You can start small by first detecting the formats and nulls and slowly augment with methods to detect complex data quality scenarios.

How is data quality defined?

Various definitions exist for data quality because there are many dimensions to data. Various articles and papers provide a list of data quality criteria. These vary slightly from article to article. Sometimes the definitions are the same but the terminology is different. Some articles skip one dimension. The following is a set of these data quality dimensions:

- **Accuracy** questions whether the value of the data is as it should be. Inaccurate account balances in a banking environment are an example. If the account balance is $100, then it should be $100 and not $99 or $101. Another example is the wrong addresses in the client dataset. `123 Elm Street` cannot be stored as `123 Elb Street`.

- **Completeness** indicates whether all the necessary data has been included. In a financial report, data for all the quarters must be included. If data for an entire quarter is missing from a financial report, it will mean wrong reporting and analytics.

- **Consistency** means that the data is consistent across systems. For example, if a dataset from a retail database shows a product as out of stock while it is in stock in the source system, this might result in the company ordering the product when it's not actually required. Alternatively, prices of stocks being shown differently on different stock exchanges can result in large losses of invested funds.

- **Timeliness** is about how recent the data is. All data has an original source. In retail, it could be the point-of-sale machine where an article is sold. In healthcare, it is the memory of the machine recording a health parameter. Timeliness is about the time difference between the time the data was at the source and the time it was read by the data product providing this data to others. For real-time or near-real-time systems involved in stock trading, hospital monitoring, or building safety systems, this can be critical. Hence, there is a threshold for timeliness that cannot be breached. For other systems such as financial forecasting, the timeliness threshold can be a few hours, as it will not make a big difference.

- **Validity** refers to whether the data is valid. Data must adhere to some business rules. For example, someone's age cannot be more than 150 years. Credit transactions cannot be negative. If data is found violating these rules, then it's considered not valid.

- **Uniqueness** means that the data should only appear once in a dataset. Duplicate customers and duplicate transactions with the same transaction ID are examples of data that violates uniqueness.

- **Reliability** ensures that data is being collected from the source of truth or from another verified data source. Revenue not matching the company's original financial report or having fluctuating sales patterns in one region while other regions show consistency with each other are examples of unreliable data.

Checking for all these elements can be a daunting task. It might involve cross-checking with multiple systems or even with publicly available information. But it is important to start somewhere, even if it's with a simple format and range checks. A data quality solution cannot be taken up as one large project. It needs to be built brick by brick. Implement the easy checks first and then tackle the complex quality requirements.

So how do you check data quality? In the next section, we will look at where and how to check for data quality.

How to manage data quality

In the previous section, we saw that there are many dimensions to data quality. So clearly it's not a simple solution or service that can be quickly put together. Data quality needs to be a company-wide strategy. In order to build this strategy and be able to design and architect a solution, let us look at each dimension of data quality and investigate how that dimension can be implemented in a real system.

Accuracy

You can check accuracy by first ensuring that the right data enters the dataset when it's written. Programmers writing stored procedures to insert or update records should know which fields are important and what the value ranges for those fields are. They should then write code to check for nulls, zeros, and data types. Early checks on quality at the source reduce quality check efforts later. For example, if there is a salary field in the database, you can run a check across the table to select all rows with zero or negative salaries, or you could check that the age field doesn't contain negative numbers or entries higher than 150. A data steward needs to define these rules and enforce the checks across all databases.

Completeness

This involves checking the dimensions and the range of the data. If a dataset is supposed to have a certain number of records only, check to make sure it does. This can be achieved by running a count query. *Are all the fields in the dataset present as they should be?* This can be checked by ensuring that the dataset fields match the schema in the data contract. These checks will also vary drastically depending on the vertical domain of the analytical system or the company.

For a financial reporting system, there should be a check for the min and max date in the dataset to ensure that data for the entire financial year is included. There should also be a check for dates for each quarter range to ensure that no quarter in the middle is missing. For a healthcare system, *completeness* might mean checking for the *completeness* of patient records such as health records, diagnosis, and treatment.

Consistency

This is probably one of the hardest dimensions to check because it involves checking against the source systems. *Consistency* issues can be contained if these checks are done across all systems as a company-wide policy and they are governed by a central data governance team that ensures that measures are followed. Depending on the data, different consistency levels or completeness need to be ensured.

For example, you might ensure that financial data is compliant with **atomicity, consistency, isolation, and durability (ACID)** standards and has proper relationship key constraints defined. Most databases provide a way to check *consistency* by maintaining a checksum for the entire data. This prevents data corruption on the disks or in memory. Azure SQL Database has a **Database Consistency Checker**

command (DBCC); `https://learn.microsoft.com/en-us/sql/t-sql/database-console-commands/dbcc-checkdb-transact-sql`. You can run this command on the entire database or a single table.

Another *consistency* check is to ensure that the data is consistent with the source. This means that after the data is copied to the target and published as a release version and before the data contract is updated, the pipeline that copied the data must initiate a check with the source system. The challenge here is that sometimes the data can be millions of records stored in a company's ERP or CRM system. Running a query such as that on a source system that is in production and is servicing users can put a burden on the source system and slow it down, impacting its users. So, this check might have to be done during off-peak hours.

There is also a method called **aggregate-based verification**, which involves storing aggregate values of certain numerical fields in another table in the source system. You then run an aggregate on the target data and check it against this field. This technique is also called **checksum verification**. Techniques such as these need to be employed to ensure that you are able to verify the consistency of data against the source system without impacting the people who are using the source systems.

Timeliness

Timeliness is ensuring that the data present in a dataset is not older than a given tolerance value. This tolerance value is stored in the data contract. So, the source pipeline needs to update three values in the contract; the `previous-update-timestamp`, `current-update-timestamp`, and `staleness-threshold`. The consuming system can now check the difference between the `previous-update-timestamp` and `current-update-timestamp` values and check to see if it is less or equal to the `staleness-threshold` value. If the difference is more than the `staleness-threshold` value, then the contract has been violated and the data should not be used.

Most importantly, the pipeline that makes this data available needs to move the `current-update-timestamp` values to the `previous-update-timestamp` values before updating the contract document.

Validity

Validity checks are probably one of the most common checks done by data engineers. Validity checks are about ensuring that the data format and range are correct. They check for null values and for counts of records that need to be a certain number to be valid. These checks can be done on source and the target systems. However, since these are the most common checks done across multiple data systems, they can also be centralized and parameterized to ensure reuse and consistency. We will discuss more on how to build such common validation systems in the *Data quality management systems* section.

Uniqueness

Unique values should truly be unique. You can easily check the uniqueness of data by running a few queries or functions depending on the development framework. In SQL, it could be running a combination of Select, Count, and Distinct commands.

```
SELECT column_name, COUNT(*)
FROM table_name
GROUP BY column_name
HAVING COUNT(*) > 1;
```

Figure 9.1 – SQL code to check the uniqueness of a column in a table

The preceding query will return more than zero rows only if it finds duplicate values in the column_name. Similarly, in Python, you can check for duplicates by using the duplicated function of the data frame, as shown in *Figure 9.2*:

```
import pandas as pd

# Assuming df is your DataFrame and 'column_name'
is the column you want to check
duplicates = df.duplicated(subset=['column_name'])

if duplicates.any():
    print("The column contains duplicate values.")
else:
    print("All values in the column are unique.")
```

Figure 9.2 – Python code to check the uniqueness of a column in a data frame

Reliability

This is another hard dimension to measure. It can mean different things for different types of data. You need to check if the source of the data and the methods used for collecting the data are reliable. You can raise questions such as these:

- Are the data owners responsible and professional?
- Do they take responsibility for the quality and accuracy of their data?

There are some steps involved in implementing reliability:

- Data stewards do the due diligence to ensure that the data is reliable by checking the sources and doing code reviews. After that, they should certify the data on the Data Catalog and tag it with a **Reliability Factor**.

- Users of the data should rate the data on the Data Catalog using the user rating feature. This will close the loop with the first step. Users will see the **Reliability Factor** and the **User Rating** and if they match, then they know they can rely on the data.

Based on these insights into measuring each dimension, we can group the measurement techniques into three buckets:

- Monitoring at the source

- Monitoring at the target

- Manual verification of monitoring at the source and target

Now that we have a good idea of how each of these dimensions can be measured, let us now look at how we can design and implement a data quality management system.

Data quality management systems

Data quality management systems, or **DQMSs** for short, play a critical role in monitoring the quality of data across all the dimensions that we looked at in the previous section. The more clean, accurate, and reliable data available across the data mesh, the speedier we can drive innovation. But considering all the points at which data is produced and consumed, it can be a daunting task to consistently ensure data quality across the entire data mesh; especially if it's a large data mesh. Smaller companies who have decided to build a data mesh have the advantage of setting up DQMSs from the beginning and are definitely at a huge advantage over a large company that is adopting a data mesh over already existing globally distributed analytical systems.

A problem of this magnitude needs to be solved systematically at different levels. The ideal place to start is data standardization.

Data standardization and **data processing standardization** are about creating a certain set of basic rules that everybody in the organization needs to follow while producing and consuming data, especially producing. These are gating rules that will have to be cleared if you want your data to be listed in the Data Catalog and be used by others. These rules are for data values, data formats, and data processing code. Some simple examples are as follows:

- Date formats stored in semi-structured files such as CSVs and JSONs should always be formatted in the YYYYMMDD format.

- Client IDs should always be in a certain format across the company. The same applies to product IDs.

- The names of people must always be in four separate fields: `Salutation`, `First Name`, `Middle Name`, `Last Name`.

- A person's age must be between 0 to 150 years.

- The state field in a US address must be a two-letter state code and must be valid.

These rules can then be categorized into generic and domain-specific rules. Generic rules such as age and address might apply to any data. But some domain-specific rules could be specific to a domain:

- Product codes must be correctly formatted

- Inventory counts must not be negative

- Sales transactions must not have a future date

Along with rules on data formats and values, you also need to create rules on data management and processing. These rules are specific to data processing frameworks. For SQL Server, you could have rules about the following:

- Mandating primary key/foreign key constraints for referential integrity

- A requirement for important transaction code to be wrapped in a **Begin Transaction** and **End Transaction** statement

Similar rules could be created for other big data and machine learning data frameworks.

All these rules need to be stored at a central location as a single source of truth. The policy should be accessible to all stakeholders, preferably on the data mesh portal organized as a set of linked searchable pages for easy access.

The policies could be stored in two ways:

- They can be a set of pages/documents that are maintained in a version control system. The big disadvantage of this method is that there is no programmatic access to the rules and policies. This can be used as a method of storing rules to begin with. It provides a central repository of rules but is not a good long-term solution.

- They can be stored in the form of a relational schema in a database. This database can then be used to populate the portal page for data quality or can be used by programs, pipelines, or DQMSs to ensure that the code to check data quality complies with the policy.

The database option is the preferred option as it can be programmatically accessed and modified through APIs.

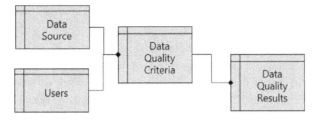

Figure 9.3 – Sample database structure for a data quality warehouse

Figure 9.3 shows an example of a relational model to store data quality rules. If you add more dimensions to it, you can even convert the model into a star schema by creating a fact table out of the data quality rules.

These data quality rules stored in a database can be made searchable through the data mesh portal. Data stewards should be able to log in to this part of the data mesh portal and browse the rules. As an added feature, they should be able to select a data source and verify the quality of the data against various data quality rules.

The quality and maintenance of these data quality rules are going to drive the level of success of data quality management in the organization. Hence, it's extremely important that you plan and build a DQMS. Once again, start small and grow as you build, slowly incorporating all the needs. *Figure 9.4* shows the interactions that various entities and teams have with the DQMS rules/policies:

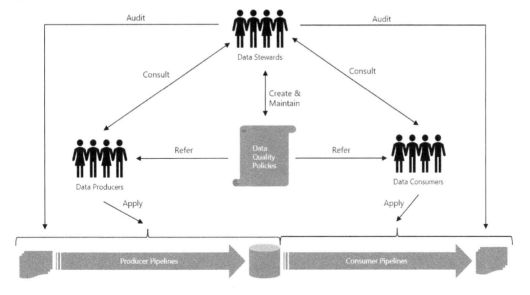

Figure 9.4 – Roles and responsibilities in data quality policies

Ideally, data stewards should be responsible for creating and maintaining the data policies. They should be the only team allowed to modify the policy. They should consult with the data consumers and producers to implement and make any ongoing changes to the policy to keep it current and in line with corporate policies and local regulations.

The data producers and the data consumers should refer to the data policy and apply those policies to their data sources, pipelines, and data targets. If they observe any important aspect of their data or their processing logic that should become a policy, they should consult with the data stewards and propose its inclusion in the policy. Data stewards will define and word the policy and modify the data policy document/record. Notifications about changes should be sent to all data mesh users who are linked to that data transaction. However, this approach could also make the data stewards the bottleneck in the data quality process. So, a decentralized or a hybrid approach can be more effective.

Implementing a data quality governance framework such as the one described might require a big cultural change in the organization. Highly regulated industries such as healthcare and pharma are usually used to such processes, but for other industries, this could mean a big change.

While the process might look very bureaucratic, it actually is not. The efficiency of the data quality management system such as the one described completely depends on the tooling and maintenance of the policy. If the policy is hosted on a portal with efficient tools to check out and check in changes with version control systems, human efforts can be minimized.

Once this policy is in place, let's focus on implementing the data quality rules across the entire producer-consumer pipeline.

There are three main approaches to implementing the policies:

- **Decentralized**
- **Centralized**
- **Hybrid**

Let us look at these approaches in detail.

Completely decentralized

This approach puts the onus on the producers and the consumers to implement all the relevant policies in their data, pipelines, and processes. They can use tools of their choice to do so. The data stewards audit and maintain the data policies.

The advantage of this method is that it's the easiest to implement. All data owners know their data well and implement the policies using tools they are comfortable with. The disadvantage is that the duplication of efforts for common policies and non-standardized implementations of common policies can lead to discrepancies and increase the workload of the data stewards as they not only have to audit the policies but they now also have to audit the implementation for all the data and processes in the entire data mesh.

Completely centralized

This approach implements all the data policy rules into one central framework or system. Every process in the data mesh must call to this central system/framework via APIs.

The advantage is that the implementation is standardized and centrally maintained so there are no discrepancies. Data stewards have to only ensure that everyone is calling these **quality APIs**. The huge disadvantage is that it's almost impossible to implement. All data will have rules and policies that only apply to it, and maintaining all these centrally can be a herculean task. This approach might work for small- and medium-sized organizations. For large organizations with globally distributed analytical teams, the central data stewards team could become a bottleneck in the data quality process.

The hybrid approach

This approach combines the preceding two approaches. All the common policies and format checks are implemented centrally. The local policies that apply to individual datasets are implemented locally by the responsible data teams. This is usually the best and preferred approach.

The hybrid implementation will look something like in *Figure 9.5*:

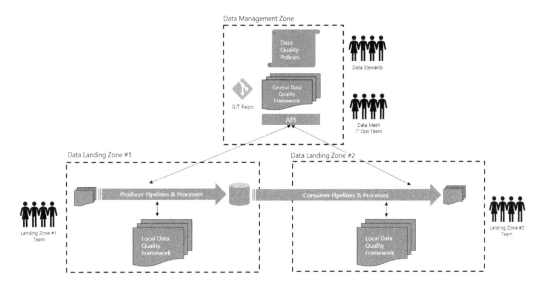

Figure 9.5 – Hybrid data quality management

There is one challenge with this architecture. The central data quality framework can create performance and scale challenges. Consider a situation where in a large data mesh, common data quality code is executed centrally. If hundreds of pipelines start calling the central data quality frameworks thousands of times during the day, it will create a major performance bottleneck in the central system. As the code executes for one pipeline, other calls will start queuing up. This will delay all these pipelines waiting in the queue to execute the data quality code. To solve this problem we will need to scale the central data quality code execution.

One solution to this problem is to only maintain the code of the central data quality framework centrally and shift the actual execution of the code to the pipeline itself. Each data landing zone pulls the code from the central GitHub repository and maintains the execution of these rules locally. Every time a change is made to the central repository, a set of auto-deploy pipelines can pull the code and deploy it locally to each landing zone, as shown in *Figure 9.6*:

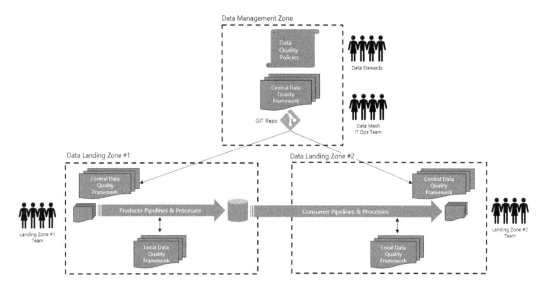

Figure 9.6 – Centralized code and decentralized execution

The model in *Figure 9.6* has some key advantages. The central ITOps team has to only maintain the code and not the infrastructure to run the code. Decentralization also eliminates performance issues for the landing zones as only their pipelines and processes are calling the central quality framework that is not set up in their environment.

The local quality framework is the responsibility of the data landing zone team. The central data quality framework can be built using a few different techniques. We can also use some ready-made third-party or open source libraries. We will discuss more about this in the next section.

Build versus buy

Build, buy, or both? In the previous section, we observed that data quality has many different aspects. It also is something that evolves over time. As you build your data mesh and as you onboard new projects, new data quality parameters need to be added. So, clearly, you need a solution that will change and grow with your requirements. If you build your data quality management system, you will not have to worry about this requirement. You will be able to change, modify, and upgrade the functionality whenever you need to.

If you build your own data quality engine, you will need the following components:

- Data quality warehouse
- Data quality engine
- User interface to manage the DQMS
- API for the pipelines and processes to call

Figure 9.7 shows the components of a data quality management system:

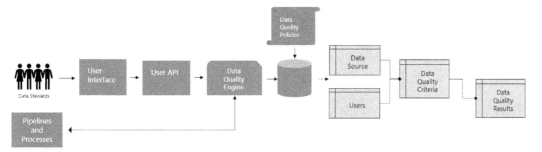

Figure 9.7 – Components of DQMS architecture

The main disadvantages of building your own DQMS are the use of resources and time. You need a team to build and maintain the DQMS.

The other option is to buy an out-of-the-box DQMS solution.

At the time of writing this book, the **Microsoft Purview Data Quality Assessment** and **Data Quality Insights** features were in Private Preview. If you have already decided to use Microsoft Purview as a Data Catalog, you will need to wait a few months before the feature goes into public preview and eventually become generally available.

The other option is to use third-party data quality tools.

To summarize the build versus buy decision, let us consider all the pros and cons of both.

The pros and cons of building a DQMS are as follows:

Pros:

- **Customization**: You can tailor the system to meet your specific needs
- **Control**: You have complete control over the system's features and updates

Cons:

- **Time and resources**: Building a DQMS from scratch can be time-consuming and resource-intensive
- **Complexity**: Managing changes is a complex task that involves many stakeholders

The pros and cons of buying a DQMS are as follows:

Pros:

- **Quick implementation**: A ready-made DQMS can be implemented quickly
- **Expertise**: Vendors often have extensive experience in data quality management
- **Features**: Many systems come with advanced features such as data security

Cons:

- **Cost**: There can be significant costs associated with purchasing and maintaining a DQMS
- **Flexibility**: A purchased system may not be as flexible or customizable as a custom-built one

A hybrid between build and buy would be to use a ready, open source framework that can be modified and extended to your requirements. It will allow you to start off the blocks quickly, and it is flexible on any new requirements.

In the next section, let's look at some of the popular frameworks available for building your DQMS.

Popular data quality frameworks and tools

In this section, we will look at some of the frameworks and products available for DQMSs. But we cannot go deep into the design and implementation of these products as that is out of the scope of this book. But I will provide links that you can use to learn more about them.

If you are using Microsoft Purview and don't want to wait for the data quality features to be generally available, you can opt to go with one of the Microsoft Partner solutions such as Profisee (`www.profisee.com`). Profisee offers a master data management and data quality solution that integrates with Microsoft Purview. Microsoft Purview and Profisee is a common combination used by many companies.

If you wish to go for an open source framework, you can consider Great Expectations (`https://greatexpectations.io/`). Great Expectations is one of the most popular open source extensible frameworks for data quality management, being used by many companies.

Great Expectations calls these data quality rules **expectations**. All expectations functions are prefixed with `expect`. For example, `expect_column_values_to_not_be_null` inspects the table or the column provided as the parameter for null values.

Great-Expectations comes with over 300 out-of-the-box expectations that can be browsed at `https://greatexpectations.io/expectations/`.

You can also build custom expectations on top of the framework or even extend existing expectations.

Going deeper into Great Expectations is beyond the scope of this book. To explore its capabilities in detail, refer to `https://greatexpectations.io/`.

Profisee and Great Expectations are two of the popular frameworks used for data quality management. Many such frameworks exist and you should go through the features and architecture of these frameworks to decide which one best meets your requirements.

As the data mesh grows and teams become dependent on each other's data, it will become critical to ensure that the chain of dependency is kept functional. Teams need to trust each other's data to accelerate collaboration and innovation. A DQMS plays a critical role here. It should not be an afterthought; it should be baked into the data mesh architecture right from the beginning.

Having said that, a DQMS can be complex to implement. It is important to start small and build and improve it over time.

Summary

We understood the importance of data quality to the data mesh and defined data quality and all of its attributes. We dived deeper into understanding these attributes and the methods of capturing them. Data quality can be implemented in multiple ways, e.g., centralized, decentralized, and hybrid. We looked at these approaches. Finally, we explored a few examples of third-party tools available for implementing data quality frameworks.

In the next chapter, we will discuss master data management—yet another important component that brings consistency to the analytical products of the data mesh.

10

Master Data Management

Every company, big or small, is made up of some common entities that are referenced across all departments. Some of the most common examples of this are customers, products, suppliers, and addresses. This data should be fixed but, unfortunately, it changes over time as it travels through the different departments and regional offices of a company.

This data is called **master data**.

As a data mesh grows and you incorporate more data products into the mesh, different versions of the master data start flowing into the mesh. This can start impacting the analytical output. Inaccuracies, errors, and redundancies will start showing up in reports leading to hours of manual debugging and lost time and money for the company.

In this chapter, we will learn about **master data management** (**MDM**) and its importance to the data mesh.

In this chapter, we will cover the following:

- Single source of truth
- What causes discrepancies in master data?
- MDM design patterns
- MDM architecture for a data mesh
- Build versus buy
- Popular MDM tools

Single source of truth

What is master data? The data of the core non-transactional entities of the business that are used across an enterprise or a company are called master data. They provide context to transactions, such as sales and purchase orders. In order to complete a sales transaction or a purchase order, we need information about entities, such as customers, products, suppliers, and address locations. These entities are the master data. In a report that shows sales by customer, sales are the transaction data, and customer is the master data.

Master data entities will vary depending on the vertical market of the enterprise. For healthcare, it will be patients, providers, medicines, and treatments. For a bank, it's the account numbers, SWIFT codes, and **know-your-customer (kyc)**) data.

As you can imagine, master data is critical, as enterprises are run around using this data. All the analytics will have the master data as dimensions to the facts. Sales reports by customers, sales reports by product, and sales reports by store can all be important analytics for any business. The sales numbers have to be accurate, but imagine having duplicate customers in the report or the same product SKU referred to with different names. It can create confusion and drive wrong decisions in the field, rendering the entire analytical process ineffective and creating doubts about the investment in analytical systems. The field teams will lose faith in analytics.

Consistency and **accuracy** are mandatory requirements of any analytical system. As a company becomes dependent on analytical systems for their business forecasts, predictions, and performance reports, it becomes crucial that the data being used to generate these analytics are consistent and accurate. This is true for transactional and master data alike.

So, what causes this discrepancy in master data? Let's look at some of the common causes and reasons in the next section.

What causes discrepancies in master data?

Every company starts with a simple database to manage its customers, products, and all other important business entities. As the company grows, these data start migrating to the different departments and regions of the company. Over time, copies of these data exist in many areas of the company. The data are changed or modified over time. These changes are sometimes planned and sometimes accidental. As a result, the data starts drifting from its original value, and you have different versions of the same data at different locations. Here are a few reasons why this master data drifts from its original values:

- **Inconsistent naming conventions**: Some countries capture the names of people, such as their last name, first name, and middle name. Some countries skip middle names. These inconsistent naming conventions can lead to duplicate records for the same product.

- **Lack of standards**: Information such as product names and account numbers are often not standardized in their formats, leading to the same information being written in different formats across the organization. Since computer systems work on exact values, queries and joins result in recognizing these values as different entities and, hence, creating duplicates in the query results.

- **Data entry errors**: Sometimes, differences between the names of entities surface because of data entry errors. Typos or cultural differences in pronunciations cause these mistakes and create erroneous duplicates. Sarah gets spelled as Sara. John can be spelled as Jon. These changes could also be typos or wrong spellings due to cultural changes.

- **Culture-friendly product names**: One of the most common reasons for the same product being called differently in different countries is because some product names translate to something offensive or derogatory, and the names of these products have to be changed. Sometimes, names are changed because they are difficult to pronounce in another country with a different local language. For example, the word "mist" translates to manure or dung in German. Several fragrances and beauty products have the English word "mist" in them. These products might get renamed and marketed under a different name in Germany.

- **External factors**: External factors, such as country-based regulatory changes, industry shifts, or organization restructuring, can force changes to the original data.

These and other reasons can create discrepancies in the master data. Some of these reasons are business-driven, and some are more to do with the siloed systems created as the company grows and issues due to a lack of data quality controls. Whatever the reasons, detecting these discrepancies and fixing them can be a complex task.

Consider the following record entered into different systems:

Name	Address	Date of birth
A Deswandikar	1 Main street, Jamestown	20-Oct-1972
Aniruddha Deswandikar	One Main Street, Jamestown	20-10-72
Aniruddha A Deswandikar	1 Main street, James Town	20-Oct-72

Table 10.1 – Example record

Within each system, each is a valid record, but are they the same person? Complex fuzzy logic lookup (https://en.wikipedia.org/wiki/Approximate_string_matching) and phonetics search (https://en.wikipedia.org/wiki/Phonetic_algorithm)-based algorithms are required to find out if these are the same entity. The ones that cannot be detected have to be manually merged by actually checking the physical references.

An MDM system will need these processing algorithms. Many of these algorithms are available as readymade libraries and don't have to be built from scratch. However, integrating and testing them requires effort. Third-party MDM solutions have these integrated into their core systems.

Let's now look at how these enterprise systems manage master data within themselves. Though source systems, such as **enterprise resource planning** and **customer relationship management**, are beyond the scope of this book, the topic will help understand the complexity of MDM and how it impacts a data mesh.

MDM design patterns

MDM has been a requirement for many decades now. Enterprise systems such as **enterprise resource planning (ERP)**, **customer relationship management (CRM)**, **supply chain management (SCM)**, **human resources management (HRM)**, and others have been around for many decades now. Invariably, these systems are set up by different software vendors, and some of them can be homegrown. Managing the master data between these systems has been a requirement for a long time now. As a result, a few industry patterns have emerged on how master data are managed. Multiple articles and papers will discuss different patterns; here, I am summing it all up into three high-level methods of managing your master data:

- **Registry-based system**: This is the traditional method where the actual master data are maintained inside the individual systems, but the data are registered with a reference in a central database. The records across the systems are matched, and duplicates are recognized and indexed with a unique identifier. This is especially useful when you have multiple enterprise systems (multiple ERPs or multiple CRMs) across the organization.

- **Consolidation-based systems**: The consolidation-based system consolidates master data from multiple systems and stores a single version of the truth in a central hub location. All surrounding systems reference this data when they need it. This consolidated master data is updated back into the source systems. Changes to the master data are also reflected in the source system. So, the job of the central master data database, in this case, is to keep all the source systems in sync with the same values.

- **Repository-based system**: In a repository-based system, the master data is created and maintained in a repository and supplied to all systems. Here, the master data becomes the system of the records. The repository system can also be implemented using a third-party MDM solution.

Irrespective of the MDM pattern you use, it still serves as a central system for your enterprise applications and your business intelligence and analytics framework. In a centralized analytics framework, it might be easier to connect the MDM and all the transactions to a data warehouse through some standard pipelines. However, in a data mesh architecture, it will have to be different. The analytics is no longer centralized:

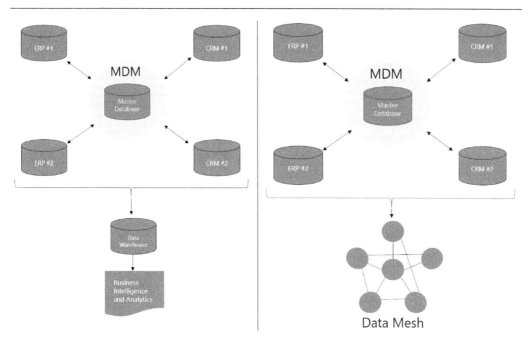

Figure 10.1 – MDM in centralized analytics versus a data mesh

In the next section, let's look at how MDM can be incorporated into a data mesh architecture.

MDM architecture for a data mesh

Given the distributed nature of a data mesh, each data product needs to ensure that the master data they are using are consistent and accurate. This mandates a need for a reference master dataset that is centrally maintained and referenced by all the data products and their pipelines that need to ensure consistency. Multiple architectures are available for managing this central reference dataset. To understand what design works best for you, you should first examine your master data. Not all master data is used by every domain in the company. Customer master data might not overlap product master data, but the sales domain might use both.

Hence, two strategies emerge for managing master data: **domain-oriented MDM** and **domain-level MDM**:

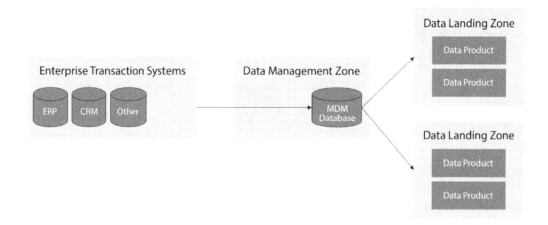

Figure 10.2 – Domain-oriented MDM

The domain-oriented technique has a single MDM domain that is referenced by all the data products across all the data landing zones, as shown in *Figure 10.2*. Irrespective of what domain the product belongs to, all master data is housed in the same database. Basically, the MDM has its domain. Often, this domain is the **data management zone**. This is a preferred method when managing MDM when the overlap in the master data across domains is large.

If the overlap between the master data is not as much, scanning through all the master data by every data product might not be an efficient way to fetch master data. In this case, it might make sense to maintain master data for each domain/product. We split the central master data into different domains and house them in different landing zones. The data products, in turn, can refer to the master data from the required domain, as shown in *Figure 10.3*.

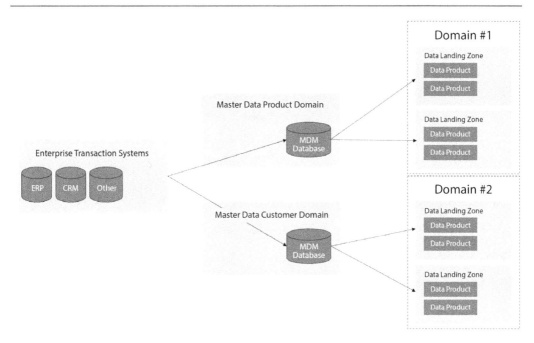

Figure 10.3 – Domain-level MDM

Another approach could be to build a domain-oriented MDM, where the created views inside each domain can be connected to each domain- level product. This approach is actually the preferred approach and is the most efficient. This is also supported by most MDM products. *Figure 10.4* shows the domain-based approach:

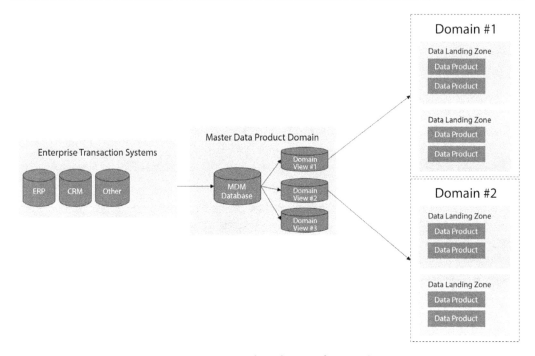

Figure 10.4 – Domain-based views of master data

MDM can become very complex if you manage too many areas of master data. You need to ensure that what is being managed in the master data is truly the master data used by multiple products. If any master data have no overlap with any domain, they're best managed locally by the product itself. This division of management is very critical and is very easily achievable in a data mesh architecture.

For example, customer, product, supplier, and employee data could be used across multiple products. However, some project-related master data or a specific marketing campaign related to master data might not be needed by any product other than these individual products. Therefore, while the former should be part of MDM systems, the latter does not need any MDM.

Build versus buy

The build versus buy discussion for MDM is the same as the one for data quality discussion. It all boils down to cost versus customization. Building your own MDM can be expensive, but it will be flexible to fit your exact needs. Buying a system might be cheaper, but you will need to adjust to its limitations.

Popular MDM tools

While there are many MDM solutions in the market, if you are using **Microsoft Purview** as your data governance tool, then there are two popular partner solutions for MDM that integrate well with Microsoft Purview:

- **Profisee** (`https://profisee.com/`)
- **CluedIn** (`https://www.cluedin.com/`)

This concludes the topic of MDM. The actual topic of MDM is quite vast and beyond the scope of this book. However, the reason I wanted to stress this topic is because it's important for an efficient data mesh implementation. Without a good MDM solution, the data products will not produce reliable analytics, and collaborative innovation will not be achieved.

Summary

In this chapter, we looked at what master data is and the importance of clean master data for generating accurate analytics. We looked at some of the main reasons why master data drifts from its original and correct values. We then looked at various patterns for maintaining master data and how master data can be accessed in a data mesh scenario with distributed analytics. MDM systems can be complex to build and maintain. We saw the pros and cons of building versus buying an MDM system.

In the next chapter, we will understand monitoring and data observability.

11

Monitoring and Data Observability

Monitoring and data observability are two sides of the same coin and are both critical for a well-managed data mesh.

Monitoring is all about proactively monitoring the health of the landing zones. As the data mesh grows and more data products start leveraging the mesh, it becomes critical to ensure that all the data products and their landing zones are up and running. This requires the proactive and reactive monitoring of the entire data mesh from a central location.

Data observability has more to do with a data mesh inherently being a collaborative framework. Data will be moving between landing zones and it's very important to observe this movement of data and any changes made to the data.

In this chapter, we will see how to think about, design, and build a monitoring system from the ground up that will make the management of the data mesh easier.

In this chapter, we will cover the following:

- The importance of data mesh monitoring and data observability
- How data mesh monitoring differs
- Baking diagnostic logging into the landing zone templates
- Designing a data mesh operations center
- Tooling for the DMOC
- Data observability
- Setting up alerts

Piecing it all together – the importance of data mesh monitoring and data observability

In my experience of working on data mesh projects with multiple customers, I have observed two uber-level patterns on how **centralized data analytics** gets funded and monetized:

- **The central cost center model**: Some companies treat centralized analytics as a requirement for the company and fund it as a central initiative. In such scenarios, an annual budget is allocated to analytics and projects are prioritized by a committee of key stakeholders that decide which analytical projects will be supported and which will be put on the back-burner for the next year. Central analytics is a cost center, and the **return on investment (ROI)** is evaluated by the overall impact of analytics on the top and bottom lines of the business. The data mesh implementation is also part of this central budget.

- **The distributed cost center model**: Many large global companies treat each zone or major product division as a profit center and expect them to fund their own analytics. Let's call them data products for simplicity. In such scenarios, the cost of any kind of central analytics is passed on to these data product teams. The data product teams now have a choice: building their own analytics framework and infrastructure and managing their collaborations with other zones or groups, or choosing to be part of the central analytical system that provides them governance, management collaboration, and data discovery out of the box. The central analytical system (data mesh) is also a cost center and passes on the costs of these services to the data products that onboard their services. The data products compare the cost and benefits of being on a centrally managed data mesh. If they don't see the benefits, they can opt out and maintain their own environment.

Both of these approaches have their pros and cons. In the first approach, inefficiency of any kind will reflect on the entire company. In the second approach, inefficiency will drive the central data mesh into the ground. In order to run an efficient data mesh in either of these scenarios, you will need to proactively monitor the efficiency and performance of the data mesh and provide monitoring output to the data product teams so that they can ensure the quality and reliability of their products. ROI is important in both of the aforementioned situations. If the data products are unreliable or produce delayed results, it can be detrimental to business and to the value of the data mesh. ROI in this era of data is the ability to make quick decisions, stay nimble to insights, and make remediations/changes as fast as we can.

In traditional centralized analytics, where there is a common set of resources and services being used by the entire company, monitoring is rather simple. The number of resources to be managed is limited and known. Changes to monitoring itself are based on changes to the architecture or the addition of services. These changes are not very frequent.

How data mesh monitoring differs

In a data mesh, the monitoring can become complex. Each data product brings its own set of resource requirements. Multiple data products churn out diagnostic data logs, and as the data mesh grows, these logs will also grow exponentially.

This is why monitoring is very important to the data mesh. It's an area that should be part of the very initial strategy and should be baked into the design of the data mesh landing zones right from the beginning. Let us see how we can do that in the next section.

How data mesh monitoring differs

In a centralized analytical system, you have a few fixed subscriptions that manage resources across the end-to-end analytical cycle. The pipelines, storage system, data warehouse, and all the analytical frameworks are common to entire the system. The monitoring system, too, focuses only on this set of resources. Any change to the analytical system's architecture is systematically added and changes are made to the monitoring system. These changes are few and far between.

A data mesh environment, depending on your data mesh strategy, can be very dynamic. New landing zones and data products can get added to the mesh more frequently than to the central system. Each data product will have a different set of tools and services for ingestion, analytics, and serving. Monitoring all the landing zones means ingesting diagnostics and logs from all the landing zones into the central data management zone and then analyzing all of them. The monitoring data and dashboards need to be made visible to each landing zone based on their resources and services, and a central dashboard is needed that shows the health of the entire data mesh to the central ops team. *Figure 11.1* shows the difference in monitoring a central analytical system as opposed to a data mesh:

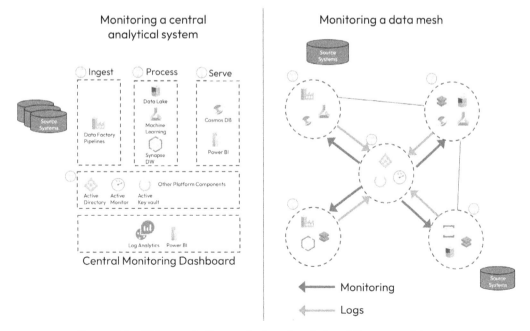

Figure 11.1 – Difference in the monitoring of central analytics versus data mesh

Clearly, monitoring a data mesh looks to be more complex, but it does not have to be. You can simplify this process by starting early and standardizing it. If each data landing zone template is designed to stream diagnostic data to the data management zone and if the analytical dashboards are designed from the beginning to reflect the health of the data mesh and resources, then onboarding any new landing zones will become exponentially easier.

In the next section, we will see how these diagnostic settings can be baked into the landing zone templates.

Baking diagnostic logging into the landing zone templates

Every Azure service has a very consistent method of collecting diagnostic logs. If you go to the Azure portal and go to the landing page of any Azure service, you will see a pane on the left side of the landing page, also called the **Resource Menu**. Under the **Monitoring** section, you will see a menu option called **Diagnostic Settings**, as shown in *Figure 11.3*. The working pane of this menu option allows users to set up diagnostics for this service.

There are different categories of diagnostics and logs in Azure. The Azure cloud service is divided into the management plane or the control plane and the data plane. The role of the control plane is to create and manage the resource (create, update, delete). The data plane is used to interact with the resource (read, write, execute). For example, if I am creating a storage account, the creation process is done via the **control plane** using the **Azure Resource Manager** to create the storage account. When I want to upload files to the storage account or read files from the storage account, these operations are performed by the data plane.

Similarly to the operations, the metrics and logs are also separated across planes. The platform metrics are part of the control plane and are collected automatically by Azure at no cost to the users. The platform logs, however, are generated and captured only when the user specifically sets up diagnostic settings and indicates the category of logs to be collected and where they should be directed for storage.

Let's now look at each of these metrics and logs in detail.

Azure Platform Metrics

Azure Platform Metrics is a feature of Azure Monitor that collects platform-level diagnostic data from monitored resources in a time-series database. These metrics, collected at regular intervals, provide insights into the performance and health of Azure resources. These metrics can be seen on the default **Metrics** page of the Azure service. This metrics collection comes at no cost to the users. Examples of platform metrics include **Egress** and **Ingress** (KBs over time), which is for a storage account, the **Succeeded** and **Failed** rates for Azure Data Factory, and the **Data Transaction Units** (**DTU**) percentage for Azure SQL Elastic pools.

You can find all the platform metrics for all Azure resources here:

`https://learn.microsoft.com/en-us/azure/azure-monitor/reference/`
`supported-metrics/metrics-index#metrics-by-resource-provider`

Figure 11.2 shows the platform metrics dashboard on the Azure portal. The metrics dashboard has a default view. It can also be customized by adding metrics to the dashboard. The **New chart** button will add a new chart to the dashboard. The **Add metric** button will add a new metric to the same chart:

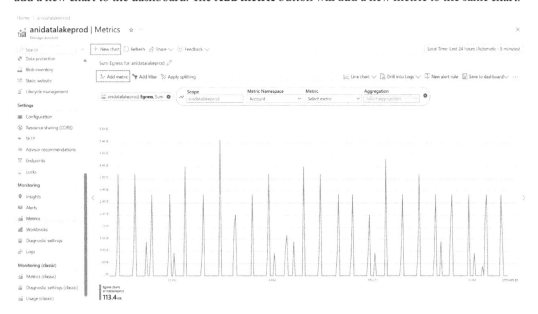

Figure 11.2 – Platform metrics in the Azure portal

Azure platform logs

Azure platform logs provide diagnostic information about the Azure resources. They are divided into three buckets: resource logs, activity logs, and Microsoft Entra logs.

Resource logs are logs of the activities produced inside the Azure resource by the data plane. **Activity logs** are logs produced by the activities performed on the resource from outside the resource, also called the control plane. **Active Directory logs** contain all the sign-in activity and any changes made to **Active Directory IDs**. These logs have been recently renamed Microsoft Entra logs (`https://learn.microsoft.com/en-us/entra/identity/monitoring-health/overview-monitoring-health`).

Examples of platform logs are the blob read, write, and delete operations on a storage account. For Azure Data Factory, there are many parameters logged, such as pipeline activity runs, trigger runs, and a number of SSIS- and Airflow-related events.

Platform logs are automatically generated by the control plane and the data plane of Azure. In order to capture these logs for analytics, however, you need to enable them.

To enable diagnostic settings and to redirect them to a destination for analytics, you need to click on **Diagnostic Settings** in the resource menu on the left and then click **Add diagnostic setting** on the working pane as shown here:

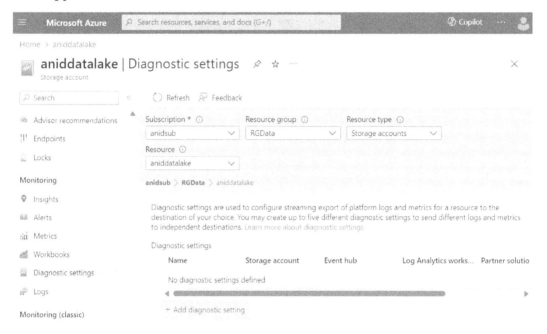

Figure 11.3 – Diagnostic settings under the resource menu

Clicking on the **Add diagnostic setting** will take you to another pane that will show you the available logs and events that can be enabled and redirected for that particular resource.

It's important to note that this is not how we will be enabling diagnostics in reality. Manually going to every Azure resource and a landing zone and enabling diagnostics will lead to accidentally missing out on important diagnostics and skipping some resources altogether. The best practice is to incorporate the diagnostics settings into the **Azure Resource Manager** (**ARM**) template for each resource. A standardized ARM template should be built for every resource with all the diagnostics enabled. This process ensures that the same diagnostic settings are enabled for every resource of a certain type. For example, all storage accounts across the entire data mesh will have the same set of diagnostic logs enabled because they would have been created from the same ARM template.

Figure 11.4 shows the diagnostic settings for a storage account on the Azure portal. The contents of the diagnostic settings will vary from resource to resource:

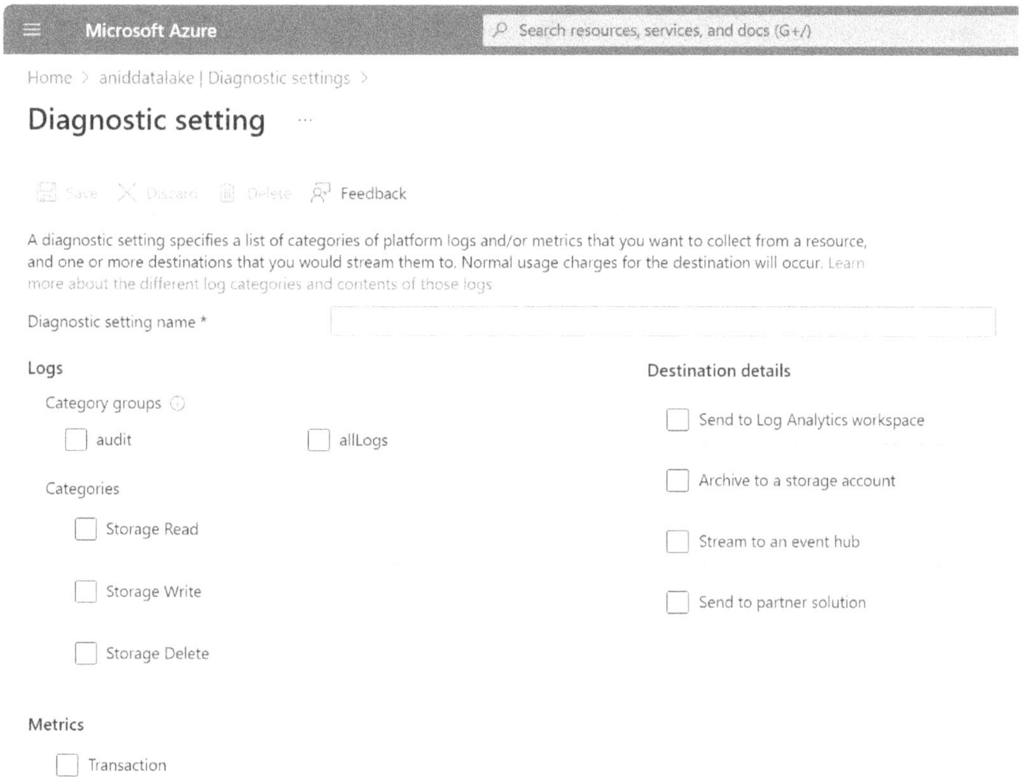

Figure 11.4 – Example of diagnostic settings for Azure data lake storage

For more details on platform metrics and platform logs, refer to the following link:

https://learn.microsoft.com/en-us/azure/azure-monitor/essentials/diagnostic-settings?tabs=portal#activity-log-settings

Before we see how these diagnostic settings can be baked into the ARM template, let us take a look at the destination options (right side of *Figure 11.4*) to where these logs can be diverted for storage and analysis:

- **Log Analytics workspace**: The Log Analytics service is part of the Azure Monitor service. It gets deployed as a workspace with its own storage and configuration. It can collect data from multiple Azure resources. The logs and metrics stored in the Log Analytics workspace can then be analyzed using the Log Analytics tool. The Log Analytics workspace is ideal for any immediate analytics over a short period of time. The Log Analytics workspace can be expensive, hence the best practice is to keep the retention periods low and move the data to an archive storage after initial analysis is done.

- **Storage account**: A storage account is preferred for the long-term storage of diagnostics data. If a resource in the data mesh is not very critical or belongs to a sandbox or a temporary landing zone, then you can move the diagnostics to a storage account. Logs and events moved to the storage account can be analyzed using tools like Azure Data Explorer (`https://azure.microsoft.com/en-us/products/data-explorer/`). This involves building a pipeline to export data to the Azure Data Explorer database where it can be analyzed.

- **Event hub**: If you wish to stream the diagnostic data for real-time analytics, you can divert it to an Azure event hub. Azure Event Hubs is a high-speed event-streaming service that plugs into multiple other Azure services for real-time analytics. For more details on Azure Event Hubs, refer to `https://learn.microsoft.com/en-us/azure/event-hubs/event-hubs-about`.

- **Partner solutions**: Microsoft has a robust partner network for analyzing logs and infrastructure monitoring. Many companies use these partner solutions as their primary monitoring solution. For such customers, Azure Monitor provides a solution for direct diagnostics and logs to these partner solutions. Popular partners such as Datadog, New Relic, and others are supported. The list is growing and you can find the most recent list of partners here at `https://learn.microsoft.com/en-us/azure/partner-solutions/partners#observability`.

The **Diagnostic Settings** menu on the Azure portal is a good way to view the options available and to experiment with the diagnostic loggings. It is not advised to use this UI to set diagnostic settings on landing zones that get deployed for the data product teams. Working with the Azure portal UI is prone to manual errors and there are no guarantees of diagnostic settings considering that the ops team responsible might forget to turn these settings on.

As we learned in *Chapter 3*, under the *Automating of landing zone deployment section*, the best practice to maintain consistency in creating and managing data mesh landing zones is to deploy them using **infrastructure-as-code** (**IaC**). This applies to any infrastructure-related settings in a data mesh. The IaC is implemented through ARM (or Bicep or Terraform) templates along with DevOps pipelines. The diagnostic settings, too, should be included in the same methodology. Let us understand how to enable diagnostic settings in an ARM template in the next section.

Enabling diagnostic settings in an ARM template

We will only cover ARM templates in this book. Bicep and Terraform are out of the scope of this book.

Diagnostic settings can be added to any ARM template in a subscription scope. It consists of a JSON template and a JSON parameter. The separate JSON parameter helps with changing the values and using the same template for multiple deployments across the mesh.

The following code snippet shows a JSON template for the diagnostic settings of an Azure SQL database. The JSON template is divided into two sections:

- **Line 1 to line 53**: The first section of the JSON document has all the details of the subscription scope, details of the Azure SQL database (server name and database name), and a set of destinations to where the diagnostics will be diverted. This template shows multiple options such as Log Analytics workspace, storage, and event hubs. In the actual template that you will build, you will only have one of these options depending on your logging and analytics strategy.

- **Line 54 to line 114**: This section defines the diagnostic settings. This template shows all the diagnostic settings as enabled. You can pick and choose the ones you want to enable. Observe that this section does not have any hardcoded values. It uses the parameter keyword instead. This means that this template is expecting these values to be populated from a parameter from the parameter template.

The code snippet is as follows:

```
1 {
2     "$schema": "https://schema.management.azure.com/
schemas/2019-04-01/deploymentTemplate.json#",
3     "contentVersion": "1.0.0.0",
4     "parameters": {
5         "settingName": {
6             "type": "string",
7             "metadata": {
8                 "description": "The name of the diagnostic setting."
9             }
10         },
11         "serverName": {
12             "type": "string",
13             "metadata": {
14                 "description": "The name of the Azure SQL database
server."
15             }
16         },
17         "dbName": {
18             "type": "string",
19             "metadata": {
20                 "description": "The name of the SQL database."
21             }
22         },
23         "workspaceId": {
24             "type": "string",
25             "metadata": {
```

```
26              "description": "The resource Id of the workspace."
27            }
28          },
29        "storageAccountId": {
30            "type": "string",
31            "metadata": {
32              "description": "The resource Id of the storage
account."
33            }
34          },
35        "eventHubAuthorizationRuleId": {
36            "type": "string",
37            "metadata": {
38              "description": "The resource Id of the event hub
authorization rule."
39            }
40          },
41        "eventHubName": {
42            "type": "string",
43            "metadata": {
44              "description": "The name of the event hub."
45            }
46          }
47        },
48        "resources": [
49          {
50            "type": "Microsoft.Insights/diagnosticSettings",
51            "apiVersion": "2021-05-01-preview",
52            "scope": "[format('Microsoft.Sql/servers/{0}/databases/
{1}', parameters('serverName'), parameters('dbName'))]",
53            "name": "[parameters('settingName')]",
54            "properties": {
55              "workspaceId": "[parameters('workspaceId')]",
56              "storageAccountId":
"[parameters('storageAccountId')]",
57              "eventHubAuthorizationRuleId":
"[parameters('eventHubAuthorizationRuleId')]",
58              "eventHubName": "[parameters('eventHubName')]",
59              "logs": [
60                {
61                  "category": "SQLInsights",
62                  "enabled": true
63                },
64                {
65                  "category": "AutomaticTuning",
```

```
66                        "enabled": true
67                },
68                {
69                        "category": "QueryStoreRuntimeStatistics",
70                        "enabled": true
71                },
72                {
73                        "category": "QueryStoreWaitStatistics",
74                        "enabled": true
75                },
76                {
77                        "category": "Errors",
78                        "enabled": true
79                },
80                {
81                        "category": "DatabaseWaitStatistics",
82                        "enabled": true
83                },
84                {
85                        "category": "Timeouts",
86                        "enabled": true
87                },
88                {
89                        "category": "Blocks",
90                        "enabled": true
91                },
92                {
93                        "category": "Deadlocks",
94                        "enabled": true
95                }
96            ],
97            "metrics": [
98                {
99                        "category": "Basic",
100                      "enabled": true
101               },
102               {
103                     "category": "InstanceAndAppAdvanced",
104                      "enabled": true
105               },
106               {
107                     "category": "WorkloadManagement",
108                      "enabled": true
```

```
109                    }
110                ]
111            }
112        }
113    ]
114 }
```

The following snippet shows the parameter file for this template:

```
1 {
2     "$schema": "https://schema.management.azure.com/
schemas/2019-04-01/deploymentParameters.json#",
3     "contentVersion": "1.0.0.0",
4     "parameters": {
5         "settingName": {
6             "value": "Send to all locations"
7         },
8         "serverName": {
9           "value": "MySqlServer"
10         },
11         "dbName": {
12             "value": "MySqlDb"
13         },
14         "workspaceId": {
15             "value": "/subscriptions/xxxxxxxx-xxxx-xxxx-xxxx-
xxxxxxxxxxxx/resourcegroups/
16             MyResourceGroup/providers/microsoft.operationalinsights/
workspaces/MyWorkspace"
17         },
18         "storageAccountId": {
19             "value": "/subscriptions/xxxxxxxx-xxxx-xxxx-xxxx-
xxxxxxxxxxxx/resourceGroups/
20             MyResourceGroup/providers/Microsoft.Storage/
storageAccounts/mystorageaccount"
21         },
22         "eventHubAuthorizationRuleId": {
23             "value": "/subscriptions/xxxxxxxx-xxxx-xxxx-xxxx-
xxxxxxxxxxxx/resourceGroups/
24             MyResourceGroup/providers/Microsoft.EventHub/namespaces/
25             MyNameSpace/authorizationrules/RootManageSharedAccessKey"
26         },
27         "eventHubName": {
28             "value": "my-eventhub"
29         }
```

```
30      }
31    }
```

If the ARM template is stored as `AzureSQLDB.json` and the `parameter` file is stored as `MySQLDB.parameters.json`, then you can deploy the ARM template using a PowerShell command as shown in the following snippet:

```
1New-AzResourceGroupDeployment -Name MyDeployment -ResourceGroupName
MyResourceGroup `
2   -TemplateFile C:\MyTemplates\ AzureSQLDB.json `
3   -TemplateParameterFile C:\MyTemplates\ MySQLDB.parameters.json
```

Every Azure resource has a diagnostic setting template like the one shown in the JSON template. Each template has the same format but different content. The service parameters and diagnostic resources change for every template. You can find more details about the diagnostics template and also find more sample templates at `https://learn.microsoft.com/en-us/azure/azure-monitor/essentials/resource-manager-diagnostic-settings`.

Once you understand these templates, follow these steps to ensure that every new landing zone or service deployed in the data mesh has diagnostics setting and routing enabled:

1. Create an ARM template for each type of Azure service, along with a parameter file.
2. Make sure you add diagnostic settings to this ARM template.
3. Check it into a Git repo and version it every time you make a change.
4. Reference this template through linking or embedding in the landing zone ARM template.
5. Ensure that you only deploy landing zones using these templates in DevOps pipelines. Simply change the values in the parameter file to match the new landing zone parameters.

If you follow these steps, you will always ensure that diagnostics for all services are being logged from the get-go.

This completes the collection part of the logs and diagnostics. In the next section, we will discuss how to build a dashboard, or a hierarchy of dashboards, to proactively and reactively monitor the entire data mesh.

Designing a data mesh operations center

People from the world of networking infrastructure must be familiar with the **Network Operations Center** (**NOC**). It is usually a physical room with screens of dashboards like the one depicted in *Figure 11.5*:

Figure 11.5 – A network operations center

A NOC is a room where the health of the entire network and infrastructure of an organization is visible. These centers typically run 24/7 for organizations that need 24/7 uptime. With networking technologies and monitoring technologies improving, these centers have reduced in size considerably.

A similar operations center is required for the data mesh. Let's call it a DMOC, though this is not an official industry term.

The data mesh can become a complex network very quickly. The complexity of the data mesh will depend on the strategy and design decisions made at the beginning, before implementing the data mesh. Some large companies have a strategy to contain the number of subscriptions by assigning a subscription to every geographical zone. After this, they don't have to add any new landing zone subscription unless a new geographical zone gets included in the company's expansion. Some companies will assign a landing zone subscription to every department. The data products in both of these cases are deployed to different resource groups within the landing zone.

What is important to note is that irrespective of your data mesh design strategy, the data products can grow very rapidly. Whether they are put into a new landing zone of their own or a resource group of their own, they still need to be monitored and managed.

A DMOC is critical to the success and growth of a data mesh. At a high level, it performs the following important functions:

- Monitoring the health of Azure using Azure Service Health. This is very important top-level monitoring that is required. If an Azure region itself is down for any reason, it impacts multiple products in your data mesh. If you have decided to keep your entire data mesh in one Azure region, then it could impact the whole mesh. Hence, monitoring Azure itself should be the priority.

- Proactively monitoring the health of the mesh, from subscriptions down to each resource.

- Providing early warnings to teams on possible future breakdowns or performance issues.

- Guiding product teams in improving their infrastructure and design.

- Providing individual dashboards to teams to monitor their own projects proactively.

- Performing efficient investigations of downtime or support instances. Using the DMOC, the ops team can quickly narrow down the impacted services and quickly investigate the issue.

- Honoring the SLAs provided to the data product teams. In the *Piecing it all together – the importance of data mesh monitoring and data observability* section, we saw the various monetization models for the data mesh. In cases where the data mesh is cross-charging the data products or departments, these SLAs can be critical to justify the cost.

One important thing to note is that the DMOC is *not* a replacement for a NOC. A NOC plays a very critical role in monitoring the networking and security of the enterprise. A DMOC only monitors the health of the data mesh and might actually depend on the NOC for network- and security-related monitoring. A DMOC can become part of the NOC.

The most logical and the most practical approach to building a DMOC is to build it from the ground up, brick by brick, and then lay those bricks on top of each other to get the big picture. Let us look at a few high-level steps to build the DMOC.

Step 1 – collection

Ensure that all the diagnostic logs and activity logs are collected centrally. This is covered in the *Baking diagnostic logging into the landing zone templates* section in this chapter. Ensure that you have studied and understood the collection of Azure Service Health data and the related APIs/queries. For more information on Azure Service Health, refer to `https://learn.microsoft.com/en-us/azure/service-health/overview`.

Step 2 – rank the critical metrics and events

Not everything that is collected needs to be on the DMOC dashboard. For example, for Azure Data Factory, `Trigger Failed Runs` is a more important metric than `Trigger Succeeded Runs`. Similarly, for each Azure service, rank the metrics in terms of severity and importance. Some metrics might be important from a denominator perspective. For example, 10 Trigger Failed Runs / 15 Trigger Succeeded Runs is definitely more worrisome than 1 Trigger Failed Run / 15 Trigger Succeeded Runs.

Step 3 – build a threshold logic for each service in a data product

For each Azure service, build a logic for when the critical metric can be considered green, amber, or red. Some thresholds might vary based on how critical the data product is. For a virtual machine, the CPU that builds the daily business KPI dashboard for the company leadership, even a single `Trigger Failed Runs` could be considered red. However, for a virtual machine in an Azure Databricks cluster, GPU usage could rise slowly and go from green to amber to red. It's a situation that can show some tolerance to higher levels of GPU usage before analytics comes to a grinding halt.

Step 4 – build a monitoring view for each resource

There are many ways to visualize metrics for the data mesh. We will discuss the different technologies for visualization in the next section. For this step, you need to aggregate all the important metrics and log the analytics query results on one dashboard. They can be displayed in the form of numbers or charts or a combination of both. The layout is completely up to you to decide. The important requirement is that, at a glance, the dashboard should be able to tell the observer whether everything is OK with this particular instance of the service; if not, then it must say which areas are amber or red. The next level of investigation should lead from here. This could involve going through the logs, analyzing the other services and users that are connecting to it, or looking for any Azure cloud downtime instances.

An example of a dashboard for an Azure SQL DB is depicted in *Figure 11.6*:

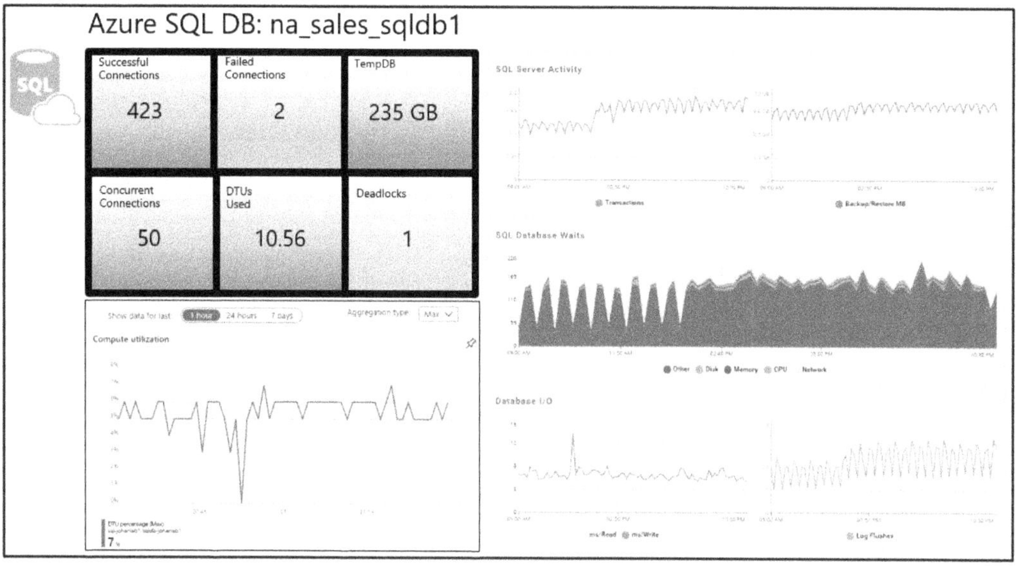

Figure 11.6 – An example of a monitoring dashboard for an Azure SQL DB

Step 5 – build a threshold logic for each data product

Similar to the service threshold, build a threshold logic for each data product:

- If one or more metrics from any service in the data product are red, then the data product should need attention and should be marked as *red*

- If the combined number of metrics on any services in a data product exceeds 10, then the data product itself should be colored *amber*

- If the combined number of metrics on any services in a data product exceeds 11, then the data product itself should be colored *red*

Step 6 – build a threshold logic for each data landing zone

Depending on how you have structured your data mesh, you will need to bubble up the health of each data product to the data landing zone, but if you have one data product per landing zone, then your dashboard needn't go further than this level.

Figure 11.7 shows the hierarchy of dashboards that you need to build:

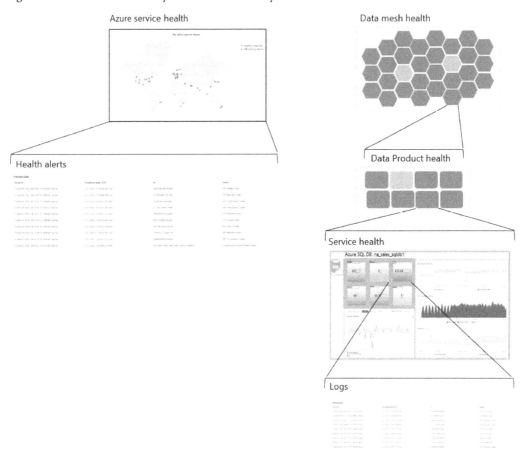

Figure 11.7 – Hierarchy of data mesh monitoring dashboards

Step 7 – set up alerts for critical metrics

Visual dashboards alone are not enough. If a certain metric hits the limit or goes amber, a set of people on different teams will have to be notified. Azure Monitor provides a feature to set alerts. Alerts have rules and actions. In the next section, we will look at Azure alerts in more detail.

Step 8 – host the dashboards in one location

The best place to house all of these dashboards is the data mesh portal. Ensure that you provide conditional access to different levels of the dashboard. Depending on the dashboarding tool that you choose to use, refer to the documentation on how to provide conditional access to dashboards for that tool. It is also good practice to build a small desk for the DMOC for continuous visual monitoring. If you already have an NOC location, you can add an extra desk in there for the DMOC.

This concludes our discussion on building a centralized dashboard for data mesh monitoring. Building a detailed data mesh monitor with drill-down options to dive into from higher-level monitoring to pinpoint issues can be a long-drawn-out process. It is best to start small and create building blocks that can be reused so that the entire effort can become easier as you progress.

In the next section, we will look at the technologies used to build monitoring and alerting in a data mesh.

Tooling for the DMOC

There are multiple ways of building monitoring dashboards in Azure. In this section, we will discuss the most popular combinations. Let us begin by summarizing the list of available tools.

Azure Monitor

Azure Monitor is one of the core services of Azure that collects, monitors, and helps analyze the metrics and logs from the cloud and on-premises services and resources. It's the core building block for any infrastructure monitoring need. It also helps you set alerts to respond to the metrics exceeding certain levels. Alerts can send messages and emails. They can also trigger runbooks to implement any autoscaling or maintenance jobs to automate escalation to the solution.

Log Analytics

As we saw in *Baking diagnostic logging into the landing zone templates*, Log Analytics is part of the Azure Monitor service. It is a tool that allows you to run queries against the logs collected by Azure Monitor. It uses **Kusto query language** (**KQL**) to query the logs.

To learn more about how to use Log Analytics, refer to the following link: `https://learn.microsoft.com/en-us/azure/azure-monitor/logs/log-analytics-overview`

To learn more about KQL, refer to the following link:

`https://learn.microsoft.com/en-us/azure/data-explorer/kusto/query/`

Azure Data Explorer

Azure Data Explorer (**ADX**) is a more generic big-data analytics tool. It runs on the Kusto query framework, which is the same framework that Log Analytics is built on. ADX and Log Analytics are very similar in that respect. The only difference is that Log Analytics works only on the logs collected by Azure Monitor, whereas ADX works on the tables in the databases that are mounted in its workspace. You need to ingest data from different sources into the ADX workspace before you can query them.

If we direct the diagnostics of Azure services to a storage account and ingest that data into ADX, we can run Kusto queries on this data and conduct analytics just the way we do in Log Analytics.

The Log Analytics workspace is a more expensive tool to use. Its costs are in GBs ingested per day and retention after 30 days. Collecting all the logs for all the services can amount to a large amount of data, making it a very expensive service to use. ADX plus a storage account provides a cheaper alternative to Log Analytics.

To learn more about how to use Azure Data Explorer, refer to the following link: `https://learn.microsoft.com/en-us/azure/data-explorer/data-explorer-overview`

Grafana

Grafana is a visualization and observability tool from Grafana Labs. It is very popular in the industry as an open framework for visualization. It is also available as a managed service on Azure. It is popular in building monitoring dashboards and integrates well with Azure Monitor services.

To learn more about how to use Grafana for monitoring, refer to the following link: `https://learn.microsoft.com/en-us/azure/azure-monitor/visualize/grafana-plugin`

Power BI

Power BI is a very popular business intelligence, analytics, and visualization tool. Over many years, it has grown from a simple dashboarding tool to a very comprehensive data analytics tool. Since Power BI is the dashboarding tool of choice for many companies, it is also a convenient choice for a data mesh monitoring dashboard, even more so because talented staff to work with Power BI are easily available in such companies.

To learn more about Power BI, refer to the following link: `https://learn.microsoft.com/nl-nl/power-bi/fundamentals/power-bi-overview`

Using the aforementioned tools, you have the following combinations/options to build a data mesh monitoring system:

- **Option 1**: Redirect diagnostics data for all the landing zone resources to Log Analytics. Use the Log Analytics workspace and Kusto queries to do any investigation/exploration work. Use Power BI/Grafana to build the visual dashboards from the Log Analytics storage.

- **Option 2**: Redirect diagnostic data for all landing zone resources to a Blob storage account. Ingest that data into Azure Data Explorer and use Kusto queries to do exploratory and investigation work. Use Power BI/Grafana to build the visual dashboards from the Log Analytics storage.

- **Option 3**: Redirect the diagnostic data to Event Hubs. Ingest the data into Azure Data Explorer and use Kusto queries to do exploratory and investigation work. Use Power BI/Grafana to build the visual dashboards from the Log Analytics storage.

- **Option 4**: Redirect the diagnostic data to Event Hubs. Write an Azure function to redirect the Event Hub data to a third-party partner product such as Datadog, Logz.io, or Dynatrace.

- **Option 5**: Directly push the diagnostic settings to a third-party partner product such as Datadog, Logz.io, or Dynatrace.

Figure 11.8 shows all of the possible options as an architecture flow:

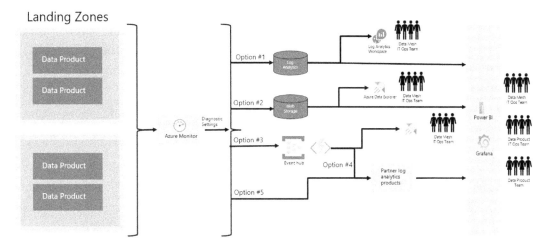

Figure 11.8 – All possible options for routing and publishing diagnostics data

This concludes the data mesh monitoring portion of this chapter. Data mesh monitoring focuses on the health of the resources in the data mesh. Next, we will look at another very important side of monitoring a data mesh: data observability. We will cover monitoring the data that passes through the data mesh and reporting on it to its producers and consumers. Though a lot of aspects of data observability, such as data lineage, data quality, and master data management, have already been covered, let's look at how to bring all these aspects together onto a single dashboard.

Data observability

The health of your network defines the health of your infrastructure. A large virtual machine with great specifications to crunch numbers at blazing speed is rendered useless if the network is not working. Similarly, data pipelines are the backbone of a healthy data mesh. Without timely and accurate data, the best analytical system is not useful to the business.

Data quality, data contracts, and master data management are some of the key tenets of the quality and accuracy of data. Along with quality and accuracy, we also need to monitor the movement of data through data lineage in Microsoft Purview as well as data pipeline health through data mesh monitoring.

Throughout multiple chapters in this book, we have looked at all of these aspects of data. As part of data mesh monitoring, you need to bring all of these different data observability metrics together onto a single pane of glass.

Setting up alerts

Being proactive about monitoring the data mesh is very important. Your stakeholders finding out about issues with data or services before you do is never a good scenario.

In order to ensure that the IT ops team is ahead of infrastructure failures, performance bottlenecks, and data quality issues, you need to ensure that alerts are triggered whenever a diagnostic setting goes beyond a threshold (amber or red). The alert has four parts:

- **Resources**: The resources on which the alerts need to be set.
- **Alert rules**: The rules that define when an alert should trigger.
- **Alert**: The alert itself.
- **Actions**: The actions that the alert should take once it triggers. This could be sending an email or mobile SMS or triggering a runbook.

For more details on how to set alerts in Azure, refer to the following link: `https://learn.microsoft.com/en-us/azure/azure-monitor/alerts/alerts-overview`

Microsoft Purview also has an alerts feature for the data compliance manager. For details on how to use those alerts, refer to the following link: `https://learn.microsoft.com/en-us/purview/compliance-manager-alert-policies`

Piecing it all together

When a pipeline goes down or a resource is reaching its limit and needs to be configured to scale further, you need to act quickly. In order to do so, you need to know where to look for the diagnostics and investigate the situation. Hence, it's very important that the monitoring system is centralized to a single pane of glass that everyone can look at. This single pane of glass should be the data mesh portal. All of the dashboards and the alert management system should be brought to the portal with granular access rights defined to have access to different levels. The higher-level dashboard should only be visible to the data mesh ops team. Individual landing zone dashboards should also be accessible to the concerned landing zone team but not to any other landing zone team. These access levels can also be easily set if everything is in one place.

Summary

This concludes the chapter on monitoring and data observability. We looked at all the complexities of monitoring a data mesh and how to integrate monitoring as part of the data mesh by adding it to the landing zone templates. We then looked at the steps for building a DMOC and briefly talked about bringing all the data monitoring aspects covered so far in this book together to build data observability.

In the next chapter, we will look at monitoring the cost of a data mesh and building an effective cross-charging system for scenarios where the central data mesh is not an independent cost center and needs to fund itself by charging for its services.

12

Monitoring Data Mesh Costs and Building a Cross-Charging Model

In the previous chapter, we discussed two broad models of how a data mesh is monetized by companies through a central or distributed cost model. In either of these models, it's important to be able to measure the cost of the data mesh broken down into individual data products. Irrespective of the cost distribution strategy that a company adopts, it will need to get the cost of each landing zone in order to ensure **return on investment (ROI)** and plan budgets at a granular level.

There are multiple aspects to the cost of a data mesh. What are these cost components? How do you measure them? How do you split the cost of common components across different data products? These and many such questions will be answered in this chapter.

In this chapter, we will cover the following topics:

- Components of data mesh costs
- Cost models in a data mesh
- Overview of cost management in Azure
- Allocating costs to different product groups and domains
- How to determine the cost of shared resources

Components of data mesh costs

In a centralized analytical platform, a set of common resources is being used for all analytics in the company. The cost of analytics is typically borne by the company. The ROI of each analytical output is bundled into the big analytical costs and returns for the company. Though some level of cost segregation can happen in a centralized analytical platform, it's difficult to get this accurately.

With the data mesh and its decentralized data ownership, the cost of maintaining, processing, and managing the data can also be decentralized. With each data product carved out into its own landing zone (subscription or resource group), it becomes easier to calculate individual costs. Well, almost easier. There are still some shared and indirect costs that need to be managed. However, the majority of the costs can be easily attributed to the individual data product.

The costs of a data mesh can be split into the following high-level elements:

- **Direct resources cost**: Cost of the Azure services, data, and any third-party services used by the data product alone.

- **Shared resources cost**: Multiple data products could be sharing a common resource. In the *Organizing resources in a landing zone* section of *Chapter 3*, we discussed the possibility of having multiple products in different resource groups under one landing zone subscription. The same landing zone subscription also has a resource group called **shared resources**. The *shared resources* group has a set of resources that can be shared by products in the domain. For example, a set of products might need a common dataset. This dataset could be piped into a common data lake that could be shared by this set of products. This pipeline could use some Databricks clusters for data processing, along with the data lake that is being used to store this dataset. The cost of these resources (Databricks and data lake) under the *shared resources* resource group comes under shared costs.

  Another shared entity across the data mesh is the data management zone. The data management zone is connected to every data landing zone in the data mesh. That is the only way a landing zone becomes a part of the data mesh. The data landing zone pushes all diagnostic data to the data management zone. The data management zone has storage and compute being used to monitor and manage the data mesh. It might also be running some common pipelines to get data from on-premises or other enterprise systems such as **customer relationship management** (**CRM**) and **enterprise resource planning** (**ERP**)systems. Almost all the cost of resources used by the data management come under shared costs.

- **Service cost**: In a distributed cost-center model where each data product team is charged for the data mesh services, the data product team might be given an option for different service levels. Depending on the level they opt for, a **service-level agreement** (**SLA**) could be offered in terms of system uptime guarantees and speed of resolution of service tickets. **Recovery time objective** (**RTO**) and **recovery point objective** (**RPO**) metrics in case of **disaster recovery** (**DR**) situations might also be part of this SLA. The higher the SLA, the higher the cost. These costs are also part of the cost of using the data mesh.

- **People cost**: The data mesh ITOps team ensures that the data mesh is managed, maintained, and monitored to a high level of performance and availability. This entails scripts and **Azure Resource Manager** (**ARM**) templates to be maintained and updated regularly, manning a **data mesh operations center** (**DMOC**) to quickly respond to outages and many other such activities that need human intervention. The people cost of the data mesh ITOps team could also be a shared cost for every data product.

Figure 12.1 shows the breakup of shared and product costs in a data mesh. These cost categories are generic and what I observe with companies I have worked with. However, there might be other cost attributes that are specific to the operations of a company that are not shown here:

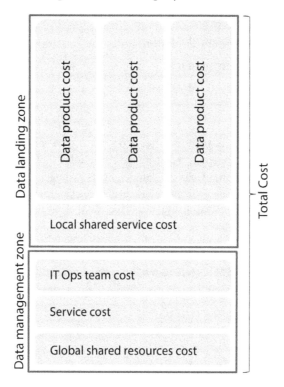

Figure 12.1 – Components of data mesh cost

Some of the service cost and people cost can also be shifted to a product team depending on the service level they choose. For example, a data product team could choose a model where their team ensures the uptime of their resources and maintains their backup scripts and ARM templates. In such cases, most of the costs of the service and people will be borne by the data product team, but some small amount of common service and people costs will still be common to the data mesh and will be categorized as shared costs.

In the next section, we will look at how shared costs can get distributed/owned in different cost models.

Cost models in a data mesh

In a *centralized cost model* where the cost of analytics is borne by the company and the ROI is calculated at a much higher level, cost modeling is simple. All costs discussed in the previous section are borne by a central cost center. The complexity is shifted to selecting projects to execute given the limited budget.

In a *distributed cost model* where the central data mesh itself is a cost center and so are all the products, the cost is borne by individual products. The individual products have to muster the budget to fund their project and provide an ROI. They could build the product in isolation or join the data mesh. The advantages of joining the data mesh are manifold, such as the following:

- Shared costs of management and monitoring

- Easy access to data from other products

- Shared governance

- Shared best practices

If they choose to join the data mesh, then they need to pay the data mesh department the charges described in the previous section. Except, in a distributed cost model, shared costs can be split in many ways. If the data product team is a small team of data scientists and data engineers and does not have the capacity to maintain and monitor their infrastructure, they can choose to completely rely on the central ITOps team to maintain and monitor their environment.

On the other hand, if the data product team does have the required resources to manage their infrastructure, they can take on those tasks and pay only for their consumed resources plus some small management costs, and then there could be multiple scenarios in between where teams can choose to take on or delegate portions of shared costs. *Figure 12.2* shows two possible options for distributing shared costs:

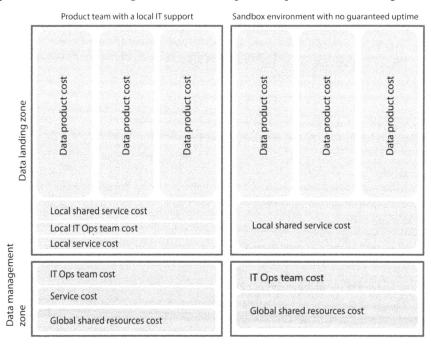

Figure 12.2 – Two sample cost models for two scenarios

There can be many combinations made where product teams and the central ITOps team can decide to split costs in different ways.

For complex situations of distributed costs, the company can come up with a **Responsible, Accountable, Consulted, and Informed (RACI)** matrix. A RACI matrix is a commonly used tool to describe the roles and responsibilities of various teams in any given system or project. It can be applied to a data mesh management, maintenance, and service scope.

Figure 12.3 shows a sample RACI matrix. In this matrix, the data product team is taking up most of the service and maintenance work except backups. They only consult the data mesh teams when required:

Process		Data mesh		Data product	
Process ID	Process	ITOps team	Data engineering team	ITOps teams	Data engineering team
DM1.1	Service monitoring	R		A/R	I
DM1.2	Pipeline monitoring		C/I		A/R
DM1.2.1	Pipeline maintenance		C	I	A/R
DM1.3	Service tickets	C		A/R	I
DM1.4	Scale requests	C		A/R	I
DM1.5	Backups	A/R		C	I
DMX.Y	Other processes...	R/A/C/I	R/A/C/I	R/A/C/I	R/A/C/I

* R = Responsible, A = Accountable, C = Consulted, I = Informed

Figure 12.3 – Sample RACI matrix for an SLA

Various cost models are possible. It is important to plan upfront for how these cost models are defined and managed. Planning the cost model and the RACI matrices for various SLAs requires teamwork. It is an iterative process of building the models and sharing them with the stakeholders for feedback. It also needs continuous improvement. As you implement and roll out the data mesh, new service requirements and service situations might be encountered that need to be incorporated into the cost model and the RACI matrix.

In order to devise a solution to distribute these costs across different data products, let us first take a look at how Azure does cost management.

Overview of cost management in Azure

There are two aspects to cost management in Azure: **Billing** and **Cost Management**.

Microsoft Azure has a large variety of resources and services, ranging from networking, storage, and virtual machines (**Infrastructure as a Service** or **IaaS**) to managed development platforms such as functions, pipelines, **machine learning** (**ML**), and analytics (**Platform as a Service** or **PaaS**) to out-of-the-box vertical software services such as Dynamics 365 and Office 365 (**Software as a Service** or **SaaS**).

All resources and services in Azure push usage data through a pipeline called the **Microsoft Commerce pipeline**. The pipeline then applies different discounts based on the price sheet that applies to your subscription (pay-as-you-go, fixed price, reservation plans, and so on). At the end, it looks for any pending credits that can be applied (service credits because of SLA violation, gift cards, and others) and, finally, publishes the bill.

For details on how billing works, refer to `https://learn.microsoft.com/en-us/azure/cost-management-billing/`.

The billing cycle in Azure is based on your agreement. 72 hours after the billing cycle date, a bill is generated. The date of payment is indicated on the invoice. By this time, if you realize the bill is too high, it's too late. This is where **Azure Cost Management** comes into play. Azure Cost Management helps you manage your costs by setting budgets and alerts so that you can avoid generating a high bill. Azure Cost Management is a set of FinOps tools that help you proactively manage your Azure cloud costs. All data used in the Billing pipeline is also provided to Cost Management. Using the **Cost Management** tool in the Azure portal, you can set budgets and alerts to ensure that you are always aware of rising costs and are able to control them before bills are generated.

The **Cost Management** portal and tools can be found in the Azure portal by typing `Cost Management` in the search bar, as shown in *Figure 12.4*:

Figure 12.4 – Searching for Cost Management and Billing in the Azure portal

The **Cost Management** portal can be seen in *Figure 12.5*. On the left menu bar, you will see tools such as **Budget**, **Cost alerts**, **Cost analysis**, and **Advisor recommendations**:

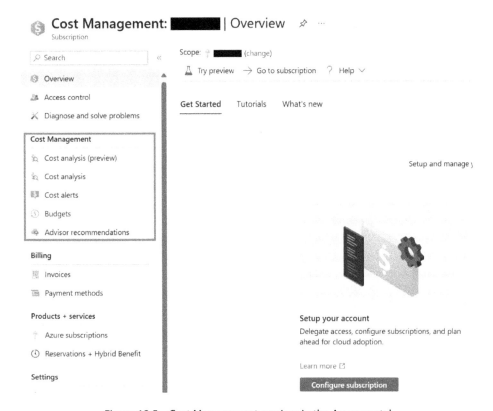

Figure 12.5 – Cost Management services in the Azure portal

For more information on Azure Cost Management services, refer to https://learn.microsoft.com/en-us/azure/cost-management-billing/costs/.

We now have a fair understanding of how billing and cost management work in Azure. We also looked at the different cost components in a data mesh and how these costs need to be distributed across different data products based on what they are consuming, along with shared costs. Irrespective of the cost-center model you follow, central or distributed, you still need to split these costs across different data products just to understand who is consuming how much and who has the most cost impact. It is also important for the data product teams to understand their costs and manage them.

While there are many complex elements to distributing costs, let us start with the simplest of them all: individual resource costs for each data product. This is the easiest to calculate and distribute as these resources are assigned and used by only one data product team, and you can attribute costs to that data product. Azure Billing also supports splitting the bill based on this attribution.

In the next section, let's look at how we can segregate the cost of resources being used by individual data product teams at the time of billing in a way that separate bills get generated. This cost will form the major component of the distributed cost of the data mesh.

Allocating costs to different data product groups and domains

Azure cloud environments can become very complex, irrespective of whether you implement a data mesh or not. Large and medium-sized organizations can easily grow into many subscriptions housing thousands of resources. Managing and maintaining these resources can be a huge challenge. To ease the job of the cloud ITOps teams, Azure has a concept called **tags**. Whenever you create an Azure resource in the cloud, it will offer you an option to create some tags for this resource. You will see a **Tags** section in most Azure resource creation wizards, as shown in *Figure 12.6*:

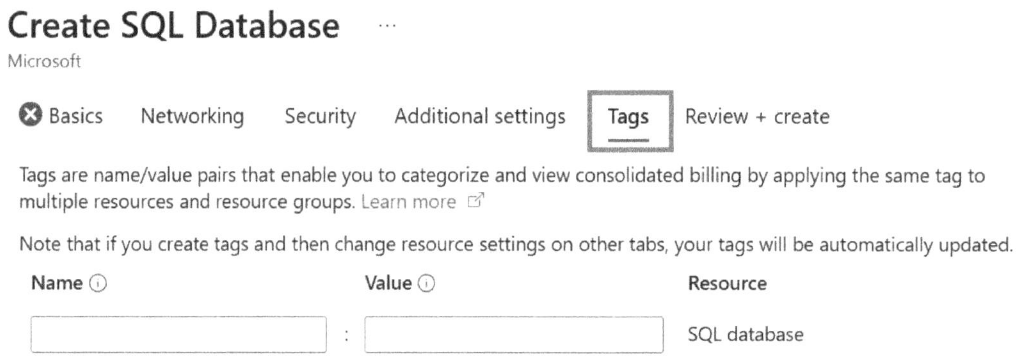

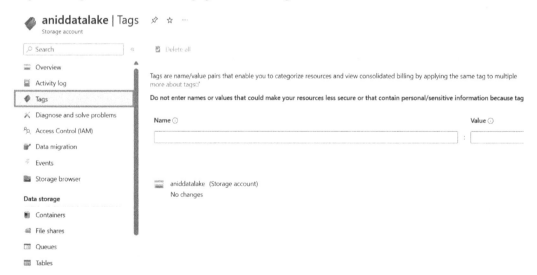

Figure 12.6 – Tags section in the Create SQL Database wizard

Tags can be changed, and new tags can be added after creating a resource too. *Figure 12.7* shows the **Tags** menu option on the resource page of the Azure portal:

Figure 12.7 – Tags menu in the Azure portal

Not all Azure resources support tags. To see a list of resources that don't support tags or partially support tags, refer to https://learn.microsoft.com/en-us/azure/azure-resource-manager/management/tag-support. From a data mesh perspective, almost all resources typically involved in data and analytics support tags.

What are these tags, and how are they used? And how are they useful to segregate resource costs?

Tags are metadata (key/value pairs) that can be attached to a resource that supports tags. These key/value pairs can be used to track resources for maintenance and management purposes. For example, let us say you have architected your data mesh to have domains, and each domain to have data products within them. Each domain gets a subscription, and the data products are organized into resource groups. You can add a tag called domain to the subscription with a value of the name of the domain. You can also add a tag named data product and give it a value of the name of the product.

Figure 12.8 shows an example of what these tags may look like. The naming conventions and the resource groups have been simplified for the example:

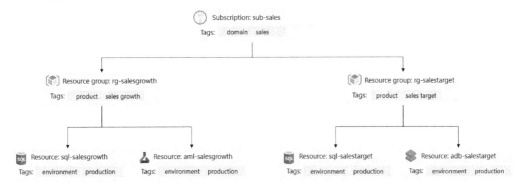

Figure 12.8 – Example of tags at the subscription, resource group, and resource levels

Figure 12.8 shows a very simple example of applying tags. In practice, this can be more sophisticated. For example, each product could have two or more resource groups for development, test, and production environments. In this case, multiple tags could be applied to each resource group.

However, applying multiple tags to each resource group or resource can be complex and prone to errors. Azure also has the option to inherit tags. It is an option that needs to be turned on. You can do this at a billing scope or a subscription scope. *Figures 12.9, 12.10,* and *12.11* show the screens for enabling tag inheritance at a subscription level:

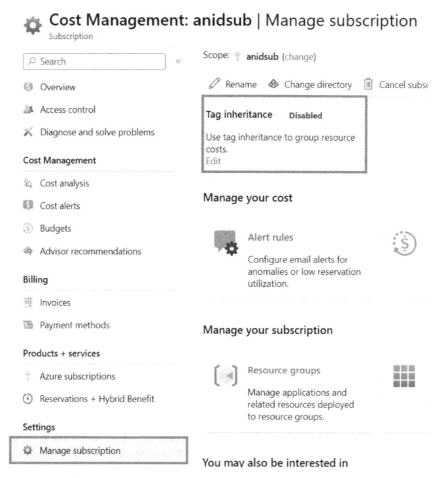

Figure 12.9 – Enabling tag inheritance at a subscription level

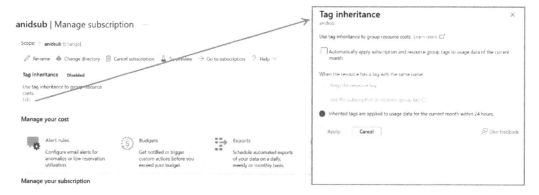

Figure 12.10 – Enabling tag inheritance at a subscription level

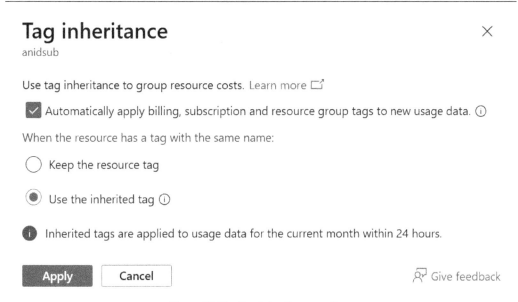

Figure 12.11 – Tag inheritance options

For more information on tag inheritance, refer to `https://learn.microsoft.com/en-us/azure/cost-management-billing/costs/enable-tag-inheritance`.

Tag inheritance will help you club billing together at the product and domain levels. The inherited tags will start showing in the billing within 24 hours. Once these costs get segregated, you can filter them on the **Cost analysis** screen by tags, as shown in *Figure 12.12*:

Figure 12.12 – Grouping costs by tags

Using tags, we will be able to segregate individual resource costs, which usually form the larger chunk of the total cost of a data product. You can also download Azure usage reports by clicking on the **Download** button on the Azure **Cost analysis** page, as shown in *Figure 12.12*. These reports can also be generated using a PowerShell script using the Azure Cost Management API. The API takes a query JSON structure to filter the report based on subscription, time period, and other parameters. One of the parameters can be a tag value, as shown in the following snippet of code:

```
1 POST https://management.azure.com/providers/../query?api-
version=2023-11-01
2
3 {
4   "type": "Usage",
5   "timeframe": "MonthToDate",
6   "dataset": {
7     "granularity": "Daily",
8     "filter": {
9       "and": [
10         {
11           "or": [
12             {
13               "dimensions": {
14                 "name": "ResourceLocation",
15                 "operator": "In",
16                 "values": [
17                   "East US",
18                   "West Europe"
19                 ]
20               }
21             },
22             {
23               "tags": {
24                 "name": "Environment",
25                 "operator": "In",
26                 "values": [
27                   "UAT",
28                   "Prod"
29                 ]
30               }
31             }
32           ]
33         },
34         {
35           "dimensions": {
36             "name": "ResourceGroup",
```

```
37                    "operator": "In",
38                    "values": [
39                      "API"
40                    ]
41                 }
42               }
43             ]
44           }
45        }
46 }
```

Now that we have covered the simpler aspect of the cost distribution of individual data products in a data mesh, in the next section, we will look at how to determine costs for shared resources.

How to determine the cost of shared resources

The pricing of Azure resources can be simple or complex, depending on the resource. A virtual machine, for example, can be one of the most simple for pricing. Once you select a virtual machine **stock keeping unit (SKU)**, you will be charged a fixed amount per hour, even if the machine is shut down (storage charges). **Azure Synapse Analytics** (formerly Azure SQL Data Warehouse) is an example of complex pricing. You have many components to look at. Dedicated SQL pools, serverless pools, data storage, data flows, and other components contribute to the cost of the resource.

Calculating the cost of a shared resource and then cross-charging the usage to individual data products that share the resource can be a challenging task. It can sometimes also involve guessing the cost to a rough amount. Sometimes, it might be easier to bake the price of some shared resources into the administrative cost of the data mesh and distribute it equally between all data products on the mesh. But you cannot do this for large resources shared by many data products. It would be unfair to smaller data products, and it will not give those teams time to find out that they are overpaying for some resources they hardly use.

In this section, we will take only two service types as an example to explain the process of analyzing usage and distributing costs of shared resources. We will take Azure Storage and Azure Synapse Analytics as these are the two most common resources that get shared in a data mesh.

Azure Storage

Azure Storage pricing is split into two broad buckets: storage and transactions.

Storage is based on the amount of storage/month and the different storage tiers: hot, cool, cold, and archive. Hot provides the fastest access to the data stored, followed by cool and cold. When you move data to the archive tier, data is moved to slow cheap storage. While storage becomes cheap in the archive tear, data retrieval costs increase. To understand more about Azure Data Lake Storage tiers, refer to https://learn.microsoft.com/en-us/azure/storage/blobs/access-tiers-overview.

Transactions are measured as read/write/query operations. These transactions are then batched and charged at different batch sizes depending on the operation and on the storage type and storage tiers. For details on what these charges look like, refer to `https://azure.microsoft.com/en-us/pricing/details/storage/data-lake/`.

In order to calculate and distribute the cost of Azure Data Lake Storage across multiple data products, we will have to measure how much storage per tier a data product is using and how many different transactions are being executed over a period of one billing cycle.

To calculate the size of storage along with other details such as the number of objects, Azure Storage has recently introduced a new feature called **inventory reports**. Inventory reports are rule-based reports that you can run to create reports in CSV or Parquet format. These reports can be based on certain filters, and the report schema can be customized. These reports can then be queried using one of the many query tools.

Let's first look at how to enable these inventory reports. You can find this resource menu on any Azure Storage account, as shown in *Figures 12.13* and *12.14*. Clicking the **Blob inventory** menu option will pop up an **Add a rule** blade. On this blade, you can define the following:

- The target location where the inventory log must be stored.
- Types of objects you want to inventory (for example, containers and blobs).
- Blob types.
- If you are collecting blob information, how recent the creation date should be.
- Columns you wish to include in the logs. Available columns will change based on whether you are collecting information at a blob level or a container level.
- Frequency of log collection (daily or weekly).
- The prefix of container names to be included or excluded. The prefix is the start of the name of the container – for example, `prodX` or `prodX/foo1`.

There is a small charge to collect inventory logs, so plan the collection frequency accordingly:

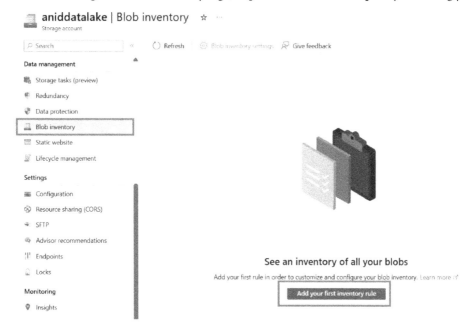

Figure 12.13 – Blob inventory user interface in the Azure portal

Figure 12.14 – Adding blob inventory rules

You can create multiple rules. If you have designed the naming convention of the shared storage account in a way that each container's name has the data product name embedded in it, then you can create one rule for every data product and include the appropriate prefix for that data product.

For more details on the fields you can include for containers and blobs, refer to `https://learn.microsoft.com/en-us/azure/storage/blobs/blob-inventory`.

A few important fields to consider for calculating usage are the following:

- `Creation-time`
- `Last-modified`
- `LastAccessTime`
- `Content-Length`
- `AccessTier`
- `AccessTierChangedTime`
- `BlobType`
- `Deleted`
- `DeletedTime`

Once you have started collecting the logs, you can slice and dice the data using one of the many analytical tools available on Azure, such as Azure Synapse, Databricks, and Azure Data Explorer.

The following code outputs the number of blobs and the total size of all blobs for a given container:

```
1 SELECT LEFT([Name], CHARINDEX('/', [Name]) - 1) AS Container,
2 COUNT(*) AS TotalBlobCount,
3 SUM([Content-Length]) AS TotalBlobSize
4 FROM OPENROWSET(
5 bulk '<URL to your inventory CSV file>',
6 format='csv', parser_version='2.0', header_row=TRUE
7 ) AS Source
8 GROUP BY LEFT([Name], CHARINDEX('/', [Name]) - 1)
```

You can modify this script to add other conditions such as storage tiers. Once you have narrowed down which containers belong to which data product and how much data is in each container, the next cost element you need to calculate for a storage account is the transactions.

To calculate the number of transactions on a storage container, you will need to query the diagnostic logs. In *Chapter 11*, we learned how to divert logs to one of the many storage and analysis options provided in the diagnostics settings for a given service. If we assume that you diverted the logs to Azure Log Analytics, you can run a Kusto query on the diagnostic logs. A sample Kusto query is shown next:

```
1 AzureDiagnostics
2 | where ResourceProvider == "MICROSOFT.STORAGE" and (Category ==
"StorageRead" or
3     Category == "StorageWrite" or
4     Category == "StorageDelete")
5 | where parse_json(Properties_s).container == "<YourContainerName>"
6 | where parse_json(Properties_s).blob == "<YourFolderName>"
7 | project TimeGenerated, AccountName=tostring(parse_
json(Properties_s).account),
8            ContainerName=tostring(parse_json(Properties_s).container),
9            BlobName=tostring(parse_json(Properties_s).blob),
10           OperationName, Status, CallerIpAddress,
11           ETag=tostring(parse_json(Properties_s).etag),
12           RequestId=tostring(parse_json(Properties_s).requestId),
13           UserAgentHeader=tostring(parse_json(Properties_s).
userAgentHeader)
```

The preceding query will filter the logs on folders and containers in the storage account for read, write, delete, and rehydration operations. **Rehydration** operations are operations of moving data from the archive tier to the hot/cool/cold tier. When a blob is moved to the archive tier, it is moved to cheap offline storage (cheap hard disk drives). When the storage tier of the archived storage is changed from archive back to hot, cool, or cold, a backend process has to first mount the offline storage and move the data from archive storage to hot, cool, or cold storage. This process is called rehydration and is indicated by an operation named `SetBlobTier`.

For details on how archiving costs work, refer to `https://learn.microsoft.com/en-us/azure/storage/blobs/archive-cost-estimation`.

You need a script that queries the storage and transaction logs and aggregates the reports into one table that looks like *Table 12.1*:

Data Mesh Product Name	Storage Location	Storage Consumed (GB)	Storage Tier	Read Operations	Write Operations	Delete Operations	Rehydra-tion Operations
Sales_fore-cast	Sales/fore-cast/2023	100	Hot	20000	123	0	0
Sales_fore-cast	Sales/fore-cast/2024	120	Hot	12000	234	0	20
Sales_KPI	Sales/KPI/2024/Q1	1453	Cool	3200	156	20	0
Sales_KPI	Sales/KPI/2024/Q2	1535	Cool	2310	162	0	10

Table 12.1 – Sample table generated from diagnostics and inventory logs

You will need to multiply the output of this script by the rate at which the storage and transactions are being charged. To get the most accurate pricing, you can use one of Azure's many pricing APIs. Different pricing APIs are available based on the Azure subscription you have. This book is going to assume an Azure **Enterprise Agreement** (**EA**) is in place before you start your analytics and data mesh journey. If you are on some other Azure pricing plan, then the pricing API will change. For EA, you can retrieve the most accurate pricing for a given billing period by using the ARM price list API to query price sheet and usage data.

The following is the URL for the Enterprise API to get the price sheet for the current billing period:

```
https://management.azure.com/{scope}/providers/Microsoft.Consumption/
pricesheets/default?api-version=2019-10-01
```

The scope can be a billing tenant ID or a subscription ID.

If you wish to get the price sheet for a specific billing period, you can use the following API URL:

```
https://management.azure.com/{scope}/billingPeriods/
{billingPeriodName}/providers/Microsoft.Consumption/pricesheets/
default?api-version=2019-10-01
```

Here, the billing period might be represented as 202304 for April 2023.

The Python code to call this API is shown next:

```
1 Import requests
2 # Set up your Azure credentials and endpoint details
3 tenant_id = 'YOUR_TENANT_ID'
4 client_id = 'YOUR_CLIENT_ID'
5 client_secret = 'YOUR_CLIENT_SECRET'
6 subscription_id = 'YOUR_SUBSCRIPTION_ID'
7 resource_scope = f"/subscriptions/{subscription_id}"
8
9 # Construct the URL
10 url = f"https://management.azure.com{resource_scope}/providers/ \
11 Microsoft.Consumption/pricesheets/default?api-version=2019-10-01"
12
13 # Get the OAuth2 token
14 token_url = f"https://login.microsoftonline.com/{tenant_id}/oauth2/
token"
15 token_data = {
16     'grant_type': 'client_credentials',
17     'client_id': client_id,
18     'client_secret': client_secret,
19     'resource': 'https://management.azure.com/'
20 }
21 token_r = requests.post(token_url, data=token_data)
22 token = token_r.json().get("access_token")
23
24 # Make the API call
25 headers = {
26     'Authorization': f'Bearer {token}',
27     'Content-Type': 'application/json',
28 }
29 response = requests.get(url, headers=headers)
30
31 # Print the result
32 print(response.json())
```

The output will look like this:

```
1 {
2   "id": "/subscriptions/00000000-0000-0000-0000/
3   providers/Microsoft.Billing/billingPeriods/201702/
4   providers/Microsoft.Consumption/pricesheets/default",
5   "name": "default",
6   "type": "Microsoft.Consumption/pricesheets",
```

```
7   "properties": {
8     "nextLink": "https://management.azure.com/
subscriptions/00000000-0000-0000/
9     providers/microsoft.consumption/pricesheets/
10  default?api-version=2018-01-31
11  &$skiptoken=AQAAAA%3D%3D&$expand=properties/pricesheets/
meterDetails",
12    "pricesheets": [
13      {
14        "billingPeriodId": "/
subscriptions/00000000-0000-0000-0000-000000000000/providers/
15        Microsoft.Billing/billingPeriods/201702",
16        "meterId": "00000000-0000-0000-0000-000000000000",
17        "unitOfMeasure": "100 Hours",
18        "includedQuantity": 100,
19        "partNumber": "XX-11110",
20        "unitPrice": 0.00000,
21        "currencyCode": "EUR",
22        "offerId": "OfferId 1",
23        "meterDetails": {
24          "meterName": "Data Transfer Out (GB)",
25          "meterCategory": "Networking",
26          "unit": "GB",
27          "meterLocation": "Zone 2",
28          "totalIncludedQuantity": 0,
29          "pretaxStandardRate": 0.000
30        }
31      }
32    ]
33  }
34}
```

This output provides the important data points for calculating cost — meterId and unitPrice.

But this is just half the solution. This data just tells you the price of a specific service type. You still need to find the actual service instance and map it to meterId. To do this, we need another API called the **usage API**:

```
https://management.azure.com/{scope}/providers/Microsoft.Consumption/
usageDetails?api-version=2023-05-01
```

Using similar Python code to that shown previously, you can execute this API call. The output will look like the following:

```
1 {
2   "value": [
```

```
3     {
4       "id": "/subscriptions/{subscription-id}/providers/
5     Microsoft.Consumption/usageDetails/{usage-detail-id}",
6       "name": "{usage-detail-id}",
7       "type": "Microsoft.Consumption/usageDetails",
8       "properties": {
9         "usageStart": "2023-01-01T00:00:00Z",
10        "usageEnd": "2023-01-01T23:59:59Z",
11        "meterId": "{meter-id}",
12        "meterName": "Standard IO - File Read Operation Units",
13        "meterCategory": "Storage",
14        "meterSubCategory": "Blob Storage",
15        "unit": "10K operations",
16        "meterRegion": "US East",
17        "quantity": 500.0,
18        "cost": 5.00,
19        "currency": "USD",
20        "instanceId": "/subscriptions/{subscription-id}/
    resourceGroups/
21      {resource-group-name}/providers/Microsoft.Storage/
22      storageAccounts/{storage-account-name}",
23        "instanceName": "{storage-account-name}",
24        "instanceLocation": "US East",
25        "product": "Azure Blob Storage",
26        "consumedService": "Microsoft.Storage",
27        "resourceRate": 0.01,
28        "offerId": "MS-AZR-0003P",
29        "isEstimated": false,
30        "subscriptionGuid": "{subscription-id}",
31        "subscriptionName": "Your Subscription Name",
32        "accountName": "Your Account Name",
33        "departmentName": "Your Department Name",
34        "costCenter": "1234",
35        "additionalProperties": {}
36      }
37    },
38    ... (more usage details for other resources)
39  ],
40  "nextLink": "https://management.azure.com/subscriptions/
    {subscription-id}/
41  providers/Microsoft.Consumption/
42  usageDetails?api-version=2019-10-01
43  &$skiptoken={token-for-next-page}"
44 }
```

As you can see in the output, you get the `meterId`, `unitPrice`, `currency`, `InstanceId`, and `InstanceName` values that you can now use to join the information across inventory logs, transaction logs, price sheet output, usage output, and the figures in *Table 12.1* to come up with a formula to calculate the cross charge for a data product.

The scheme of the formula will look like this:

```
(Storage consumed X Unit Price for storage tier) +

(Read operations X Unit Price for storage read operations) +

(Write operations X Unit Price for storage write operations) +

(Delete operations X Unit Price for storage write operations) +

(Archive operations X Unit Price for storage retrieval operations) +

(Management cost) +

(IT Ops cost)
```

The formula is a high-level formula. Depending on how your central data lake is shared, you will need to adjust the formula accordingly. You might also choose to add a multiplication factor for the admin costs based on the amount of storage per data product. The more the storage, the higher the management and admin costs. The cost of backups, **high availability** (**HA**), and DR also need to be added to this cost if applicable.

We have learned how to distribute costs for a shared data lake or storage. Let us look at how to distribute the cost of a shared data warehouse using Azure Synapse Analytics dedicated pools.

Azure Synapse Analytics dedicated pools

Azure Synapse Analytics is a popular big-data processing platform that provides compute, storage, and workspace to process big-data sources for analytics. It converges multiple data analytics frameworks such as SQL, Python, and Kusto into one single workspace, allowing data engineers and data scientists to collaborate better.

Azure Synapse Analytics provides multiple processing engines such as SQL Data Warehouse, Apache Spark, and Azure Data Explorer to process the data. A deep discussion on Azure Synapse Analytics is beyond the scope of this book. To read and understand more about Azure Synapse Analytics, refer to `https://learn.microsoft.com/en-us/azure/synapse-analytics/`.

One of the commonly shared resources on a data mesh is a data warehouse, and the most common data warehouse solution on Azure is Azure Synapse Analytics dedicated SQL pools. It is a collection of computing resources and engines required to do data warehousing operations using a **Massively Parallel Processing** (**MPP**) architecture. The MPP architecture distributes compute across multiple nodes and spreads the data across the nodes either through replication or hash distribution, keeping all required data close to its compute.

To learn more about the dedicated SQL pool MPP architecture, refer to `https://learn.microsoft.com/en-us/azure/synapse-analytics/sql-data-warehouse/massively-parallel-processing-mpp-architecture`.

Just like any other service, Azure Synapse also supports the collection of diagnostic data. Synapse dedicated pool diagnostic data provides data on active queries, query steps, and query compute per query step through diagnostic logs called **Execute requests**, **Request steps**, and **SQL requests**.

To understand more about these diagnostic log parameters, refer to the following links:

`https://learn.microsoft.com/en-us/azure/synapse-analytics/sql-data-warehouse/sql-data-warehouse-manage-monitor`

`https://learn.microsoft.com/en-us/azure/synapse-analytics/monitoring/how-to-monitor-using-azure-monitor#dedicated-sql-pool-logs`

Monitoring these log parameters will be similar to what we did with Azure Storage in the previous section. So, we will leave this as an exercise for you. We will cover the part that is the most tricky to evaluate individual product usage of the Azure Synapse dedicated pool, which is measured as **Data Warehouse Units** (**DWUs**).

A DWU is a combined unit of CPU, memory, and I/O used by the dedicated SQL pool for executing a query. You provision an Azure Synapse instance by setting the maximum DWU capacity that it should use. Synapse is available in two versions: **Gen1** and **Gen2**. **Gen1** uses DWU and **Gen2** uses **compute DWU** or **DWUc**. The Azure Synapse instance is created with a **service-level objective** (**SLO**). This is the setting that determines how many DWU or DWUc instances will be provisioned. **Gen2** allows a minimum of 100 and a maximum of 30,000 DWUc instances.

For more information on DWUs, refer to `https://learn.microsoft.com/en-us/azure/synapse-analytics/sql-data-warehouse/what-is-a-data-warehouse-unit-dwu-cdwu`.

In a typical analytical setup, data warehouses are set up as shared resources because they allow teams to use data from different products and **business units** (**BUs**) to run analytics. Each product or BU loads its data into the data warehouse and then runs analytical queries against this data. The data warehouse SQL engine (provisioned DWUc) is shared by all these queries.

This means that if all the DWUc capacity is being used by a set of queries at any given time, then other queries that are not executing yet have to wait in a queue until some DWUcs free up. This can cause problems. An important query that runs critical daily business reports for the executives could be stuck in the queue. Hence, Azure Synapse also provides a feature called **workload management**. Workload management helps data warehouse operators classify, prioritize, and isolate the execution of queries. This ensures that important queries get prioritized and no query completely takes over all available DWUc instances. To learn more about workload management, refer to `https://learn.microsoft.com/en-us/azure/synapse-analytics/sql-data-warehouse/sql-data-warehouse-workload-management`.

Assuming that you have put all the best practices in place, including a good workload management strategy, how do you measure and distribute the cost of the data warehouse that is being shared by so many data products running queries? Well, it is almost impossible to come up with the exact DWUc instances used to execute a specific query unless that was the only query running. In a real-world scenario, for a large organization, multiple queries would be executing and many would be waiting in the queue to be executed.

What can be done to get a close estimate of the usage per data product? The idea here is not to be accurate but to be fair in terms of cross charges.

In order to distribute the cost of the data warehouse, we will have to start looking at the SQL dedicated pool and other Azure logs. Let us look at all the logs we will need to determine this cost estimation.

The Synapse SQL dedicated pool diagnostic log is the first log to look at. Assuming that you have enabled diagnostic logs and pushed them either to Log Analytics or an Azure Storage account, you can get some important usage information in these logs.

For a list of all diagnostic log events captured for a Synapse dedicated pool, refer to `https://learn.microsoft.com/en-us/azure/synapse-analytics/monitoring/how-to-monitor-using-azure-monitor#dedicated-sql-pool-metrics`.

Events of particular importance are the following:

- `DWULimit`: The provisioned size of the SQL pool.
- `DWUUsed`: This is the count of the average DWU usage percentage, measured as `DWU limit * DWU percentage`.
- `ActiveQueries/WLGActiveQueries`: The number of active queries at a given time. If you are using workload management, then use `WLGActiveQueries`.

To get this data for the last month, you could execute a Kusto query, such as the one shown next:

```
1 let last_month_start = startofmonth(now(-1m));
2 let last_month_end = endofmonth(now(-1m));
3 AzureDiagnostics
4 | where ResourceType == "SQLPOOLS"
5 | where TimeGenerated >= last_month_start and TimeGenerated < last_month_end
6 | project TimeGenerated, DWULimit_s, DWUUsed_s
7 | project ActiveQueries_s, WLGActiveQueries_s
```

The next step is to find queries running in the same period. The `ExecuteRequest` category of diagnostics can give you this information, as shown in the following code:

```
1 let last_month_start = startofmonth(now(-1m));
2 let last_month_end = endofmonth(now(-1m));
3 AzureDiagnostics
4|  where Category == "ExecRequests"
5|  where Databaseid == "<Database Name>"
6|  where Status == "Completed"
7|  where TimeGenerated >= last_month_start and TimeGenerated < last_
month_end
8|  project ResourceGroup, LogicalServerName,
9|  project DatabaseId, StartTime,
10| project EndTime, Category,
11| project Status, RequestId,
12| project Command
```

You could also further get aggregated data for the longest-running queries, as shown in the following code:

```
1 let last_month_start = startofmonth(now(-1m));
2 let last_month_end = endofmonth(now(-1m));
3 AzureDiagnostics
4  | where Category == "ExecRequests"
5  | where type_s == "SqlQuery"
6  | where Status = "Completed"
7  | where TimeGenerated >= last_month_start and TimeGenerated < last_
month_end
8  | extend duration = endDateTime_t - startDateTime_t
9  | summarize max_duration=max(duration) by command_s
10 | top 5 by max_duration desc
```

The `summarize` keyword in Kusto can help you aggregate data in the logs.

Do note that these are just one of many ways to get this data. Here are two other methods:

- **Dedicated SQL Pool Dynamic Management Views** (**DMVs**): DMVs are ready-made views in the dedicated SQL pool instance that can be queried using SQL. The data in these views is the same as diagnostic logs in Azure Monitor.

  For more information on dedicated SQL pool DMVs, refer to `https://learn.microsoft.com/en-us/azure/synapse-analytics/sql-data-warehouse/sql-data-warehouse-manage-monitor`.

- **SQL Server audit logs**: These logs are also available for Azure dedicated SQL pools. You can enable them in the Azure portal, as shown in *Figure 12.15*:

Figure 12.15 – Enabling security logs on a dedicated SQL pool

The Kusto code in the Log Analytics workspace to query these SQL audit logs is shown next:

```
1 AzureDiagnostics
2 | where Category == "SQLSecurityAuditEvents"
3 | project ResourceGroup, LogicalServerName_s
4 | project database_name_s, event_time_t
5 | project Category, tobool (succeeded_s)
6 | project tostring (session_id_d), client_ip_s
7 | project host_name_s, server_principal_name_s
8 | project tolong (duration_milliseconds_d)
9 | project statement_s, TenantId, _ResourceId
```

The advantage of querying SQL audit logs is that you get a few other details, such as who executed the script, the hostname, and the service principal. Audit logs, as the name suggests, are good for investigation. In our experience, many times, data product team members want proof they executed an SQL script that they are being charged for. The audit logs will provide that proof.

Using data from all these logs, you can create custom tables that accumulate costs for each data product across various dedicated and shared resources in their landing zones and across the data mesh. *Figure 12.16* depicts the high-level architecture of this cost management setup:

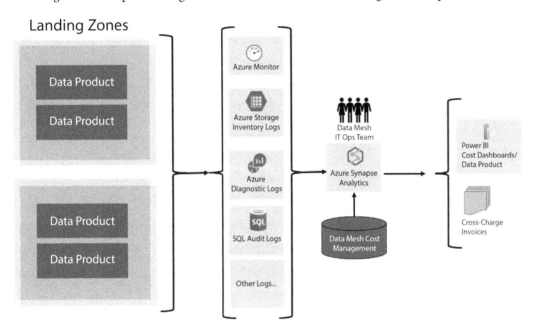

Figure 12.16 – Data mesh cost management architecture

Recommendations

The following are some recommendations for centralized cost calculations and centralizing cost dashboards:

- **Azure Synapse Analytics**: Considering the number of logs and different format files that you will deal with when it comes to managing and distributing data mesh costs, it is recommended that you build your cost management system on Azure Synapse Analytics. Azure Synapse Analytics provides SQL, Python, and Kusto notebooks and has the Data Warehouse engine, Spark engine, and Azure Data Explorer all bundled into one environment. Azure Synapse will allow you to query, slice and dice, and aggregate data. This data can then be stored in a separate cost management database in Azure Synapse.

- **Data mesh portal**: Bring all cost dashboards and invoices into the data mesh portal. All data product teams will have a central location to go to monitor and look at their costs.

Summary

This concludes the chapter on data mesh cost management. We broke down the costs into multiple large buckets of direct, shared, service, and people costs. We looked at how these costs are measured and ways of capturing these costs. Some of these costs can be captured accurately, such as direct costs, but some need to be estimated, such as shared costs. We also looked at sample queries and code snippets to find out costs from log files. Finally, we looked at ways of bringing all these costs together and distributing them to individual landing zones and projects.

As you must have observed, cost management is a complex topic with many variables. Planning and organizing from the beginning will be key to ensuring that the complexity does not overwhelm you later. Start early and start simple. Initially, it may be a simple dashboard or just a report. As the mesh grows, you can make it more sophisticated with custom alerts and dashboards.

Next, we will look at organizing and managing data access and data security while accessing data from a shared data lake or data warehouse. While it sounds simple, it can get complex and difficult to manage if you don't put enough designing and planning effort in upfront.

13

Understanding Data-Sharing Topologies in a Data Mesh

In my experience of helping Microsoft customers implement a data mesh, the part that concerns the customers the most is data sharing. The concept of **in-place sharing** is completely new to most customers, and they wonder how it will actually work. In-place sharing is a way of sharing data with others without moving the data from its source system. Well, it's important to understand that while in-place data sharing is key to avoiding data movement through the mesh, it's not mandatory. So, when do we use in-place sharing, and when do we move data? Are there any other ways of sharing data? And when should we use which sharing technique?

This chapter will answer all these questions. It will lay out clear topologies of data-sharing techniques and scenarios that need each of these sharing topologies.

In this chapter, we will cover the following topics:

- What is in-place sharing?
- Understanding data-sharing challenges in a data mesh
- Exploring different methods available for sharing data
- Picking the right data-sharing topologies

What is in-place sharing?

In-place data sharing is a method of sharing data where the data remains in its original location. It is not physically copied or moved to a different location when another data product wants to access it. Instead, access is granted to the data where it resides. This approach contrasts with traditional data-sharing methods such as data copy pipelines, which involve copying the data to a new location.

The way the data is accessed depends on the way the data is stored. If the data is stored in a data lake, you can provide a connection string to the data lake that the consuming data product can use to directly read the data and load it into its processing space (a Python DataFrame or SQL query result). Security can be managed using temporary keys or authenticated service principals.

Azure Databricks has a feature called **Delta Sharing**. It's an open protocol and is supported by its Unity Catalog service. The shared metadata is stored in Unity Catalog. Access security is also managed by Unity Catalog.

Key aspects of in-place data sharing include the following:

- **Access control**: In-place data sharing requires robust access control mechanisms. This is especially important because direct access to the source data is provided in many scenarios. Permissions and access rights are managed to ensure that only authorized users or systems can access the right data.

- **Data governance**: Effective data governance policies are crucial to manage how data is accessed and used. This includes defining who can access the data and for what purposes, and ensuring compliance with relevant regulations and standards.

- **Real-time data access**: In-place data sharing allows for real-time or near-real-time access to data, as there is no delay caused by data movement. This is particularly beneficial for applications that require up-to-date information.

- **Reduced data redundancy**: By avoiding the need to copy or replicate data, in-place data sharing helps in reducing data redundancy and storage costs. It also minimizes the risks associated with data synchronization issues, such as inconsistencies or outdated information.

One key challenge with in-place sharing is latency. The data is loaded from the source directly by the processing code. This works well if the code and the source data are in the same data center. If the code is in Western Europe and the data is in Central United States, the latency of loading a large dataset will make the data product very slow.

But before we further understand more about in-place sharing and the various techniques to implement it, let us look at the challenges of data sharing in a data mesh.

Understanding data-sharing challenges in a data mesh

A data mesh is an architecture that proposes decentralizing data ownership and centralizes governance of these decentralized data products or landing zones. While it provides agility and independence to the products and the product teams, it does raise multiple new challenges. In many previous chapters, we have discussed these challenges: deploying and managing multiple landing zones, managing data access across different data products, discovering decentralized data, and many other such challenges. We found solutions to make them easier and more manageable.

When we propose a data mesh architecture to companies, the very first thought that comes to their mind is, how will data be shared across this mesh? Will each data product pull data from across the mesh? Will that not create duplicate copies of data across the mesh? What about security across different **access points (APs)**?

To answer these questions and many more, let us first look at some of the challenges of data sharing in a data mesh.

Latency

When you transfer data across a source and a destination, one of the important aspects to consider is **latency**. To understand latency in the context of a data mesh and in-place sharing, let us consider the scenario depicted in *Figure 13.1*. Every landing zone has one or more data stores. These stores can be of different types (Databricks, a data lake, or a SQL database). Landing zone 4 shares data with three other landing zones:

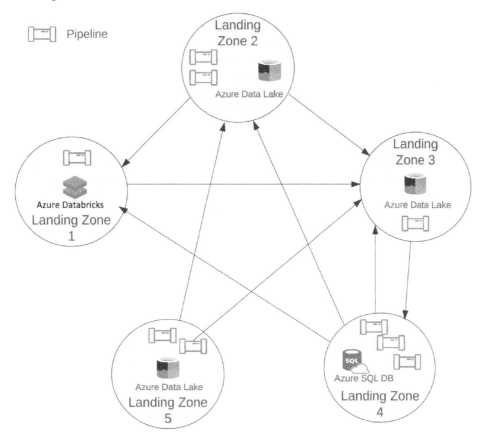

Figure 13.1 – Pipeline-driven data sharing

For every data-sharing requirement, we implement a pipeline with the appropriate source and sink. This approach has the following challenges:

- The same data is replicated at multiple locations (data duplication).

- The consumer landing zone is not sure whether it is using the most recent copy of the data. The freshness of data is dependent on the frequency of pipeline runs.

- The source landing zone has to maintain multiple pipelines.

- As sharing across the data mesh grows, the number of pipelines keeps growing.

- If the pipeline goes down, then data sharing stops.

To solve these challenges, the data mesh proposes in-place sharing. This means that the source data does not leave its landing zone and is directly accessed by the processing code, as depicted in *Figure 13.2*.

This ensures no duplication of data and avoids building and maintaining pipelines. It definitely seems like a great way of sharing data between different data products:

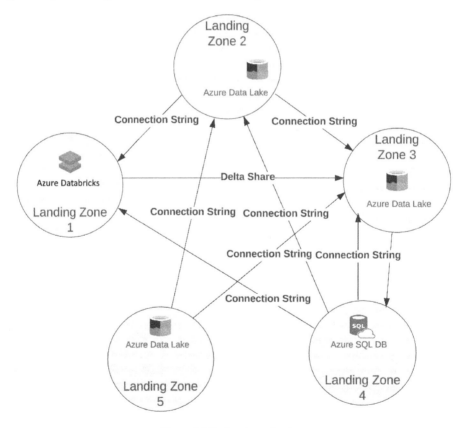

Figure 13.2 – In-place sharing

Now, let's imagine a scenario where the resources of landing zone 1 are in a different region of the world than the other landing zones, as shown in *Figure 13.3*.

The data shares marked in red (please see the e-book for the color version of the image) will now run on an intercontinental network. This will introduce latency resulting from the distance between the source and the destination. This could mean that the products using landing zone 1 data will now face a performance issue with loading the data into their code. If the code has to load this data multiple times, it will multiply the impact on the performance of this analytical code. The same is true for landing zone 1, which is using data from landing zones 2 and 4. While the performance of this data exchange will depend on the size of the data being loaded, let us assume that for this scenario, the data being shared is large. One other important aspect to consider here is the egress charges of data moving between two Microsoft Azure regions:

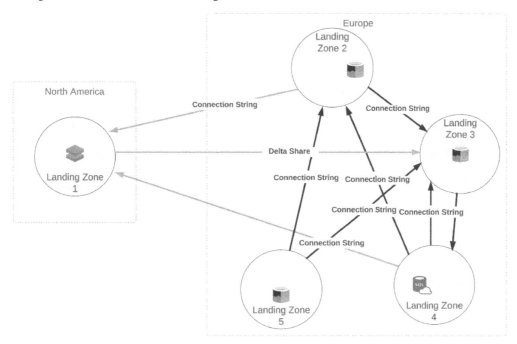

Figure 13.3 – In-place sharing with data shares

In order to solve this problem, we could take a hybrid approach. Only for the red lines (lines connecting landing zone 2 to landing zone 1, landing zone 1 to landing zone 3, and landing zone 4 to landing zone 1), we implement the data share as a pipeline that periodically pushes data to the destination landing zone, as shown in *Figure 13.4*. The data pushed is stored locally and referenced locally by the code.

While this introduces pipelines back into the topology, the number of pipelines is very small and hence manageable. The only scenario where this will not work is if the data is needed in real time by the processing code, but for batch-processing scenarios, hybrid can be a good solution.

The conclusion is that as a best practice, the data mesh proposes in-place sharing to minimize data movement and pipeline management. However, it's not always practical to do in-place sharing. Depending on the distance between the source and the target product, the size of the data being loaded, and anything else that can impact data latency, we can choose to implement a pipeline-based data share:

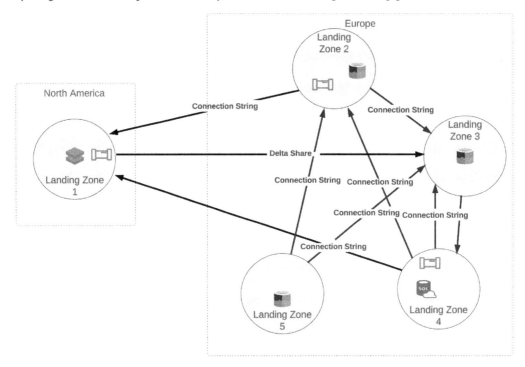

Figure 13.4 – Hybrid data-sharing approach

Next, let's look at security and access control concerns that most customers have with a data mesh.

Security and access control

In a centralized analytics system where data is piped and stored centrally, only data that is required for analytics is brought into the central data lake. This data is also preprocessed to remove any **personally identifiable information** (**PII**) or sensitive information as required. The central data lake can be designed keeping security and access in mind.

With in-place sharing in a data mesh environment, data is stored and managed in a distributed environment, based on the requirement of the data product that is being built on that data. Providing direct access to this data without any preprocessing may not be agreeable to the team that owns the data. The privacy and security council in the company will also not agree to access data directly from its source data product without proper privacy controls.

To solve this problem, consider the following:

- **Plan ahead**: When designing the landing zone for the data product, assume that some data will be shared with other products. This data should be copied into two places by the processing logic: local and shareable stores.

- **Create a separate shareable store**: For any on-demand requirements of sharing data, create a separate store and provide external access to only this store. Any data that needs to be shared must be copied to this store. Direct access to the actual business will not be allowed. Data stored in the shareable store can be preprocessed to remove PII. Additional access security can also be implemented on this shareable store.

- **Share using APIs**: If the amount of data to be shared is small, expose the data through an **application programming interface** (**API**). The program will preprocess data and ensure that sensitive data is masked or removed. APIs also allow you to use technologies such as API Management to better control access security. For more details on API Management, refer to `https://learn.microsoft.com/en-us/azure/api-management/`.

As we read in the *What is in-place sharing?* section, in-place sharing is implemented in different ways by different storage systems. Some consumers may not be able to consume these sharing protocols and formats seamlessly. In the next section, let us look at some of these challenges of data format and protocol incompatibility.

Data formats and protocols

Each data store will have a data format it stores data in. Databricks Delta Sharing stores data in Parquet format. Data Lake might have data in JSON or CSV format. Similarly, different protocols might be used to provide direct access to this data. Azure Data Lake specifies the **Azure Blob File System** (**ABFS**) protocol in its connection string. Microsoft SQL Server uses **Tabular Data Stream** (**TDS**) over a TCP protocol. Azure Databricks Delta Sharing uses its own open protocol to share data.

The target system that is consuming the data must be able to seamlessly connect to these protocols or formats. If it is not able to, then it will need a separate system to read and convert the data into a format and a protocol that is supported. This might make the whole purpose of in-place sharing redundant.

These are the main challenges that a company could face when sharing data across different data products and landing zones. This also means that different techniques might have to be used other than in-place sharing to minimize the duplication of data and maintain access control and security across the data mesh. We need a data-sharing strategy and set of standardized methodologies to share data for different data-sharing scenarios.

In the next section, let us discuss different topologies that can be implemented to share data across data products.

Exploring different methods available for sharing data

One of the challenges most companies face is deciding on a data-sharing best practice that standardizes one standard technique to share data. However, while discussing the challenges of data sharing in a data mesh, we realized that there are multiple ways of sharing data. Let us spend some time organizing all these data-sharing techniques and the different components and layers involved in their implementation. This will help in aligning the different methods to different data-sharing scenarios.

In-place access

As discussed in the *What is in-place sharing?* section, in-place sharing provides direct access to the data from the code that needs to process that data.

As an example, let's assume a file called `data.csv` is stored in a data lake of a European finance data product in a company, as shown in *Figure 13.5*.

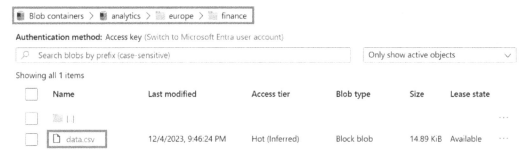

Figure 13.5 – data.csv file location

An executive dashboard team in Europe needs real-time access to `data.csv` without copying the data into their landing zone. The executive dashboard team is using Synapse Analytics to build their dashboard. The executive dashboard has a managed identity that it uses to access European finance data. The finance team has assigned a read permission **access control list** (**ACL**) entry to `data.csv` for this managed identity. The ACLs applied to the file are shown in *Table 13.1*:

/	/europe	/finance	data.csv
--X	--X	--X	R--

Table 13.1 – ACLs for read access to data.csv

The Python code running in the executive dashboard data product that needs this data can directly read it using an `adfss` connection string, as shown in the following code:

```
#read data file
df = pandas.read_csv(\
```

```
'abfs[s]//analytics@financedatalake.dfs.core.windows.net/europe/
finance/data.csv',\
storage_options = {'linked_service' : 'linked_service_name'})
print(df)
```

In the preceding code, we are using an abfs[s] URL to directly read the data.csv file from the source location. The output of this code will look like this:

```
   Year  Sales
0  2018    100
1  2019    150
2  2020    200
3  2021    250
```

Figure 13.6 shows the in-place sharing topology between two data products:

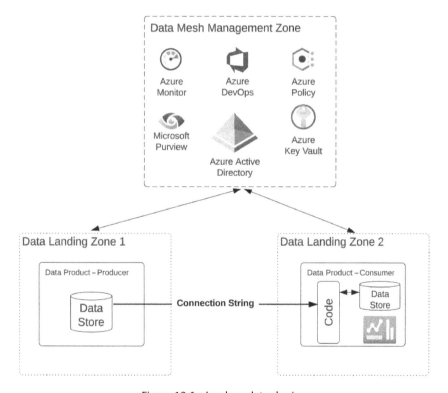

Figure 13.6 – In-place data sharing

Similar code can be executed for reading a SQL database using a SQL connection string and the pyodbc library. The pyodbc library can be downloaded from https://pypi.org/project/pyodbc/, or if your analytics code is in SQL, then through a SQL code editor, you can directly load the CSV file using the `openrowset` command. Details on how to query CSV files in Azure Synapse Analytics can be found here: `https://learn.microsoft.com/en-us/azure/synapse-analytics/sql/query-single-csv-file`. As long as the target coding environment has a way to connect to the source data directly, you can implement in-place sharing.

The process and steps to implement in-place access are set out here:

1. The data product consumer team raises an access request to the data producer team.

2. The data producer team accepts/rejects the access request based on company policies and data-sharing guidelines.

3. If the request is approved, the data producer requests a managed identity that will read the data.

4. The data consumer provides the managed identity.

5. The data producer builds a data contract document and submits it to the data steward.

6. The data producer and consumer agree on the data contract.

7. The data producer grants relevant access to the managed identity and provides the connection string details.

8. The data consumer starts reading the data using the details provided in *step 7*.

But what if direct access to data is not possible? There can be many reasons for direct access being difficult or not possible. We will discuss these reasons in the next section as we discuss different scenarios for using each of these sharing topologies. The most common method of sharing data in the cloud across different systems and products is building a data pipeline. Let us look at data pipelines and how they are used as a way to share/move data across different systems.

Data pipelines

A pipeline is used to share data by moving the data from the source to the target location. A pipeline can be built in Azure Data Factory or Azure Synapse pipelines, or it could even be code executing in an Azure Databricks job. *Figure 13.7* shows the topology of this pipeline-based data sharing:

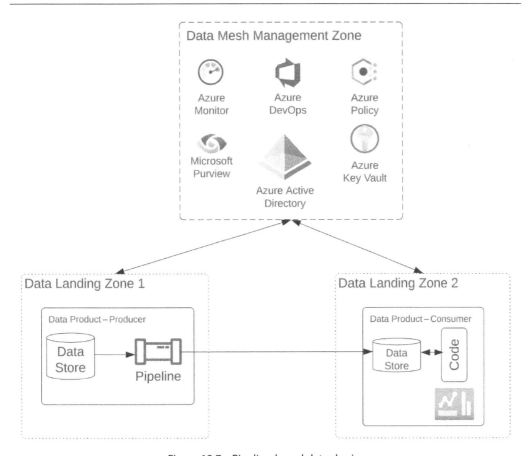

Figure 13.7 – Pipeline-based data sharing

In order to implement a pipeline, the initial steps of requesting and granting access to the data remain the same as in-place sharing. Once access to the data is granted, the steps to implement a pipeline are the following:

1. The data producer builds a pipeline with the managed identity, performing any transformations if required (data masking; removing PII).

2. The data producer builds a data contract document and submits it to the data steward.

3. The data producer and consumer agree on the data contract.

4. The data producer schedules the pipeline run based on the contract.

The scenarios we covered are ideal for medium to large volumes of data that need to be read and processed by the data consumer, but what if the data required is a small piece of information – for example, a prediction or a forecast value, or a small table of data generated by some complex market analysis algorithm? Do we need to provide direct access or build a pipeline for such small amounts of data? Let us look at a way of sharing such small amounts of data in the next sharing methodology called data APIs.

Data APIs

To understand the application of APIs to data, let us take an example. A company has a team building an executive sales report. Their job is to collect sales-related data from different teams, process it, and assemble it into a report. This is the data consumer. Another team in the company works on a statistical analysis of the sales pipeline and the actual sales to calculate the forecast accuracy. This is the data producer team.

The sales forecast accuracy is an important **key performance indicator** (**KPI**) to be included in the report. The data required is just a few numbers: time period, forecasted sales, actual sales, and forecast accuracy. Instead of providing direct access to this data or building a pipeline just to transfer these four numbers, the producer team can build an API. Building an API also helps provide more functionality, such as providing data for different time periods based on parameters passed to the API. The producer can also write APIs to provide the forecast data in different formats. It's value added for the consumer.

The steps to implement a data API are set out here:

1. The data producer team designs and builds a program that reads the required data, performs the required processing, and exposes it as an API. Different APIs are designed and built for different data outputs they wish to provide.

2. The data producer documents these APIs and creates a data contract. The contract explains the use, access policy, access request process, and the **service-level agreement** (**SLA**).

3. The data producers share this document with the data stewards and make their APIs discoverable.

4. Data consumers discover these APIs. They read the data contracts and understand the functionality and limitations.

5. If the contract and the data output are in accordance with their requirement, data consumers request access by following the request process and providing a managed identity to the producer.

6. The data producer grants access to the required APIs to the managed identity provided in *step 5*.

7. The data consumer starts calling the API to consume the data and use it in their analytics product.

Figure 13.8 depicts the design of exposing data as an API:

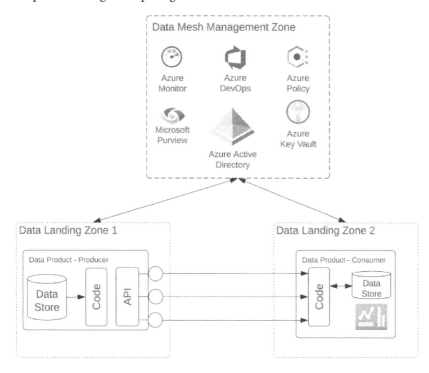

Figure 13.8 – Sharing data using a data API

Companies often work with multiple vendors and partners to run their business. They need to share data across different globally distributed departments, organizations, or companies (external partners). It could be a joint venture between two companies or a third-party analytics company that produces analytical reports using the source company's data. For such scenarios, the data-sharing methods discussed thus far won't work because these users are outside the organization and cannot be given access to internal data sources. Azure has a special service called Azure Data Share for such scenarios. Let us explore Azure Data Share as the next method of sharing data.

Data Share

Often, when companies want to share data outside their department or company, they bundle it in an Excel file, attach it to an email, and send it. This method has a lot of flaws. It duplicates data, data can be stale, and it is not secure. To solve this problem, Azure has a service called **Azure Data Share**. Azure Data Share allows companies to share data with multiple external partners securely by creating a share. The producer defines the terms and the frequency of sharing the data. The consumer must agree to these terms to receive data. The producer can also revoke access to the share at any time.

There are two ways to share data using Azure Data Share:

- **Snapshot-based sharing**: In snapshot-based sharing, the producer creates a snapshot of the data they want to share. They send an invite to the consumer to the data share. The consumer must accept the invitation. Once accepted, they will be provided with a link that triggers a full snapshot of data that will be shared with them. The data is physically moved from the producer's store to the consumer's store. Both of these stores must be on an Azure subscription. The producer can now send regularly updated snapshots to all consumers.

- **In-place sharing**: In this method, the invitation to share data is sent to the consumer. However, the data is not moved to the consumer. Instead, a symbolic link is shared with the consumer. They can use this link to read the data directly from the source.

The steps to implement Data Share are set out here:

1. The data producer prepares the data to be shared.

2. The data consumer requests data from the producer.

3. The data producer decides how to share the data: through snapshot or in-place sharing. Accordingly, they create an Azure data share of that type.

4. The data producer creates a snapshot schedule if the sharing type is a snapshot.

5. The data producer adds the recipients to the Azure data share.

6. The consumer will receive an email. They can also open the invitation from the Azure portal.

7. The consumer accepts the invite and follows the instructions to receive the data.

Figure 13.9 shows how Azure Data Share works:

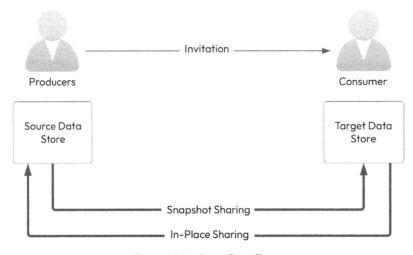

Figure 13.9 – Azure Data Share

To learn more about Azure Data Share, refer to `https://learn.microsoft.com/en-us/azure/data-share/`.

This concludes all the topologies or methods of sharing data across a data mesh and outside a data mesh.

Now, let's look at how to pick the right sharing method for a given scenario. In the next section, let us look at all the pros and cons of each method and understand the scenarios for using each sharing topology.

Picking the right data-sharing topologies

To understand the scenarios under which each of these topologies should be used, let us look at the pros and cons of each data-sharing method.

In-place sharing

Here are the pros and cons of in-place sharing:

Pros	Cons
Real-time data-sharing	Prone to network latency and heavy payload-related performance issues
No data duplication	Direct access to source data needs higher security monitoring and complex policies

Table 13.2 – Pros and cons of in-place sharing

The following are ideal scenarios for using in-place sharing:

- Real-time access that needs the most recent version of the data
- Small or medium-sized reference data (**exploratory data analysis** or **EDA**; real-time APIs)
- The source and target are in the same or neighboring Azure regions
- The source and target are in the same company

Data pipelines

Here are the pros and cons of data pipelines:

Pros	Cons
Better control over what data is shared	Data freshness is a factor in the frequency of pipeline runs
The frequency of sharing can be controlled	Added administration and management of pipelines

Simpler security setup as data is not directly exposed	
Distance- and volume-related latency can be controlled by pipeline run frequency and dividing large data into smaller batch pipelines	

Table 13.3 – Pros and cons of data pipelines

The following are ideal scenarios for using data pipelines:

- The source and target are in different geographical regions

- The volume of data is very high

- Real-time data is not a requirement

- The producer wants to control the access and flow of data

Data APIs

Here are the pros and cons of data APIs:

Pros	Cons
Real-time sharing of small datasets	Cannot handle large payloads
Ability to provide different flavors of data depending on consumer's needs	Higher effort to code, build, and maintain
Better security structure	

Table 13.4 – Pros and cons of data APIs

The following is an ideal scenarios for using data APIs:

- Ideal for sharing KPIs, real-time aggregated data, and output of **machine learning** (**ML**) models

Data sharing

Here are the pros and cons of data sharing:

Pros	Cons
Enhanced data-sharing controls	Producer and consumer must be on Azure
Highly secure	The added cost of the Azure Data Share service
Better security structure	

Table 13.5 – Pros and cons of data sharing

The following is an ideal scenario for using data sharing:

- Sharing data with third-party partners, customers, consortiums, or outside of your organization

Based on these pros and cons, you can devise your data-sharing strategy and build landing zone templates based on data-sharing requirements.

Let us summarize the data-sharing methods.

Summary

We started with understanding the challenges of data sharing in a data mesh and what in-place sharing is, defined by the data mesh architecture as the best way to share data to reduce data movement. There are many ways of sharing data across the data mesh and beyond the data mesh. We saw four of the most popular topologies for this: in-place, data pipelines, data APIs, and data sharing. We looked at the pros and cons of each along with their ideal application. One important takeaway from this chapter is that there is no one preferred way to share data. You need to understand the pros and cons of each method and then form a best practice across the data mesh for data product teams to pick the right method for their requirements.

This ends the important topics of designing and implementing a data mesh. The next four chapters will cover some common data analytics workloads and the required architecture to implement these analytical solutions on Microsoft Azure. The first scenario will cover advanced analytics using Azure Machine Learning, Databricks, and the Lakehouse architecture.

Part 3:
Popular Data Product Architectures

After working with multiple customers on implementing a data mesh, we found that there are a few common architecture patterns used to process different data and analytics workloads. Most companies build common templates for these workloads so that they can be reused with minor modifications. This part of the book covers four of these common architectures. Architectures for a particular solution can be built in many different ways, so these are just suggestions. Your actual architecture might look different. However, you can use these chapters for guidance.

The structure and format of these chapters are very different from the previous chapters. There are more reference materials, and hence they are very to the point with plenty of links to point you to the documentation of different Microsoft Azure services used to build these templates.

This part has the following chapters:

- *Chapter 14, Advanced Analytics Using Azure Machine Learning, Databricks, and the Lakehouse Architecture*

- *Chapter 15, Big Data Analytics Using Azure Synapse Analytics*

- *Chapter 16, Event-Driven Analytics Using Azure Event Hubs, Azure Stream Analytics, and Azure Machine Learning*

- *Chapter 17, AI Using Azure Cognitive Services and Azure OpenAI*

14

Advanced Analytics Using Azure Machine Learning, Databricks, and the Lakehouse Architecture

Advanced analytics involves analyzing enterprise data that stretches beyond traditional **business intelligence** (**BI**) reports. It extends beyond structured and relational data warehouses and analyses semi-structured and unstructured data such as user interactions on a website or free-flowing text inputs such as social media feeds.

In this chapter, we will look at the tools, techniques, and a sample architecture template for implementing advanced analytics in your organization. This architecture can be converted into a standardized data mesh landing zone template and offered to any product team wanting to build a product that uses advanced analytics.

In this chapter, we will look at the typical requirements for advanced analytics scenarios. We will walk through a typical architecture for implementing advanced analytics, along with all the Azure services involved. We will see how data and processes flow through this architecture. Finally, we will consider some scenarios of advanced analytics and any variations that can be made to the architecture to fit these scenarios.

In this chapter, we will cover the following main topics:

- Requirements
- Architecture
- Components
- Data flow
- Scenarios

> **Note for Chapters 14, 15, 16, and 17**
>
> The format of *Chapters 14, 15, 16*, and *17* is different from all the previous chapters. This is because these chapters are architectural references. These chapters aim to provide guidance on how to set up analytics for a given workload. You might also observe portions of text being repeated across these chapters. This is also by design. At a later point, you might want to refer to one of these chapters directly. To make sure you have everything you need in these four chapters, we will be repeating some of the text across these chapters. These chapters are designed to be quick reads and let you explore all the components using the reference links provided for each component of the architecture.

Requirements

Advanced analytics involves processing data from source business/enterprise applications such as **customer relationship management** (**CRM**), **enterprise resource planning** (**ERP**), finance data, human resources data, and many other similar sources. These sources can vary, depending on your industry. Pharmacies or hospitals, for example, will have patient data, medical procedures, insurance data, and radiology and imagery data.

Traditionally and even to date, these kinds of analytical systems involve a central data warehouse. In *Chapter 1*, in the *Exploring the evolution of modern data analytics* and *Discovering the challenges of modern-day enterprises* sections, we observed how the nature of data and the requirements of data analytics have changed. A traditional data warehouse is built on strong relationships between data entities. This provides the ability to slice and dice the data in different ways without worrying about the consistency of the data as the relationship rules ensure consistency. However, these rules and their related processing requirements hinder the ability of data warehouses to scale linearly as the data and analysis requirements grow.

Three notable changes started, making the data warehouse a difficult architecture to work with:

- **Data formats**: Modern systems need to analyze data from sensors (**internet of things** (**IoT**)), customer clicks on a website (clickstream), dynamic customer and product profiles, free text such as social media feeds, images, voice, and other such data formats.

- **Machine learning**: Machine learning allows companies to run predictive trends on their data. These algorithms need to be improved iteratively by continuously tweaking data and parameters. They need direct access to the raw data/semi-processed data.

- **Analytics platforms**: With the advent of machine learning, SQL was no longer the only language for analyzing data. Python, Scala, R, and Java are used to process data and build machine learning algorithms.

Hence, a new technology and architecture needed to be developed and adopted that supported these three fundamental shifts by shifting compute toward distributed data nodes. While doing this, it also needed to provide the benefits of a data warehouse, such as consistency and transactions.

This brought around an innovation of combining the data lake (semi-structured data) and data warehouse (transactions and consistency) into a merged architecture called the **lakehouse**.

Before we dive into the lakehouse architecture and its building blocks, let's understand the requirements of such an architecture:

- **Ingest**: The data itself is housed in different source systems. These could be web logs, enterprise systems, or document repositories. Some pipelines or processes need to be built that can connect to this data and pull it and either transform it into a different format or simply store it in its raw format.

- **Store**: The data from these sources needs to be pulled into a storage system that supports a more flexible data format. Such stores are called data lake storage. These stores need to be categorized into different buckets, depending on the stage of data being processed through the system. They also need to support granular access control to ensure only the authorized people and processes have access.

- **Process**: The ingested data needs to be cleaned and formatted so that it can be used for analytics or machine learning. The type of processing that's used will depend on the type of analytics to be performed. For business intelligence processing, data needs to be aggregated or transformed into a different schema to alter relationships that are more convenient for running analytics. For machine learning processing, data just needs to be cleaned in terms of null values being removed or substituted with a default. Date formats also need to be standardized. Sometimes, additional synthetic columns need to be added to help machine learning algorithms.

- **Serve**: This stage is sometimes divided into two – model and serve. However, in the case of a lakehouse, the model portion overlaps between process and serve. The processed data needs to be served to the end users. This can either be in the form of processed data, machine learning models, or business dashboards.

Next, let us look at the architecture for the analytics.

Architecture

While there are many architecture possibilities, it will always be divided into four buckets: ingest, store, process, and server. The components inside these buckets can change based on individual preferences. Components are often chosen based on the team's skills – for example, a team that has experts in Databricks might prefer to use it for ingestion. *Figure 14.1* shows one possible architecture for this workload:

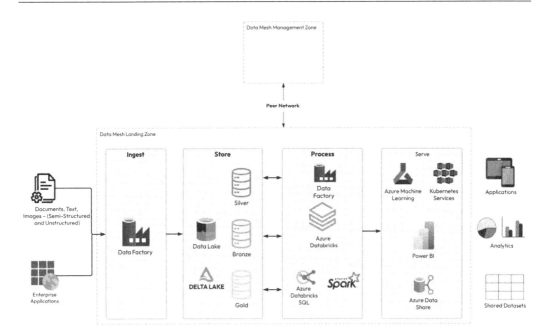

Figure 14.1 – Advanced analytics with Databricks and Azure Machine Learning

Take a moment to study this architecture diagram; then, move on to the next section to learn more about the components involved and their functionality.

Components

In *Figure 14.1*, starting from left to right, let's look at each component and understand their functionality/attributes.

Source data

Source data can be document repositories, social media feeds, images, or voice recordings. Semi-structured data is typically stored in **comma-separated files** (**CSV**) or the JSON format. These could be customer profiles or product details.

Azure Data Factory

Azure Data Factory is a cloud-scale **extract, transform, and load** (**ETL**) framework. It has ready-made connectors to over a hundred different sources. It can connect to SAP, Oracle, SQL Server, and many more enterprise systems and data stores. It can have connectors for various cloud services that extend beyond Azure to **Google Cloud Platform** (**GCP**) and **Amazon Web Services** (**AWS**).

The following are some resources that can help you learn more about Azure Data Factory and its connectors:

- Azure Data Factory documentation: `https://learn.microsoft.com/en-us/azure/data-factory/`

- Azure Data Factory connectors: `https://learn.microsoft.com/en-us/azure/data-factory/connector-overview`

Azure Data Lake Storage Gen2

Azure Storage is one of the key services of Azure that helps you store semi-structured and unstructured data for cheap yet fast access. It's **Platform as a Service** (**PaaS**), so you don't need to run virtual machines to support storage. Azure Storage accounts come in many flavors, depending on your storage needs – for example, Azure files, blobs, queues, and tables. Azure blobs have a variation called **Azure Data Lake Storage Gen 2** (**ADLS Gen2**). This is the most commonly used storage system for analytics. The fundamental difference between blob storage and ADLS Gen2 is that blobs store the data as large blocks for fast access. ADLS Gen2 provides a hierarchical filesystem with folders and subfolders with granular access control to these folders and subfolders. There are many other differences, such as Hadoop-compatible file access and others. However, it is beyond the scope of this book to detail all the differences and features of ADLS Gen2. Please refer to the documentation for more details: `https://learn.microsoft.com/en-us/azure/storage/blobs/data-lake-storage-introduction`.

In this architecture, ADLS Gen2 will store the ingested data and move it from one processing layer to another. This movement and maintenance of different levels of processed data is called the **Medallion architecture**. Raw data is stored as-is in the **bronze layer**. The bronze layer's data is then moved through additional cleaning and formatting and moved to the **silver layer**. The silver layer data is ready to be used by some analytical systems so that the base data is in a good format. Machine learning algorithms will almost always use data from the silver and bronze layers. Advanced reports and dashboards might need to further transform and aggregate the data in the silver layer. This can be done using Python or SQL code. The transformed and aggregated data is then moved to the **gold layer**. The gold layer's data can be directly used by dashboards as imported datasets.

Processing data as it moves through the bronze, silver, and gold layers can be done with a combination of technologies. Let's take a look at those technologies, all of which can be found in the process layer of the architecture.

Azure Databricks

Azure Databricks is a first-party service on Azure. It's a service built by Databricks, which is a first-party partner with Microsoft Azure. It's also a fully managed and supported service in Azure. Azure Databricks is an advanced machine learning, analytics, and AI framework built on the distributed processing architecture of Apache Spark (`https://spark.apache.org/`). Databricks has taken the Apache Spark distribution and built its own custom Spark engine, making it one of the fastest on the market.

The initial framework focused on machine learning and AI workloads and supported Python and Scala. Around 2020, Databricks introduced the concept of lakehouse architecture. A combination of semi-structured data and transaction logs is stored in a format called a Delta Lake. This Delta Lake stores data in Parquet format (`https://parquet.apache.org/docs/overview/`) and provides a set of log files that record transactions made to the data. This technique of storing data in columnar Parquet format and maintaining the transaction logs gives Delta Lake the advantage of providing the functionality of a relational database on top of semi-structured data, not to mention that it uses a distributed processing engine such as Spark. This is a winning combination and an alternative to the traditional monolithic data warehouse.

The Delta Lake technology allows Databricks to run SQL queries on top of the Delta Lake, giving users a combination of a data lake and a data warehouse, hence the term lakehouse.

Delta Lake, the lakehouse architecture, and how Databricks provides a platform to implement all this is a vast topic. Here are a few resources so that you can read up on these topics:

- Azure Databricks: `https://learn.microsoft.com/en-us/azure/databricks/`
- Databricks lakehouse: `https://www.databricks.com/blog/2020/01/30/what-is-a-data-lakehouse.html?itm_data=lakehouse-link-lakehouseblog`
- Delta Lake: `https://delta.io/`

Azure Databricks is the core processing engine in this architecture. It provides a framework for advanced machine learning workloads, as well as SQL-based data warehouse workloads. It can also be used in combination with Azure Data Factory to execute complex transformations in data movement pipelines.

Azure Data Factory can also be used as an orchestrator of multiple Databricks processing jobs. Let's consider a situation where data has to be moved through a complex set of transformations and needs to be stored at a temporary location between these processing jobs. The processes are complex Python code written and maintained by multiple teams. Azure Data Factory can call these Databricks notebooks by using Azure Data Factory in a pipeline with multiple steps/tasks (`https://learn.microsoft.com/en-us/azure/databricks/delta-live-tables/workflows#azure-data-factory`).

Azure Machine Learning

Spark is good for large-scale data processing and large model training processes that need large amounts of data to be processed in memory. For some workloads, such as deep learning, or algorithms that need specialized hardware, you need to run them on a cluster of specialized machines. Azure Machine Learning can help you run these workloads. Azure Machine Learning also has a **software development kit** (**SDK**) that helps you programmatically manage machine learning environments and pipelines. This SDK can also be used from Azure Databricks. This allows you to leverage the Azure Machine Learning SDK but run the algorithms on a Spark cluster.

Azure Kubernetes Service (AKS)

Azure Machine Learning is also good for inferencing workloads. Inferencing workloads are scenarios where you train a machine learning algorithm and then host it as an API that can be called by an application. These can be prediction algorithms that predict the next value, such as a sales price, given a future date. It can be any type of real-time activity that needs machine learning models. These workloads can demand dynamic scale as many users will use the models simultaneously. Azure Machine Learning allows you to host models on AKS. Kubernetes allows you to build containers of the trained models, along with all their dependencies, and scale them across a cluster of machines (`https://kubernetes.io/`). AKS is a managed Kubernetes cluster on Azure (`https://learn.microsoft.com/en-us/azure/aks/`).

Power BI

Power BI is a data visualization and analytics tool. It allows you to import data into its workspaces. Then, using its powerful query language, **Data Analysis Expressions** (**DAX**), you can slice and dice the data and present it with compelling visualizations. Power BI is a vast platform with many options for importing data. Each option supports different scenarios. To learn more about Power BI, please refer to `https://learn.microsoft.com/en-us/power-bi/`.

Power BI is a dashboarding tool in this architecture. All the analytics that need to be presented as charts or **key performance indicators** (**KPIs**) with interactive drill-downs can be surfaced through Power BI.

Azure Data Share

One of the key tenets of a data mesh is to share data. Sometimes, the data needs to be shared with partners outside of the company. For example, a consumer retail organization might want to share recent sales numbers of a shop with the company that owns the shop daily. Or perhaps you need to form a consortium of your customers to share some market or research data with all of them. Most importantly, you want to do this without giving them access to your data store.

These scenarios are enabled by Azure Data Share. As mentioned in *Chapter 13*, in the *Understanding data-sharing challenges in a data mesh* section, Azure Data Share provides two options: you can perform snapshots-based sharing, where a snapshot of data moves from your Azure subscription to the partner's Azure subscription, or you can do in-place sharing, where data is shared from its original place using a symbolic link that points to the data.

For more information on Azure Data Share, please refer to `https://learn.microsoft.com/en-us/azure/data-share/`.

With that, we've covered all the components you need to build this architecture. Now, let's understand how the data flows through the system.

Data flow

1. Data is ingested into the bronze layer by the Azure Data Factory pipelines of the Azure data lake and stored in its raw format.

2. Azure Data Factory pipelines or a combination of Azure Data Factory and Azure Databricks cleans and formats the data and moves it to the silver layer of the data lake.

3. The data in the silver layer can be directly consumed by machine learning algorithms via Azure Databricks or Azure Machine Learning.

4. For advanced analytics that needs analytical cubes or a star schema of fact and dimension tables (`https://learn.microsoft.com/en-us/power-bi/guidance/star-schema`), data from the silver layer is further transformed using Azure Data Factory and Azure Databricks before being moved to the gold layer.

5. Machine learning models trained on data from the silver layer are hosted on an AKS cluster for inferencing by applications.

6. Power BI reads data from the gold or silver layer to build visual dashboards.

7. Data that needs to be shared with external parties is shared using Azure Data Share.

Scenarios

-   **BI and reporting**: Any kind of reporting requirement where historical data needs to be analyzed and presented to key stakeholders to analyze the state of the business.

-   **Predictive analytics**: This architecture can be used to predict the maintenance of machines. Here, historical data is used to build predictive models for possible failures/breakdowns or service requirements. A similar application involves predicting the price of goods to build a pricing strategy for a consumer goods company.

Summary

In this chapter, we looked at a possible architecture for building a lakehouse. We discussed all its layers and components, as well as some scenarios. It is important to note that this is just one of the possible architectures. You can build a similar architecture using Azure Synapse Analytics. But what we have presented here is a popular architecture that's typically used by many companies.

The next three chapters are architecture references and will be in a very similar format as this chapter.

In the next chapter, we will look at big data processing using Azure Synapse Analytics.

15
Big Data Analytics Using Azure Synapse Analytics

Traditional analytics done on structured and relational data helps with analyzing transactional data. This worked well until the dotcom revolution, which saw an influx of large volumes of semi-structured data such as shopping carts, customer profiles, and ad clicks. A new type of technology was needed to process big data considering its volume. Due to this, data processing methods such as MapReduce became popular (to learn more about MapReduce, please refer to `https://learn.microsoft.com/en-us/azure/hdinsight/hadoop/apache-hadoop-introduction`). This led to technologies such as Hadoop and – later – Apache Spark becoming the new big data processing engines.

In this chapter, we will look at Azure services that can help you build a data mesh landing zone template for big data processing. We will cover one possible architecture for handling and analyzing big data by covering these topics:

- Requirements
- Architecture
- Components
- Data flow
- Scenarios

Requirements

To understand the requirements of a big data processing architecture, let's consider an example. Let's say there's a situation where a consumer goods company wants to understand its customers' preferences and behavior to optimize its product placement, inventory management, and targeted marketing. To achieve this, the company will have to collect data from the following sources:

- **Sales transactions**: These are transactions that are made either at the physical store or through online website purchases.

- **Online behavior**: Tracking which products are frequently viewed and searched as customers browse the company website.

- **Customer feedback**: Customers are often offered to provide feedback through surveys, reviews, and feedback forms. This data needs to be collected and processed to improve business performance.

- **Social media interactions**: Consumers react to company products and their experiences by adding comments and posts on social media and adding the company's hashtags to get attention. Consumers also react to online campaigns. These interactions and reactions need to be tracked to get a pulse of the consumer sentiment for the company and its products.

- **Supply chain data**: Inventory levels at warehouses and stores, as well as supplier performance and logistics information, need to be constantly monitored to ensure that the stock levels of the right products are always maintained.

All these sources can have different storage systems and formats. Data such as online behavior will not have a fixed format. Customer feedback forms could be modified over time to improve feedback, but we cannot go back and fix and back-fill all the historical data according to the new format. This means customer feedback data will also have missing fields. Social media is all free-flowing text data.

Other than formats, the rate at which the data is generated also varies. Online events can be in the millions per second. Sales transactions might occur at a rate of thousands per second and inventory data might get updated at the end of every day.

Data processing needs are also different for each data source. Online customer behavior data will be processed in real time and at the same time so that ads can be swapped dynamically. However, historical trends will also have to be analyzed to improve the marketing algorithm. Supply chain data might need a data warehouse to be used for processing. Customer feedback surveys will have to be processed using document database technology such as NoSQL.

In short, the data has multiple dimensions and they all need to be processed using different methods. This type of multi-dimensional processing of streaming, batch, and structured datasets is called **big data processing**. Big data defines these dimensions of data as the **four Vs** – **volume**, **velocity**, **variety**, and **veracity**.

To simplify the contents of this chapter, we will only look at structured and semi-structured data processing in this architecture. We will cover streaming data analytics in the next chapter.

Now that we understand what big data processing is, let's look at the different requirements across the data flow, from the source to the analytical output:

- **Ingest**: Data can come from different sources in different formats. Website data could be stored in web logs, customer feedback forms could be present in JSON files, and the store and supply chain data could be collected by connecting to the local warehouse or store system and pulling data into the analytical store. We need a mechanism to pull data from all these sources.

- **Store**: The data from these sources needs to be pulled into a storage system that supports a more flexible data format. Such stores are called data lake storage. These stores need to be categorized into different buckets, depending on where the data is being processed through the system. They also need to support granular access control to ensure only the authorized people and processes have access.

- **Process**: The ingested data needs to be cleaned and formatted so that it can be used for analytics or machine learning. The type of processing will depend on the type of analytics to be performed. For **business intelligence** (**BI**) processing, data needs to be aggregated or transformed into a different schema to alter relationships that are more convenient for running analytics. For machine learning processing, data just needs to be cleaned. Null values should be removed or substituted with a default and date formats need to be standardized. Sometimes, additional synthetic columns need to be added to help machine learning algorithms.

- **Server**: The server layer could offer data to applications for searching products or deals. Analytics can be displayed on these dashboards. The processed and aggregated datasets can be shared with other teams or with partners such as suppliers and logistics partners.

Now, let us move to the next section on understanding the architecture.

Architecture

Let's look at the architecture for implementing the preceding requirements. This architecture is divided into four stages: ingest, storage, processing, and server. It's depicted in *Figure 15.1*:

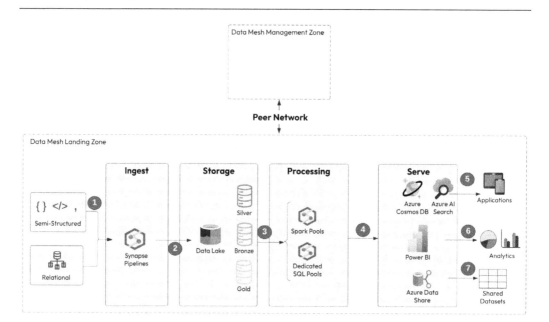

Figure 15.1 – Big data processing using Azure Synapse Analytics

Take a closer look at this architecture; in the next section, we'll learn about the components that are used and their functionality.

Components

In *Figure 15.1*, starting from left to right, let's look at each component and understand their functionality/attributes.

Source data

Source data can be semi-structured data such as web logs in JSON or comma-separated files or structured data from sales, marketing, and inventory databases.

Azure Synapse pipelines

Azure Synapse pipelines function the same as Azure Data Factory, except that they are integrated into Synapse Studio. This allows data engineers and data scientists to share the same workspace for preprocessing and analyzing the data. Azure Synapse pipelines will ingest the semi-structured logs and structured data from company databases into the data lake. They have the same number of connectors as Azure Data Factory to connect to different data sources. For more information on Azure Synapse, please refer to the following links:

- Azure Synapse documentation: `https://learn.microsoft.com/en-us/azure/synapse-analytics/get-started-pipelines`
- Azure Data Factory connectors: `https://learn.microsoft.com/en-us/azure/synapse-analytics/get-started-pipelines`

Azure Data Lake Storage Gen2

Azure Storage is one of the key services of Azure that helps you store semi-structured and unstructured data for cheap yet fast access. It's a **Platform-as-a-Service** (**PaaS**) offering, so you don't need to run virtual machines to support storage. Azure Storage accounts come in many flavors, depending on your storage needs – for example, Azure files, blobs, queues, and tables. Azure blobs have a variation called **Azure Data Lake Storage Gen 2** (**ADLS Gen2**). This is the most commonly used storage system for analytics. The fundamental difference between blob storage and ADLS Gen2 is that blobs store the data as large blocks for fast access. ADLS Gen2 also provides a hierarchical filesystem, with folders and subfolders and granular access control to these folders and subfolders. There are many other differences, such as there being Hadoop-compatible file access (Hadoop Distributed File System) and others. It is beyond the scope of this book to detail all the differences and features of ADLS Gen2. Please refer to the documentation for more details: `https://learn.microsoft.com/en-us/azure/storage/blobs/data-lake-storage-introduction`.

In this architecture, ADLS Gen2 will store the ingested data and move it from one processing layer to another. This movement and maintenance of different levels of processed data is called the **Medallion architecture**. Raw data is stored as-is in the **bronze layer**. The bronze layer's data then goes through additional cleaning and formatting and is moved to the **silver layer**. The silver layer's data is ready to be used by some analytical systems and ensures it's in a good format. Machine learning algorithms will almost always use data from the silver and bronze layers. Advanced reports and dashboards might need to further transform and aggregate the data in the silver layer. This can be done using Python or SQL code. The transformed and aggregated data is then moved to the **gold layer**. The gold layer's data can be directly used by dashboards as imported datasets.

Processing data as it moves through the bronze, silver, and gold layers can be done with a combination of technologies. Let's look at these technologies, all of which can be found in the process layer of the architecture.

Azure Synapse

Azure Synapse is an umbrella technology for running data warehouses and big data workloads. It includes multiple engines to process different types of data. These include a SQL engine, Spark clusters, and Azure Data Explorer for time series-based analysis. Azure Synapse also provides pipelines to enable data movement and transformation. It bundles all these services with a friendly user interface called **Azure Synapse Studio**. To learn more about Azure Synapse, please refer to `https://learn.microsoft.com/en-us/azure/synapse-analytics/`.

Azure Cosmos DB

Azure Cosmos DB is a globally distributed, multi-model database service that also supports document databases. It allows for fast reads and writes with very low latency-supported semi-structured data. Since it's a document database, it does not adhere to a schema. In the context of this architecture, it will be used to store documents such as products and customer profiles. These can then be searched through and surfaced on a mobile app or a website. For more information on Azure Cosmos DB, please refer to `https://learn.microsoft.com/en-us/azure/cosmos-db/`.

Azure AI Search

Azure AI Search (formerly known as **Azure Cognitive Search**) is a keyword and semantic search service that's used on a wide range of enterprise data. It directly works with data sources such as Azure Blob Storage, Azure Data Lake, Azure SQL Database, and Azure Cosmos DB. It can create a keyword-based index or a vector-based index. It also provides a very sophisticated index configuration where you can fine-tune how each data column will participate in the index search.

For more information on Azure AI Search, please refer to `https://learn.microsoft.com/en-us/azure/search/`.

Power BI

Power BI is a data visualization and analytics tool. It allows you to import data into its workspaces. Using its powerful query language, **Data Analysis Expressions** (**DAX**), you can slice and dice the data and present it with compelling visualizations. Power BI is a vast platform with many options to import data. Each option supports different scenarios. To learn more about Power BI, please refer to `https://learn.microsoft.com/en-us/power-bi/`.

Power BI is a dashboarding tool in this architecture. All the analytics that need to be presented as charts or **key performance indicators** (**KPIs**) with interactive drill-downs can be surfaced through Power BI.

Azure Data Share

One of the key tenets of a data mesh is to share data. Sometimes, the data needs to be shared with partners outside the company. For example, a consumer retail organization might want to share recent sales numbers of a shop with the company that owns the shop daily. Or perhaps you need to form a consortium of your customers to share some market or research data with all of them. Most importantly, you want to do this without giving them access to your data store.

These scenarios are enabled by **Azure Data Share**. Azure Data Share provides two options: you can do snapshots-based sharing, where a snapshot of the data moves from your Azure subscription to the partner's Azure subscription, or you can do **in-place sharing**, where data is shared from its original place using a symbolic link that points to the data.

For more information on Azure Data Share, please refer to `https://learn.microsoft.com/en-us/azure/data-share/`.

With that, we've looked at all the components you'll need to build this architecture. Now, let's understand how the data flows through the system. Refer to the numbers in blue circles in *Figure 15.1* to follow the data flow.

Data flow

1. Data from semi-structured and structured sources is read using Azure Synapse pipelines and written into the bronze layer of the data lake.

2. Data is then moved between the bronze, silver, and gold layers using more pipelines.

3. Data from the Medallion storage system is used by Synapse Spark clusters or Synapse SQL pools to further conduct analytics on it.

4. Analytical data from Synapse is pushed to Cosmos DB and Azure Data Share and read by Power BI to expose the data to various consumers, such as applications, dashboards, and other teams.

5. The data in Cosmos DB can be searched using Azure AI Search through the mobile app or website.

6. Power BI surfaces the analytics in the form of dashboards.

7. Azure Data Share shares the data with external parties that need the data for their processing purposes.

Now, let's look at some scenarios where this architecture can be applicable.

Scenarios

- **BI and strategy**: Analyzing market trends, consumer behavior, and pricing strategy

- **Healthcare**: Predict epidemics, personalized treatment plans, and manage healthcare resources

- **Energy and utility**: Predictive maintenance and optimizing energy distribution

Many other sectors, such as agriculture, retail, sports, government, and telecommunication can use big data analytics to analyze structured and semi-structured data to optimize their business and operations.

Summary

In this chapter, we looked at a possible architecture for big data analytics. We discussed all the different data dimensions (the four Vs) and how to ingest data coming at different speeds. We also looked at various processing engines to process real-time and batch time series data before we can surface the processed data and analytics to applications and dashboards and share with the other teams. It is important to note that this is just one of the possible architectures. You can build a similar architecture using Azure Databricks or Azure HDInsight. But what we have presented here is a popular architecture that's typically used by many companies.

In the next chapter, we will look at event-driven analytics using Azure Event Hubs, Azure Stream Analytics, and Azure Machine Learning.

16

Event-Driven Analytics Using Azure Event Hubs, Azure Stream Analytics, and Azure Machine Learning

In the previous chapter, we discussed the four dimensions of data in modern-day data analytics – **volume, velocity, variety,** and **veracity.**

We also looked at an architecture that covers volume and variety. We left out the velocity part to make the architecture simpler. In this chapter, we will architect for the last **V, velocity**.

Data is dynamically changing in today's fast-paced world. It's a world of instant gratification and split-second actions. You want to understand how your customers are interacting with your website so that you can dynamically swap ads or provide dynamic, relevant offers. You want to monitor the machines you make and sell to predict failures and provide proactive service and maintenance. You want to detect banking fraud before it happens. There are many such scenarios across multiple industries that need real-time processing of data.

In this chapter, we will build an architecture to process real-time events and data. We will also learn how to combine this architecture with the big data analytics architecture if you wish to build one system that covers all three Vs.

In this chapter, we will cover the following topics:

- Requirements
- Architecture
- Components
- Data flow

- Scenarios
- Combining architectures for real-time and big data analytics

Requirements

Let's look at a few examples of real-time events and data in some industries:

- A retail company wants to monitor its customers' behavior on its website in real time. It wants to see what its customers are clicking, browsing, and adding or removing from their baskets. This will help them understand customer behavior so that they can personalize ads and offers.

- A manufacturing company wants to monitor the machines they sell for usage and health. They place multiple sensors on the machine that transmit data every second. This data is then put through machine learning models to predict failures.

- A vineyard wants to monitor soil moisture, sunlight intensity, and other such parameters to ensure the right time for harvesting, preventing disease, and producing good quality wines. They place sensors on their vineyards to collect and process this data.

- A city wants to monitor its traffic and public transportation data in real time to provide better traffic control and monitor the safety of its citizens.

Scenarios for event-based and real-time processing are endless. Every industry can use this technology to stay ahead of the curve.

To achieve this, the company will have to collect data from the following types of sources:

- Business data that's transmitted in real time from systems such as point-of-sale, inventory, stock trading, and credit cards. This data is generated by triggers that have been set to detect changes to the records in the database (create, update, or delete). Every time a record is updated, inserted, or deleted, an event is triggered that calls a function that transmits a message to another system. This converts database transactions into real-time events.

- Data from sensors that monitor temperature, vibration, pressure, movement, and many other such physical and environmental parameters.

Irrespective of the source, one thing that's common about this data is that it arrives at a high speed. The data is pushed into the analytical system, not pulled. Let's look at the different requirements across the data flow, from the source to the analytical output:

- **Ingest**: Streaming data from sensors and database update triggers has to be ingested in a way that there is no loss of data. If the processing systems are slower, then the ingestion mechanism should be able to queue and buffer the data before it's processed. The data can be in JSON format or some custom device format that's supported by the sensors and hardware gateways.

- **Store**: The data storage system should support high write and read throughput to allow for real-time analytics at the speed of data ingestion.

- **Process**: The ingested data needs to be immediately processed for threshold values and patterns. Small sets of data in the near past need to be analyzed for any anomalies that need immediate attention. At the same time, some time series analysis might also be needed over a longer period to detect long-term data trends.

- **Enrich**: Some machine learning models could be built and run on this data for real-time predictions.

- **Serve**: The stored data can be supplied to mobile applications or published on real-time dashboards.

Let's look at an architecture for implementing these requirements.

Architecture

An architecture for implementing this real-time streaming of large volumes of data is depicted in *Figure 16.1*:

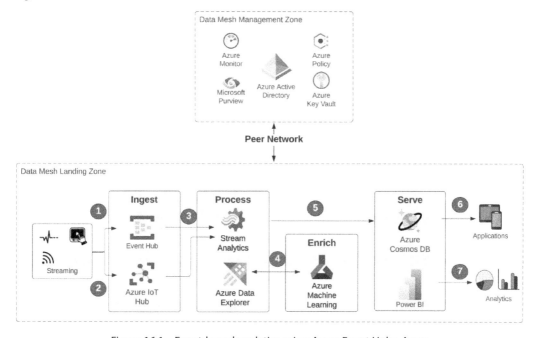

Figure 16.1 – Event-based analytics using Azure Event Hubs, Azure
Stream Analytics, and Azure Machine Learning

Take a closer look at this architecture; we'll learn about its components and their functionality in the next section.

Components

Let's look at the components of this architecture in greater detail.

Source data

Clickstream data can be collected using multiple **software development kits** (**SDKs**). These are typically JavaScript scripts that are embedded in the web pages that transmit click data to an API.

IoT data can be collected using a network of sensors connected to a gateway. The gateway can call an API in the analytical system (IoT Hub) to push the data.

Azure Event Hubs

Azure Event Hubs is a data streaming service that can scale to millions of messages per second. It is the preferred event ingestion service in Azure. It provides message/events queues to ingest and temporarily store messages/events from a producer until an event consumer pulls the event off the queue for processing. It also maintains a schema registry that the producer and consumer can refer to maintain interoperability. Event Hubs can be configured and scaled in many ways. For more details on Azure Event Hubs, please refer to the following sources:

- Azure Event Hubs: `https://learn.microsoft.com/en-us/azure/event-hubs/`
- Event Hubs scalability: `https://learn.microsoft.com/en-us/azure/event-hubs/event-hubs-scalability`
- Azure Data Factory and Azure Synapse Analytics connector overview: `https://learn.microsoft.com/en-us/azure/data-factory/connector-overview`

Azure IoT Hub

Azure IoT Hub is a managed service that's hosted on Azure and designed to manage all communication between IoT devices and sensors and Azure services. It can scale to millions of devices streaming data to Azure. It also supports bi-directional communication and can send updates back to devices. Azure IoT Hub also offers secure communication and device management.

For more details on Azure IoT Hub, please refer to `https://learn.microsoft.com/en-us/azure/iot-hub/`.

Azure Stream Analytics

Azure Stream Analytics is a data processing service that can process data in motion with sub-millisecond latencies. It is typically used to determine patterns in the buffered data. It can then trigger workflows and functions to take immediate action on what it finds. Azure Stream Analytics has a SQL-like query language to query the flowing data. You can also define functions that call **Azure Machine Learning endpoints** or create **user-defined functions** (**UDF**) in Java or C#.

For more details on Azure Stream Analytics, please refer to `https://learn.microsoft.com/en-us/azure/stream-analytics/`.

Azure Data Explorer

Azure Data Explorer (ADX) is a big data processing engine that's designed to process large streams of real-time data. It has its own query language called **Kusto Query Language** (**KQL**). This language is designed to analyze patterns, conduct time series analysis, and produce quick plots for quick visual analysis. It is an extremely powerful tool that's used by many internal Microsoft Teams to perform log analytics.

ADX can connect to Azure Storage blobs, files, tables, Event Hubs, and many other data sources. For a list of connectors, please refer to `https://learn.microsoft.com/en-us/azure/data-explorer/integrate-data-overview?tabs=connectors`. When using Python libraries, it can also connect to Azure Machine Learning to train machine learning models. For more information on ADX, please refer to the following sources:

- **Azure Data Explorer**: `https://learn.microsoft.com/en-us/azure/data-explorer/`

- **Kusto Query Language**: `https://learn.microsoft.com/en-us/azure/data-explorer/kusto/query/`

- **Using the KQLMagic library to run Azure Machine Learning notebooks on ADX data**: `https://learn.microsoft.com/en-us/azure/data-explorer/kqlmagic?tabs=code`

Azure Machine Learning

Spark is good for large-scale data processing and model training that needs large amounts of data to be processed in memory. For some workloads, such as deep learning, or algorithms that need specialized hardware, you need to run them on a cluster of specialized machines. Azure Machine Learning can help you run these workloads. In this architecture, it is used as a machine learning modeling tool to get forecasts and predictions that can saved back in a data store and served to the data consumers.

Azure Cosmos DB

Azure Cosmos DB is a distributed document database service from Azure. It allows for fast reads and writes of data documents with very low latency. Since it's a document database, it does not adhere to a schema. In the context of this architecture, it's used to store events and data being streamed from Stream Analytics. This data can be used to perform historical analysis. For more information on Azure Cosmos DB, please refer to `https://learn.microsoft.com/en-us/azure/cosmos-db/`.

Power BI

Power BI is a data visualization and analytics tool. It allows you to import data into its workspaces. Using its powerful query language, **Data Analysis Expressions** (**DAX**), you can slice and dice the data and present it with compelling visualizations. Power BI is a vast platform that provides many options for importing data. Each option supports a different scenario. To learn more about Power BI, please refer to `https://learn.microsoft.com/en-us/power-bi/`.

Power BI is a dashboarding tool in this architecture. All the analytics that need to be presented as charts or **key performance indicators** (**KPIs**) with interactive drill-downs can be surfaced through Power BI.

This completes all the components you need to build this architecture. Now, let's understand how the data flows through the system. Refer to the numbers in blue circles in *Figure 16.1* to follow the data flow.

Data flow

1. Clickstream data is sent to Azure Event Hub.

2. IoT data is sent to Azure IoT Hub.

3. Azure Event Hub and Azure IoT Hub push data to Azure Stream Analytics. Azure Stream Analytics processes the data for simple patterns and threshold values.

4. Azure Data Explorer can pull data from Stream Analytics for time series analysis. Azure Data Explorer can also pull data directly from Event Hubs and/or IoT Hub.

5. Azure Machine Learning can use data from Azure Data Explorer to build machine learning models. These models can stored as binary files in blob storage or a Data Explorer database and can be executed in Data Explorer to perform real-time inferencing.

6. After analysis, data can be pushed to Cosmos DB. Cosmos DB provides high-performance storage for documents.

7. Cosmos DB data can be consumed by mobile applications, websites, or other marketing or analytical applications.

8. Power BI can build real-time dashboards from Stream Analytics.

This architecture can also qualify as a big data analytics architecture. We are processing large volumes of semi-structured data. The only difference is the streaming nature of data. Often, this architecture is clubbed with the big data analytics architecture. So, can we combine this architecture with the big data analytics architecture? We'll find out in the next section.

Combining architectures for real-time and big data analytics

Streaming and batch data deal with large volumes of data. While the ingestion techniques for streaming and batch data are different, how these large volumes are processed is very similar.

Often, the batch and streaming data are related, and having them together as part of one system provides the advantage of being able to analyze them together. The two architectures can be combined into one to simplify the management overheads of two separate systems and also benefit from the combined analytics of streaming and batch data.

Additionally, ADX has been integrated into Synapse Analytics, thereby eliminating the need to maintain a separate Azure Data Explorer instance. This combination gives us even greater power when it comes to analyzing streaming and batched data together and correlating them. We can correlate customer behavior with a drop or rise in sales. We can do more accurate sales forecasting. Many such combined scenarios can open up across different industries. The combined architecture would look as follows:

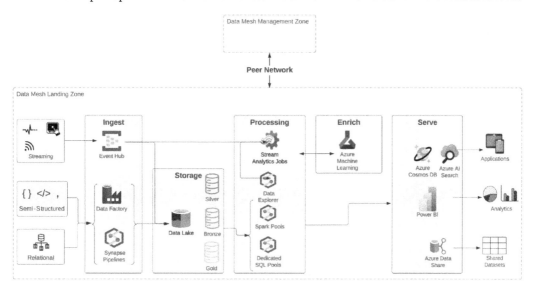

Figure 16.2 – Combined architecture for streamed data and big data analytics

Now, let's at some common scenarios for real-time analytics.

Scenarios

Here are some scenarios to consider:

- **Customer behavior analytics**: Analyze browsing and shopping trends, provide customized ads and offerings, and offer dynamic pricing

- **Detect fraud**: Monitor credit card transactions in real time to detect fraud patterns and prevent them from happening

- **Predictive maintenance**: Analyze data from machine sensors and detect future failures, provide better customer service, and adhere to uptime service-level agreements

Many other sectors, such as agriculture, retail, and smart city projects, can use real-time analytics to analyze streaming data to optimize their business and operations.

This brings us to the end of this architectural pattern. Now, let's summarize what we've learned.

Summary

In this chapter, we covered the third "V" – velocity – in the "Four Vs" of data. We discussed the different real-time data sources and ways of ingesting them. We also looked at how to process this data in real time over smaller and larger periods. To analyze small chunks of streaming data, we used Azure Stream Analytics, while for time series analysis over larger periods of historic data, we used Azure Data Explorer. Optionally, machine learning models can be built on the Data Explorer data using Azure Machine Learning. Finally, data can be served in Cosmos DB or as real-time dashboards on Power BI.

In the next chapter, we will look at more recent technologies, such as generative AI, and the architecture needed to leverage this revolutionary AI technology.

17

AI Using Azure Cognitive Services and Azure OpenAI

At the end of November 2022, OpenAI, an AI research lab, launched ChatGPT. ChatGPT is a piece of software that uses **large language models** (**LLMs**) trained on large amounts of data from the internet to generate text-based content that mimics human responses. This was followed by Microsoft providing managed OpenAI services on Azure in January 2023. Azure OpenAI provides the same OpenAI models on an enterprise-ready secure **Platform as a Service** (**PaaS**) offering. Since then, many companies have started building solutions using Azure OpenAI.

OpenAI and Azure OpenAI, as well as their models and capabilities, are a vast topic and beyond the scope of this book. If you wish to learn more about OpenAI and Azure OpenAI, refer to the following links:

- **OpenAI**: `https://platform.openai.com/docs/introduction`
- **Azure OpenAI**: `https://learn.microsoft.com/en-us/azure/ai-services/openai/`

Companies are now working on integrating OpenAI into their internal systems. Many innovative solutions are unleashed by Azure OpenAI that allow companies to run natural language conversations with their internal documents and data.

OpenAI-based solutions need many supporting services to manage, store, and process data. They also need other supporting AI services from the **Azure Cognitive Services APIs**. In this chapter, we will cover the architecture required to build a landing zone for Azure OpenAI and AI-based data products.

We will cover the following topics in this chapter:

- Requirements
- Architecture
- Components
- Data flow
- Scenarios

Requirements

OpenAI has opened a pandora of solutions for the industry. The applications of OpenAI are many and often demand different types of data and processing techniques. The requirements of an OpenAI/AI data product will vary, depending on the solution you are building. Let's look at some common OpenAI/AI solution scenarios:

- **Text summarization**: Summarizing research papers, financial reports, and policy documents
- **Question and answer chatbot**: A human resources chatbot for employees, a product chatbot for product inquiries, and a healthcare bot to answer common healthcare questions
- **Text generation**: Copywriting in marketing, drafting legal documents, and auto-generating emails for common customer support issues
- **Data interpretation**: Generating data analysis in natural language for natural language queries

Other than these solution scenarios, various architectural patterns are emerging. One such example is **Retrieval Augmented Generation (RAG)**, which allows you to augment an information retrieval system for the OpenAI model that's used for your application. There are other patterns, such as **Memory Augmented Pattern**, where external memory is used to store information for long conversations. Many other patterns are being developed as the tools and technology around generative AI are being developed further.

The most common scenario I observe customers building with OpenAI are chatbots that can query internal documents and data. So, we will consider this as the common scenario for the architecture. Let's look at the requirements of such a scenario:

- **Ingest**: Several company documents and a select set of data might have to be ingested and pre-processed so that it can be used by OpenAI. Unlike regular analytics and machine learning, data needed by OpenAI can be quite large and needs to be chunked into smaller pieces.
- **Process**: For a Q&A type of scenario, the OpenAI model needs to search content based on a natural language query. These models are called embedding models. To search the documents for semantic similarity, the document needs to be stored as a vector. A vector is a representation of text as a sequence of numbers.

For example, *data mesh democratizes analytics for an enterprise* can be represented as the following vector:

```
[0.035262, -0.059674, 0.17754, -0.070262, -0.12656, 0.32735,
-0.032857, -0.063218, 0.039455, -0.21434, -0.042003, 0.032256,
0.020303, 0.068654, -0.0080214, -0.044005, -0.057847, 0.040986,
0.025173, -0.013645, -0.021803, 0.031225, -0.029835, 0.031738,
-0.080593, -0.10895, 0.0081945, 0.035554, -0.12808, -0.082521,
-0.013485, 0.20134, -0.12462, -0.035543, -0.064829, 0.058222,
0.054504, 0.097423, -0.044764, 0.030039, -0.082868, 0.10948,
0.11184, 0.060466, -0.063482, 0.14461, 0.174, -0.010298,
-0.1169, -0.072154, -0.031333, -0.029686, -0.036285, 0.038486,
0.032921, -0.016649, -0.065111, 0.0063231, -0.0021278, -0.10516,
0.11176, -0.020062, -0.00014234, 0.0063467, -0.004582, -0.16316,
-0.12918, -0.042619, -0.063896, -0.0019468, -0.12917, -0.056189,
-0.05573, 0.080789, 0.027131, -0.069989, -0.013765, -0.078516,
0.05648, -0.090416, 0.028758, 0.046792, -0.015064, 0.024023,
-0.011394, -0.042465, -0.054132, -0.017902, -0.041468, -0.10646,
0.044888, 0.10107, -0.0037654, -0.048462, -0.049019, -0.018749,
-0.058081, -0.012742, -0.0076725, 0.041029, -0.063893,
-0.053924, 0.043986, 0.010289, -0.020448, 0.045378, 0.079902,
0.073616, 0.0056635, -0.032151, 0.034066, 0.010439, -0.087089, 0
```

It uses techniques such as word embedding, where each word is assigned a numerical vector representation based on its context and meaning. These embeddings are then compared for similarity using similarity algorithms such as cosine similarity. For more details on embeddings and cosine similarity, please refer to `https://learn.microsoft.com/en-us/azure/ai-services/openai/concepts/understand-embeddings`.

- **Chaining and task flow**: OpenAI solutions involve taking a user's query and augmenting it with additional information called **prompts**. These prompts help guide the OpenAI model to get the most accurate and relevant output. It also involves fetching data from multiple sources and vector databases and augmenting the output to the prompt. For example, if we have a chatbot that allows users to ask questions about the products of a company, we need to tell the OpenAI model to stick to products and not to answer any other questions. To ensure that the OpenAI model does not answer questions that are not relevant to products, we need to create something called a **system prompt**. So, let's say we have the following query from a customer:

`"Can you list the mountain bikes you sell?"`

The gets submitted like so:

```
You are an intelligent assistant for the Cosmic Works Bike
Company.
```

```
You are designed to provide helpful answers to user questions
about
```

```
product, product category, customer, and sales order (salesOrder)
information provided in JSON format below.
```

```
Instructions:

- Only answer questions related to the information provided
below,

- Don't reference any product, customer, or salesOrder data not
provided below.

- If you're unsure of an answer, you can say "I don't know" or
"I'm not sure" and recommend users search themselves.

Based on this information and instructions, answer the following
query:

"Can you list the mountain bikes you sell?"
```

Similarly, we might have to extract data from the product database and add it to the prompt.

Sometimes, the scenario might be more complex – for example, customers might ask the chatbot to recommend a product. In such cases, the chatbot must fetch the last few orders from the customer and add that to the prompt so that the most appropriate product can be recommended by the chatbot.

These scenarios call for chaining tasks and prompts together.

- **Execution**: Finally, the prompts need to be executed on an OpenAI model, along with some plugins such as Bing Search. Almost all solutions will also need content filtering and security to ensure that inappropriate and insecure content does not pass through the system. We need infrastructure to host and execute these OpenAI models, plugins, and libraries.

- **Interaction**: We need a user interface that interacts with the user and the chatbot engine.

Now, let's look at an architecture for implementing these requirements.

Architecture

As you might have observed, the processing stages for an OpenAI-based solution are different than those of a traditional analytical system. The architecture of an enterprise chatbot is shown in *Figure 17.1*:

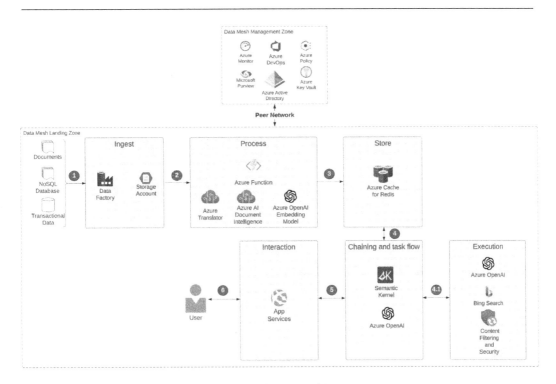

Figure 17.1 – OpenAI architecture

Take a moment to study this architecture diagram; we'll learn about the components that are used and their functionality in the next section.

Components

In *Figure 17.1*, starting from left to right, let's look at each component and understand its functionality/attributes.

Source data

Data can be company documents stored on SharePoint sites, NoSQL databases for product catalogs, Customer 360 information, or even transactions in a database.

Azure Data Factory

Azure Data Factory is a cloud-scale **extract, transform, and load** (ETL) framework. It has ready-made connectors to over a hundred different sources. It can connect to SharePoint files, NoSQL databases such as Cosmos DB or MongoDB, and transactional databases such as SQL Server or Oracle. Here are some resources that can help you learn more about Azure Data Factory and its connectors:

- Azure Data Factory documentation: `https://learn.microsoft.com/en-us/azure/data-factory/`

- Azure Data Factory connectors: `https://learn.microsoft.com/en-us/azure/data-factory/connector-overview`

Azure Translator

Azure Translator is a cloud-based managed translator service. It is used by many Microsoft products and is also available as a public service. This is an optional component in case you need to translate documents from different regional offices into one language and store them centrally. Any component where you need to pre-process the data before it is vectorized belongs to this block.

Azure AI Document Intelligence

Azure AI Document Intelligence can read documents in PDF format, image formats such as TIFF, JPEG, and others, and Microsoft document formats such as Excel, Word PowerPoint, or even HTML files. It can break the document down into logical sections and read text on images. While Azure AI Document Intelligence can be used for many different applications, in this scenario, it is used to chunk and break large documents into logical pieces so that they can be vectorized and stored.

For more information on Azure AI Document Intelligence, please refer to `https://learn.microsoft.com/en-us/azure/ai-services/document-intelligence/`.

Azure OpenAI embedding models

Azure provides a text embedding model called `text-embedding-ada-002` (version 2) and `text-embedding-ada-002` (version 1). Logically, it is best to use version 2. Version 1 is outdated and is only being maintained because some customers might still be using it. This embedding model will convert a given text into embeddings (or vectors) that you can then store in a vector database.

For more information on Azure OpenAI embedding models, please refer to `https://learn.microsoft.com/en-us/azure/ai-services/openai/concepts/models#embeddings-models`.

Azure Redis Cache

Azure Redis Cache supports storing vectors and running similarity searches. There are other services, such as **Azure Cognitive Search**, that also support vector databases and semantic search over these vectors.

For more information on these topics, please refer to the following sources:

- Redis Cache vectors: `https://redis.io/docs/interact/search-and-query/advanced-concepts/vectors/`

- Azure Search vector support: `https://learn.microsoft.com/en-us/azure/search/vector-search-overview`

Azure App Service

Azure App Service can host the user interface so that users can interact with the chatbot engine. To learn more about this, please refer to `https://learn.microsoft.com/en-us/azure/app-service/`.

Semantic Kernel

Semantic Kernel is an open source SDK that's been developed to help combine different AI models such as OpenAI, Azure OpenAI, and Hugging Face, along with plugins such as Bing search, ChatGPT, or Microsoft 365 Copilot. Semantic Kernel is the orchestrator or the brains of your engine that wires all the skills together to produce the best response. To learn more about Semantic Kernel, please refer to `https://learn.microsoft.com/en-us/semantic-kernel/overview/`.

Azure OpenAI

Azure OpenAI models are called by Semantic Kernel to search for similar text in the vector database that matches the query. It can also summarize text or generate new text, depending on the functionality you wish to support.

Bing search

Bing search is a set of APIs that provide a host of search functionality. You can use it to search the web or search your company website. It also provides services such as spellcheck, visual search, and video search. It is an optional component but can be an important plugin to enhance the functionality of your chatbot. For details on Bing search APIs, please refer to `https://learn.microsoft.com/en-us/bing/search-apis/`.

Content filtering and security

The Azure OpenAI API allows you to set up content filtering. This allows you to ensure that content is categorized as **hate**, **violence**, **sexual**, and **self-harm**. It can also help detect jailbreaks and other types of content in the prompt that can be a security threat. Furthermore, it can help detect protected content to ensure that code or text found in the public domain can be filtered out to prevent any copyright violations. Microsoft has also released a set of libraries for responsible AI that has a host of APIs that allow OpenAI to be used responsibly. These libraries can also be included in this block. Details on these topics can be found here:

- Content filtering: `https://learn.microsoft.com/en-us/azure/ai-services/openai/how-to/content-filters`

- Responsible AI: `https://learn.microsoft.com/en-us/azure/ai-services/responsible-use-of-ai-overview`

- AI-based search over company data: `https://learn.microsoft.com/en-us/azure/ai-services/openai/how-to/use-your-data-securely`

In the next section, we'll look at how data moves through this architecture.

Data flow/interactions

1. Data from documents, NoSQL databases, and transactional databases are pulled using Azure Data Factory and stored in an Azure Storage account.

2. Any change to the Azure Storage triggers an event that runs an Azure Function App.

3. The Azure Function App calls various processing APIs, such as translation and chunking, before calling the embedding model to convert it into a vector. These vectors are then stored in an Azure Redis Cache vector database.

4. Semantic Kernel interacts with and runs queries on the Azure Redis Cache vector database and searches for content with semantic similarity. Semantic Kernel can also use Azure Redis Cache to store chat history for context and memory:

    I.   Semantic Kernel also interacts with other plugins, such as Bing search, ChatGPT, or content filters.

5. The chatbot user interface, which is hosted on Azure App Service, calls Semantic Kernel with queries that have been submitted by the user and returns the response.

6. The user interacts with the chatbot's user interface.

Now, let's look at some common scenarios for this architecture.

Scenarios

- **Human resources bot**: An employee-facing bot that interacts with employees and answers their queries based on internal documents and other personal information (leaves, travel, and so on) in internal databases

- **Product catalog bot**: A product catalog on a retail company's page that helps customers find products and product recommendations

- **Procurement bot**: Analyzes purchase orders and helps the procurement team with better and well-informed negotiations

Many scenarios can be found across every industry, including summarizing documents, exploratory analysis, and recommendation engines.

This brings us to the end of this section on architecture patterns for a data mesh. Let's summarize what we've learned.

Summary

In this chapter, we learned how OpenAI solutions are different. We understood that the need for data and processing is different from a standard analytical solution. We also learned about the tools that are available for processing this data and storing it as vectors in a vector database. We now know the importance of tools such as Semantic Kernel. They are the glue that ties all the different pieces of OpenAI processing modules together in a manageable way. Finally, we looked at various plugins that can be used to enhance prompts and protect users from harmful content.

Index

W

www.packtpub.com

Subscribe to our online digital library for full access to over 7,000 books and videos, as well as industry leading tools to help you plan your personal development and advance your career. For more information, please visit our website.

Why subscribe?

- Spend less time learning and more time coding with practical eBooks and Videos from over 4,000 industry professionals

- Improve your learning with Skill Plans built especially for you

- Get a free eBook or video every month

- Fully searchable for easy access to vital information

- Copy and paste, print, and bookmark content

Did you know that Packt offers eBook versions of every book published, with PDF and ePub files available? You can upgrade to the eBook version at packtpub.com and as a print book customer, you are entitled to a discount on the eBook copy. Get in touch with us at customercare@packtpub.com for more details.

At www.packtpub.com, you can also read a collection of free technical articles, sign up for a range of free newsletters, and receive exclusive discounts and offers on Packt books and eBooks.

Other Books You May Enjoy

If you enjoyed this book, you may be interested in these other books by Packt:

Azure Data and AI Architect Handbook

Olivier Mertens, Breght Van Baelen

ISBN: 9781803234861

- Design scalable and cost-effective cloud data platforms on Microsoft Azure
- Explore architectural design patterns with various use cases
- Determine the right data stores and data warehouse solutions
- Discover best practices for data orchestration and transformation
- Help end users to visualize data using interactive dashboarding
- Leverage OpenAI and custom ML models for advanced analytics
- Manage security, compliance, and governance for the data estate

Practical Guide to Azure Cognitive Services

Chris Seferlis, Christopher Nellis, Andy Roberts

ISBN: 9781801812917

- Master cost-effective deployment of Azure Cognitive Services
- Develop proven solutions from an architecture and development standpoint
- Understand how Cognitive Services are deployed and customized
- Evaluate various uses of Cognitive Services with different mediums
- Disseminate Azure costs for Cognitive Services workloads smoothly
- Deploy next-generation Knowledge Mining solutions with Cognitive Search
- Explore the current and future journey of OpenAI
- Understand the value proposition of different AI projects

Packt is searching for authors like you

If you're interested in becoming an author for Packt, please visit `authors.packtpub.com` and apply today. We have worked with thousands of developers and tech professionals, just like you, to help them share their insight with the global tech community. You can make a general application, apply for a specific hot topic that we are recruiting an author for, or submit your own idea.

Share your thoughts

Now you've finished *Engineering Data Mesh in Azure Cloud*, we'd love to hear your thoughts! Scan the QR code below to go straight to the Amazon review page for this book and share your feedback or leave a review on the site that you purchased it from.

`https://packt.link/r/1-805-12078-6`

Your review is important to us and the tech community and will help us make sure we're delivering excellent quality content.

Download a free PDF copy of this book

Thanks for purchasing this book!

Do you like to read on the go but are unable to carry your print books everywhere?

Is your eBook purchase not compatible with the device of your choice?

Don't worry, now with every Packt book you get a DRM-free PDF version of that book at no cost.

Read anywhere, any place, on any device. Search, copy, and paste code from your favorite technical books directly into your application.

The perks don't stop there, you can get exclusive access to discounts, newsletters, and great free content in your inbox daily

Follow these simple steps to get the benefits:

1. Scan the QR code or visit the link below

https://packt.link/free-ebook/9781805120780

2. Submit your proof of purchase
3. That's it! We'll send your free PDF and other benefits to your email directly

www.ingramcontent.com/pod-product-compliance
Lightning Source LLC
LaVergne TN
LVHW081517050326

832903LV00025B/1521

* 9 7 8 1 8 0 5 1 2 0 7 8 0 *